Art in Education

Landscapes: The Arts, Aesthetics, and Education

VOLUME 1

SCOPE

This series aims to provide conceptual and empirical research in arts education, (including music, visual arts, drama, dance, media, and poetry), in a variety of areas related to the post-modern paradigm shift. The changing cultural, historical, and political contexts of arts education are recognized to be central to learning, experience, and knowledge. The books in this series present theories and methodological approaches used in arts education research as well as related disciplines - including philosophy, sociology, anthropology and psychology of arts education.

ART IN EDUCATION

Identity and Practice

by

Dennis Atkinson

Department of Educational Studies,
Goldmiths University of London, U.K.

KLUWER ACADEMIC PUBLISHERS
DORDRECHT / BOSTON / LONDON

A C.I.P. Catalogue record for this book is available from the Library of Congress.

ISBN 1-4020-1084-2 (HB)
ISBN 1-4020-1085-0 (PB)

Published by Kluwer Academic Publishers,
P.O. Box 17, 3300 AA Dordrecht, The Netherlands.

Sold and distributed in North, Central and South America
by Kluwer Academic Publishers,
101 Philip Drive, Norwell, MA 02061, U.S.A.

In all other countries, sold and distributed
by Kluwer Academic Publishers,
P.O. Box 322, 3300 AH Dordrecht, The Netherlands.

Printed on acid-free paper

Printed in the Netherlands.

CONTENTS

ACKNOWLEDGEMENTS

I want to thank a number of people who, over the years, have helped me to develop my thoughts in relation to the contents of this book. Tony Brown, Paul Dash, Alex Moore, Anna Horsley, Sheila Cox, John Matthews, John Willats, John swift, Jacquie Swift, John Johnston, Steve Herne, Rosalyn George, my PGCE, MA and MPhil students at Goldsmiths University of London, Keith Walker. Special thanks must go to Bill Brookes my former tutor who has always supported my work and provided constant advice, comment and stimulation. Thanks must also go to Tony Brown, Paul Dash and Rosalyn George for reading and commenting on drafts of the manuscript.

I want to thank a number of teachers and their children and students for allowing me to reproduce art work. John Johnson and his students at Thomas Moore School and Crofton School, Folami Bayode, Jonathan Archibald, Andy Gower and his students at Fortismere School, Carla Mindel and her students at Highgate Wood School, Sarah Dore and Robin Tipple. I am also grateful to John Johnson, Folami Bayode, Jonathan Archibald and Andy Gower for participating in a series of interviews contained in Chapter 7.

I am grateful to the *International Journal of Art and Design Education* for allowing me to reproduce images from previous publications. I thank Irene van den Reydt and Michel Lokhorst from Kluwer for their initial encouragement and enthusiasm for the project and their constant support. A final but special mention for my wife Karen, my daughter Emma and my son Luke.

Dennis Atkinson
September 2002

ABOUT THE AUTHOR

Dennis Atkinson studied art at Cardiff College of Art and art and education at Bretton Hall College of Education from where he received his Certificate in Education in 1971. This was followed by three years of teaching art at Batley High School for Boys. In 1974 he moved to Southampton where he taught art at Glen Eyre Comprehensive School becoming Head of Art Department in 1977. He began studying for a part-time Masters Degree in Education in 1979 at the University of Southampton. This led to further study culminating in 1987 when he received his PhD, which focussed on the relationship between language and action in teaching art and design. In 1988 he was appointed to the Department of Educational Studies at Goldsmiths College, University of London, as a tutor for the PGCE Art and Design (secondary) course. He became course director in 1992. He is now Senior Lecturer with responsibilities for masters degrees and research supervision. His research interests include art and design in education and initial teacher education. He has a particular interest in employing hermeneutic, post-structural and psychoanalytic theory to explore the formation of pedagogised identities and practices within educational contexts. He is currently Principal Editor of The International Journal of Art and Design Education and has published regularly since 1991 in international academic journals such as The Journal of Curriculum Studies, The International Journal of Inclusive Education, The International Journal of Art and Design Education and Discourse: Studies in the Cultural Politics of Education.

INTRODUCTION

MEMORY SEED

My introduction to teaching art began in September 1971 when I took up a post as art teacher in a secondary school in the West Riding of Yorkshire. Apart from my desire to survive and establish myself amongst students and staff I remember holding firm ideas about what I should be teaching. In relation to drawing and painting I had clear expectations concerning practice and representation. Students' art work which did not correspond to these I rather naively) considered as weak and in need of correction. I assumed wrongly that when students were making paintings and drawings from observation of objects, people or landscape, they should be aiming to develop specific representational skills associated with the idea of 'rendering' a reasonable likeness. I was reasonably familiar with the development of Western art and different forms of visual representation and expression and I knew, for example, that the projection system perspective is only one and not the correct representational system for mapping objects and their spatial relations as viewed from a particular point into corresponding relations in a painting or drawing. Nevertheless I still employed this mode of projection as an expectation or a criterion of judgement when teaching my students.In retrospect the consequence of my approach to teaching observational drawing or painting practices was that in expecting students to be able to produce a particular representational form I could be accused of assuming that all students had the same perceptual experience. That is to say, that all students viewed the world in a similar way and therefore in order to produce a good representational drawing it was a matter of them acquiring the appropriate representational techniques. My teaching practice was, therefore, grounded upon the idea of a universal vision that could be represented, given sufficient degrees of perception and drawing skill, which it was my job to teach and develop. Looking back, in many ways my teaching was a strange mixture of unquestioning acceptance of specific cultural traditions of visual representation that I had received in my training and education, coupled with my awareness of contemporary art practices and their eclectic use of representational form.

It was during this early period that I had to teach whole classes of boys from India and Pakistan, who spoke very little English. I introduced a variety of art activities to these students including printmaking and collage, however lessons concerned with observational drawing and painting left me feeling quite bewildered but also fascinated. The work they produced in these lessons was quite different to those of Western students to whom my training allowed me to respond. Essentially the Asian students' drawings and paintings were

1

highly decorative, there was no indication of depth representation (or so I thought) and the proportions of objects represented (such as plants or people) seemed exaggerated from my western viewpoint. These students appeared to be more concerned with design and decoration as opposed to representing views from particular viewpoints. My training did not allow me to respond to this work with any degree of confidence and I remember feeling a sense of muddling through even though I was struck by the remarkable difference of their drawings and paintings.

During this time in the early 1970s these students were generally unsuccessful in the GCE (16+) Art examination and many were not even considered for examination entry. The consequence for many was that their art practices went unrecognised by the examination system. Their work was frequently viewed with interest but not treated seriously within the institutional framework of formal examinations where ability in art practice was defined and identified. In terms of identity, these students' identities as learners appeared to be produced within two kinds of discourses, one in which their *difference* as students of art practice was acknowledged through a curious pedagogic voyeurism, and another in which their ability as art practitioners was unacknowledged and often pathologised (see Atkinson 1999a). In retrospect this was perhaps my first encounter with what writers in contemporary cultural and social theory refer to as 'the other'. Although as a newly qualified teacher my thoughts on pedagogy were inchoate, my experiences with these Asian students remains unforgettable and I believe they taught me a great deal about the teacher's need to be able to respond effectively to the different ways in which children and students make art. The need for teachers to be eternally vigilant of the criteria used to evaluate and assess students' art work is an important theme of this book.

In later years my interest in developing approaches to teaching art that accommodated the diverse practices of students grew and was given a strong impetus in 1980 when I was accepted for a part-time Masters Degree at the University of Southampton. There I worked with W.M. Brookes who introduced me to a host of ideas concerned with exploring the relationship between language and action that I found I could apply to my professional work teaching art. In many ways this book is the outcome of these initial explorations. It attempts to raise some of the professional issues with which art teachers are confronted, largely those concerned with the interpretation of children's and students' art practices, and offers a variety of theoretical tools which might inform appropriate responses. I was always unhappy with examination and assessment structures which valued particular forms of practice and representation over others, even though as a teacher I participated in these institutionalised judgements. My attempts to value all students' forms of representation and expression in art practice conflicted with my political and professional awareness of the need for students to be able to produce particular forms of representation in order to gain success in the public examination system. My early experience of teaching the Asian students indicated powerfully the cultural basis and bias of examination and assessment practices in which ability in art practice is classified. In later years it taught me that as a teacher examining and assessing art work I was actually involved in a form of cultural politics, (see Williams 1977; Eagleton 2000), even though I thought I was involved in identifying or recognising students' 'natural' abilities.

My concern for valuing *difference* in students' forms of representation and expression continued throughout my teaching although I made frequent mistakes and even though I knew the examination system, of which I was a part, marginalized the art work of many students. It is important to note that my interest in the difference of students' art practices is not simply concerned with formal qualities; rather, it is to do with the representational or expressive logics, the semiotics of art practice, which underpin these formal structures. This interest runs alongside that concerning the frameworks of interpretation which we employ in order to try to understand the art work of children and students we teach. I will show that conflicts of interpretation can arise between the significance of the art work for the student who makes it and its significance for the teacher who has to assess it.

Particular issues that emerged during my early years of teaching art have remained with me, in modified form, throughout my work. This book is largely about these issues. Working with young people in school has taught me that the ways in which they explore and represent their experiences through art practice are diverse. A central focus of the book therefore will be upon representation (signification) and meaning in art practice in the context of art education. How do children and older students structure and give meaning to their art practices, and, in contrast, how do teachers interpret and give meaning to their art work? Consider the drawing in Figure 1. What is it about? How can we understand it and, further, how is our understanding formed? On first glance it seems a rather strange drawing and perhaps we can make little sense of it. However, knowing something about the context in which it was made allows us to make a reading. It was produced by a young boy who was fascinated by high structures and also with the letter 'r'. Looking closely at the drawing we can pick out numerous tall 'r' linear structures joined together in a complex matrix.

Although the drawing has significance for the boy it is not easy for others to interpret and understand. What can we deduce about the process of the drawing practice that led to the production of this drawing; is it possible to understand the dynamics of production? Can we say anything about the dialectical relationship between the emerging drawing and the boy's ongoing response to it? Do meaning and signification change for the boy as he makes his drawing? In my experience, art teachers are often faced with mysterious drawings and paintings and these can raise interpretational difficulties for their professional practice and result in different ways of responding.

Such issues lead into a major concern that is to do with how teachers and students acquire and develop their identities as teachers and learners in the

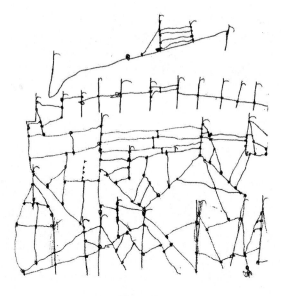

Figure 1.

context of art in education. I shall explore how such identities are developed within specific discourses of practice and representation that constitute pedagogic contexts. I will argue therefore that the construction of what I call *pedagogised identities* arises as a consequence of valuing and legitimising particular kinds of teaching and learning experiences in art. I will also argue that in different contexts of teaching and learning art different pedagogised identities are formed. For example, a secondary school art department that places great emphasis upon developing skills in observational drawing and painting and on students acquiring a series of skill and techniques in other areas such as printmaking, ceramics and collage, will precipitate different pedagogised identities to a department where the emphasis is placed upon using art practice to explore personal and social issues; where the emphasis is not upon skill and technique but upon exploring ideas and developing personal responses. This situation raises questions about the notions of universal provision and standardisation which underpin the National Curriculum for Art in England and indicates that in reality art education is comprised of a wide range of discourses and practices in which students' work is positioned and regulated.

One of the most complex issues in teaching arises when we try to reconcile what appear to be opposing ideas. How far can art be viewed as a personal practice when programmes of study and practice in art education prescribed by curriculum policies are culturally derived and framed? Teachers are concerned with getting their children or students to develop personal responses and personal investigation but equally teachers are expected to initiate students and children into conventional practices and techniques. In many ways this

seems to be an irreconcilable but inevitable project. Is it possible to reconcile the idea of developing self-expression with cultural determinism?
Connected to this pedagogical dilemma are other difficulties that concern firstly
the teacher's interpretation of the child's or student's work. How can the teacher
empathise with the work from the child's or student's perspective without
letting his or her expertise, or traditions of practice, influence judgement?
Secondly, how can we initiate work in art education that is relevant to and
located within children's and student's socio-cultural life-worlds whilst simultaneously expanding their understanding?

THEORIES OF LEARNING

The tension between the personal and the cultural is reflected within different theories of learning and development. Vygotsky's (1962, 1978) work
on learning and child development, for example, foregrounds social and cultural
factors that affect and condition learning, whilst Piaget (1950, 1956) on the
other hand stressed the internal evolving cognitive processes that facilitate
learning. Thus whilst Vygotsky's work provides a socio-cultural model of
learning and development, Piaget proposes a biological model. Ideally it seems
that we need to reconcile these two major theorisations of learning: we want
to understand the context of learning but we also want to understand the
learner's *modus operandi*, his or her learning processes.

In general terms Piagetian constructivist theory of learning argues that
children, equipped with internal processes, actively construct their knowledge of the world. This is not a rejection of an external world beyond the mind
of the learner but the child's knowledge and understanding of the world is
an active construction determined by inner processes and representations that
organise and give sense to experience. The child's construction of the world
occurs in a series of different stages which Piagetian theory proposed as
universal stages of development. Knowledge is therefore actively constructed
and the educative task is to create an environment conducive to different stages
of learning, practice and expression. Inherited techniques and traditions of
practice guide the child or student but he or she creates her own independent understanding. In social constructivist theories of learning based on the
work of Vygotsky or Mead (1934), knowledge and practices are inherited
and reconstructed by the child. Individual learning is governed by structures
of knowledge and practice that already exist and are culturally defined. Both
constructivist and social constructivist theories of learning suggest a determinism which can be reduced respectively to nature or culture.

Hermeneutic theory, particularly the work of Gadamer (1989) and Ricoeur
(1976, 1981), when applied to processes of learning, would blur the distinction between the individual and the social. For hermeneutics the individual
is always already part of the world she perceives. That is to say perception
of the world stems from how the world presents itself to consciousness which
in turn is formed within social processes. We can't stand outside the world

therefore to get a detached and objective view of it because any conception of the world depends on how it is consciously conceived and socio-cultural processes form that consciousness. By acting in the world both individual and the world as conceived are changed.

Post-structural approaches to learning present a more radical form of hermeneutics (see Gallagher 1992) that would deconstruct the nature-culture dualism even further and abandon the traditional separation between the individual and the socio-cultural by seeing such categories as determined by the symbolic (see Henriques et al. 1984; Peters 1998; Aronowitz and Giroux 1993; Apple 1990; Usher and Edwards 1994). Such radical theories claim that we can only understand, discuss or theorise issues, such as learning, within the symbolic order of language and further that language does not reveal essential meanings or provide direct access to a prior reality, but in fact produces meaning and reality. For example, post-structural theory would oppose the biological determinism of Piaget and the cultural determinism of Vygotsky on the grounds that both theories assume a biological or cultural origin which can never be attained. In contrast both theories can be viewed as *discourses* that construct particular readings of learning and development, which *create the illusion* of either biological or social origins, they do not reveal the truth about learning and development. Some argue against the transcendence of learning theories claiming that they simply reflect the social contexts in which they are produced. Walkerdine (1984) argues this case in relation to Piaget's experience of the inhumanity of war and his subsequent desire to support learning and development of rational and sympathetic human beings.

From a post-structural perspective, the Piagetian or Vygotyskian *child* is not to be viewed as a *natural* or *social* entity but as an ideological product of particular discourses in which the child is constructed accordingly. Post-structural theory would therefore reject the idea of stable bodies of knowledge that exist independently of socio-historical processes and in its more radical guise it even problematises the idea of experience by viewing it as a production of discursive practices. When post-structural theory is applied to teaching and learning contexts, teaching practices, subject knowledge and students' abilities are seen only as productions of those discourses and practices perpetuated and valued by the institution of educational practice. That is to say, teachers and learners attain their identities through the ways in which they are constructed within educational discourses and practices. This approach to teaching and learning suggests therefore that teachers and students are not independent agents, but gain their identities within practices and discourses that are ideologically construed.

LEARNING THEORY IN ART EDUCATION

The development of children's and student's learning in art practice has been theorised from a range of perspectives but the influence of psychology, particularly the work of Piaget, was pre-eminent during the 20th century. Herbert Read (1943), was influenced particularly by the work of Jung which he employed to describe and analyse children in terms of different psychological and emotional subjects. As a consequence of a moving epiphany when he came across an image produced by a five-year old girl that she entitled, 'Snake around the World and a Boat,' he became convinced that this was an example of Jung's archetypal imagery. As Thistlewood (1984) states,

. . . an association between child art and Jungian theory affected the status of art teaching, an activity considered generally to be peripheral to the fundamental business of art education. It gave meaning and new purpose to the work of many thousands of art teachers: instead of merely assisting hobbyist or recreational skills, their role would be to help integrate innate creative abilities with the levels of intellection demanded in a modern world, for the sake of individual equipoise and well-being, and also, through this, for the health of a collective social harmony (p. 113).

Read's point was that social problems of his time were the consequence of an educational system that gave priority to intellectual development and that what was required was a system of education through art that would develop individual creativity. Read's work, similar to Piaget, is also based upon a presupposition of innate ability and that it is the teacher's task to reveal this creative potential. Read's ascription of a psychological typology to drawings and paintings of particular childen in his book, Education Through Art (1943), make interesting reading, particularly in relation to the production of learner identities with which I shall be concerned. Lowenfeld's and Brittain's book, Creative and Mental Growth (1970), relies upon a Piagetian model of learning and development to inform a lively analysis of teaching and learning practices. In their view learning is viewed as a staged process for which teaching strategies have to be developed. Their approach to education and development in art education is supported by Barrett (1979) who analyses and evaluates a series of rationales for art in education.

Other approaches to art education include Elliot Eisner (1972) who discusses the ongoing socio-cultural dimension to learning in art, in which he articulates the inter-relation between the individual, the subject discipline and the socio-cultural context. Taylor (1986) argues for the value of critical thinking in the evaluation of art practice and the importance of bringing artists into the educational sphere to work with children and students. Mason (1988) and Chambers (1998) are strong and articulate advocates of inter-cultural approaches to art education. Matthews (1994, 1999) combines a universal idea of development in early drawing within socio-cultural support structures, which could be viewed as an effective reconciliation of constructivist and social constructivist traditions of learning theory.

Much contemporary social and cultural theory is concerned with exploring life-world contexts of experience and understanding and in education this means trying to attend to the ways in which teachers and learners experience classroom practices that are culturally derived. There have been few major publications in the field of art and design education that have attempted to employ contemporary social and cultural theory to explore practices in this field (but see Efland, Freedman and Stuhr 1996; Chalmers 1998; Mason 1986). But there has been a growing body of action research or professional enquiry in the wider field of educational practice that attempts to investigate the perspectives of teachers by applying these contemporary theoretical frameworks (Elliott 1991; Carr and Kemmis 1989; Brown and Jones 2001). This book is largely about exploring practices of teaching and learning in art education by applying theory from hermeneutics, semiotics, post-structuralism and psychoanalysis to teachers' professional concerns. It does not attempt to revisit and evaluate to any great extent debates about art in education that are grounded in constructivist or social constructivist perspectives. But it builds upon this theoretical history in order to develop descriptions and theorisations of identity and practice in art education which see these processes as social and cultural constructions but which also seeks to embrace a notion of human agency. One problem with constructivist or social-constructivist theory in education is that whilst the former pays little attention to social processes the latter questions the idea of individual agency. The position I wish to adopt is one in which whilst it is difficult to deny that reality and our understanding of it is a symbolic construction, the symbolic is 'not all', that there is a pre-symbolic domain which pushes against the boundaries of the symbolic and can effect change.

Many teachers are able to reconcile the conflict mentioned earlier, between personal practice and cultural tradition, in teaching art, but they do so in very different ways and so construct teaching and learning identities differently. How do teachers perceive their task of teaching art? How do they understand and assess children and students art work? How do they understand learning and development according to the evidence available? How do they guide and shape future learning and practice? These are all essentially hermeneutic issues because they relate to the teacher's construal of his or her practice, that is to say, their constructions of the world in which they function and themselves as practitioners. My interest in the formation of pedagogised identities involves an interrogation of some discourses of art in education around which teaching art in school is structured, organised and seen as meaningful. This will include an examination of curriculum discourses, such as the National Curriculum for Art in the UK (DFE 1995, 2000) according to which art education in schools in England is conceived. My intention is to show that such curriculum discourses construct art practice as a particular kind of practice in which teaching practices and student's art work are understood, positioned and regulated. Similarly these discourses produce students' abilities in art practice, they do not discover them as natural endowments.

REPRESENTATION AND SIGNIFICATION

The idea of representation will be discussed in relation to visual experience in order to challenge naturalist understandings of representation. The *natural attitude* (Bryson 1983) to representation will be contrasted with a semiotic analysis of children's and student's art practices. I shall consider how young children's and older student's art work in the form of drawings or mixed media constructions function as visual signs. By employing the term *signification* I will move from an understanding of representation seen as the reproduction of prior visual or imaginary experience, to signification seen as a visual *production* that develops out of such experience. This shift of emphasis from representation to signification removes meaning from any natural association between a representation and its referent and understands visual productions such as drawings, paintings and other art work, as a series of signifiers whose meanings are constructed within the logic of the student's visual semiotic practice. This is to argue for a shift from representation concerned with the 'fidelity of registration of the world (Bryson 1983, p. 3),' where representation is concerned with reproducing as closely as possible the appearance of a world *out there*, to an idea of signification where the emphasis is placed upon the production of a reality.

IDENTITY AND DIFFERENCE

The impact upon my thinking of contemporary theorisations of social and cultural processes has been significant in my attempts to untangle issues of representation, signification, meaning, identity and practice in art education. Of central concern are questions of discourse, identity and difference in relation to art practice and this includes a critical examination of language and other classificatory systems in which understanding and meaning are constructed. I will discuss some of this growing body of theory in order to indicate its relevance for developing a more inclusive approach to pedagogy for art in education. Issues of identity and difference emerge in potent form in the discourse of assessment practices in which student's art work and students' abilities in art practice are classified. I will show that assessment of art practice constitutes a particular instance of what Foucault (1980) describes as power-knowledge which invokes processes of surveillance, normalisation, discipline and regulation of student's art work.

Part of my exploration of identity in art education involves a consideration of expected pedagogised identities anticipated by the National Curriculum for Art in England which prescribes particular forms of knowledge and practice that children and students are expected to acquire. For example, to record and analyse first-hand observations, to use sketchbooks, to investigate and manipulate different materials and processes such as drawing, to refine and control the use of tools and techniques, to experiment with different methods and approaches to make images and other artefacts, to evaluate their own and the work of others, to learn about the visual and tactile qualities of materials and processes, to learn about the work of artists, craftspeople and designers from Western Europe and the wider world. This curriculum also provides a series of level descriptions of children's and students' levels of attainment in art practice and understanding which they are expected to achieve by the end of stipulated age phases. As such these descriptions of attainment in art practice constitute identifications of ability and learning. It is reasonable to argue, I believe, that this curriculum outlines a particular understanding of art practice and a particular way of understanding ability and attainment in art practice. In other words this curriculum produces a particular epistemology of art education in which both teaching and learning practices are epistemologised. Put another way, this curriculum organises, identifies, disciplines and regulates a particular body-in-practice. There are those who believe that it has produced an orthodoxy of planning, teaching and learning (see Hughes 1998; Swift 1999; Steers 1999) and there are those who argue that they are able to function creatively within this curriculum framework (see Allen 1996). I will attempt to contrast this epistemologising of teaching and learning with the different ontological orientations of children's and student's art practices.

I argue that the National Curriculum for Art is concerned with establishing a particular discourse of levels of attainment and achievement in which specific standards are articulated according to certain norms of practice and understanding. One consequence of this kind of curriculum is that it creates a form of inclusion and exclusion that generates a specific politics of ability, representation and identity. This can be contrasted with a curriculum which foregrounds the ontological orientation of children's and students' experiences in their search for expressive form. Such a curriculum is concerned with heterogeneity, variety, diversity and heterodoxy. This kind of art curriculum is more ecumenical; it does not prescribe or pre-determine an individual's search for expression and representation, which is able to find a place of value. The task for the teacher however becomes more complex in that he or she has to be able to respond effectively to this diversity. To use Vygotskian terminology, in this form of curriculum the teacher is involved in numerous *zones of proximal development*, or to use a term from Bruner, the teacher is required to adopt diverse forms of *scaffolding*.

THE IDEA OF EXPERIENCE

The theorising of art practice in education through the notions of identity and difference is the prelude to establishing my argument for an art curriculum that is grounded in experience. This is not a new concept and can be found in the much earlier work of Dewey (1958), Read (1943), Langer (1953) or Lowenfeld and Brittain (1970), for example, but recent theoretical work on subjectivity and identity invites us to question how we understand the term *experience*, such work demands that we question how experience has become epistemologised, that is to say, how experience has become understood through particular ways of knowing in which we construct or conceive experience. Post-structural theory (see Easthope 1991) questions naturalist or essentialist notions of experience found in earlier writers. It rejects the idea that we can reveal the essence of experience by arguing that our understanding of experience is always mediated through language or other representational media. Thus experience is always textualised (Derrida) or visualised. The difference then between earlier concerns with experience and education is that recent theory attempts to deconstruct normalised or essentialist understandings of experience by revealing its epistemologised and ideological construction within specific socio-cultural frameworks (discourses, images, practices). This practice of deconstruction suggests that access to direct experience-in-itself is not possible because any attempt to gain such access has to involve the mediation of signification. In the light of such claims notions of self-expression or uniqueness, often used to justify expression and representation in art practice, become problematised.

Through the concept of *difference*, post-structural theory attempts to acknowledge and legitimate different significations of experience in a more localised and context-dependent sense. This is not to admit essentialist ideas by the back door but to focus attention upon a *semiotics of difference*. Running through such theoretical work is a concern to show how normalised constructs of experience exert dominance over marginalized constructs, particularly in institutional sites such as schools and their internal classificatory systems of examination and assessment. This book attempts to disrupt normalised and essentialist understandings and classifications of experience and practice in the field of art in education in order to show their constructed, and by implication, their contingent nature. Consequently the task is to recognise the legitimacy of other forms of practice in the signification of experience that often appear mysterious or incomprehensible.

Perhaps it is easier to think of the normalising of experience as a kind of patterning process. We can understand our ways of thinking as patterns of thought and a pattern can be viewed as a form in space and time, or a form that creates a space and a temporality, which furthermore implies that a pattern has a boundary. That which lies beyond the boundary is difficult to conceive, to comprehend, and the tendency is therefore to marginalize. Paul Dash (2000 personal communication) has used this pattern metaphor to explore the delimiting processes of culture, particularly with respect to people whom he describes as existing or straddling *between* cultures, that is African Caribbean, Asian and other diasporic peoples. His task, and one which is also central to this book, is to develop teaching strategies and curriculum policies for art in education which allow a greater sense of inclusivity for those *on the margins* through an interrogation of the cultural politics of inclusion. In his use of the term *heterotopias* Foucault (1970) has also discussed the incommensurability that arises between contrasting cultural orders and practices. In some ways my struggle here can be viewed as an exploration of the cultural politics of teaching and assessing children's and students' art work, for these are practices in which students identities as makers of art and teachers identities as teachers of art are formed.

OUTLINE OF THE BOOK

The book consists of three parts; in Part One I introduce the theoretical frameworks of semiotics and hermeneutics in order to discuss the ideas of interpretation and meaning that arise throughout the book. Then I apply these frameworks to children's and student's drawing practices. My intention here is to develop the idea that such art practices consist of complex semiotic processes that require commensurate hermeneutic positions on the part of educators who need to interpret them. Underlying Part One is a shift from the idea of representation viewed as an attempt to copy or reproduce views of the world, towards the idea of signification and semiotic production. In making this shift I establish the possibility of comprehending drawing practice as a local semiotic process which avoids ideas of natural correspondence, optical truth or representational accuracy. Rather drawing is viewed as part of a dynamic process of *semiosis* whereby drawings do not represent an external world directly but as a production of visual signifiers, they construct visual worlds that relate to other visual signifiers and signification systems. The legitimacy or efficacy of a drawing therefore does not rest upon some external arbiter of judgement such as an accurate view or depiction, but rather upon how it functions for the child or student as a visual sign. In Part Two I turn my attention away from the interpretation of drawing practices in order to consider the very discourses that constitute such interpretations. My point is to show how such discourses construct pedagogised identities of teachers and learners. I argue that students' identities as learners in art and design education are not discovered, for example, as natural talents but that they are constructed within particular kinds of cultural, linguistic and representational codes and practices. Drawing upon post-structural and psychoanalytic theory I show how discourses of assessment and curriculum policy in art education can be considered as material practices in which both teachers and learners are constructed as particular pedagogised subjects in the field of art in education. I also present extracts form a series of conversations with secondary school teachers in England who describe their different attitudes and approaches to teaching art. Their descriptions can be viewed as teacher narratives in which each teacher constructs his or her practice of teaching and, by implication, their student's identities as learners. In Part Three I return to my concern with the semiotics of art practice developed in Part One in order to describe mixed-media art practices produced by secondary school students. My purpose here is to contrast normalising epistemological constructions of art practice described in examination assessment criteria and curriculum policy and their subsequent pedagogised identities, with the diverse ontological structures of learning as manifested in students' different approaches to art practice. This contrast highlights the dilemma of a requirement for assessment and the desire to acknowledge and legitimate individual forms of expression and world making through art practice. Such a move is informed by a radicalising of the idea of experience, which disrupts the ground of certainty that assessment systems rely upon, and it introduces a more chaotic and shifting ground to art practice and the ways in which we understand such practice.

The contemporary explosion of new forms of visual expression and visual production in a variety of media almost begs the question how is it possible to understand or theorise art practice today, what does this term mean? Indeed what was once thought of as a discrete and fundamental body of knowledge and practice which students studying art should receive, has now become, in the words of John Swift (1999), a more 'contested field of study.' This visual explosion invokes a questioning of traditional values and practices; it introduces different semiotic orders that feed off themselves constantly thereby generating an ever-increasing process of visual iteration. The implications of this explosion of visual culture are significant for art in education. Firstly in the sense that we need to re-examine our attitudes and understanding of representation and expression and the value systems which underpin them in order to be able to embrace this growing visual field. Secondly in the sense that visual education needs to move from its traditional tertiary or marginal position on the school curriculum to a place more central, this is because learning through visual practice generates a powerful means though which children and students are able to explore and understand the social and cultural worlds in which people live. The power of the visual to generate exploration and understanding can be seen in both early drawing practices and in older student's mixed-media work described in Chapter 7.

INTERPRETATION AND PRACTICE

In Part One I provide a description of semiotic and hermeneutic theory in order to provide the theoretical framework for my analysis of some children's and student's drawing practices. I concentrate on drawing because it is a familiar art activity in schools, particularly drawing from observation. I will argue that drawing is a semiotic practice and when viewed as such this calls into question conventional understandings of visual representation as an attempt to represent or reproduce views of a prior reality. If drawing is concerned with signification rather than a conventional mimetic idea of representation, then any direct relation between representation and reality is fractured. This is because, I will argue and demonstrate, that as a semiotic practice, a drawing qua signifier relates not to a fixed external referent in the world which exists prior to the drawing, but to other signifiers which consist of other images and discourses in which we understand visual structures. By choosing drawing as a practical focus for extrapolating art action as a semiotic process I establish both a practical and a theoretical ground for Part Three, where I describe more complex and innovative art practices in secondary schools in England.

CHAPTER ONE

SEMIOTICS AND HERMENEUTICS

INTRODUCTION

This chapter is concerned with the ideas of signification, interpretation and meaning and their application to the task of interpreting children's drawing practices. To begin I present a brief introduction and discussion of semiotics, the study of signs and signification systems, because I argue that drawings can be profitably viewed as semiotic processes and structures which children organise and construct for specific signification or representational purposes. An important task for those needing to interpret children's drawings is to understand how they signify for the child. If we return to the drawing in Figure 1, it is difficult to understand how it is meaningful for the child unless we have some knowledge of the child's interests and concerns which lead to the production of the drawing. Even then it is difficult to gain a clear understanding of those affective, cognitive and physical processes that constitute the dynamics of the drawing process. This is not a representational drawing in the conventional sense of depicting a view of an object or event. However it is a drawing in which the child is attempting to represent his specific idiosyncratic interests in tall structures and the letter form 'r', further, it is a drawing in which these interests are visualised according to the child's idiosyncratic graphic logic.

In many ways my discussion of this drawing helps to make the distinction between representation and signification. Representation can be understood in the conventional sense of a re-presentation, in a formal structure, of a prior view or experience of objects or events, so that these can be recognised in the representational form. John Willats (1997, p. 22) writes that:

If a picture is to provide an effective representation it must be possible to recognise in it the shapes of the objects that the artist or draftsman intended to represent. I shall therefore define an effective shape representation as a pictorial representation in which the three dimensional shapes of objects that the artist or draftsman intends to portray can be see, clearly and unambiguously.

Here representation consists of a direct association between the representational image as signifier, and the objects represented as signified. This is not unlike the sign relation, consisting of signifier and signified, postulated in structural linguistics by Saussure (1916). For Willats (1997) and Wollheim (1973) there are clearly pictorial representations which are more effective than others in conveying information about three-dimensional form. For example, some pictorial representations, such as orthographic projections, only provide information of two-dimensional shapes, whilst others such as isometric projections or linear perspective, depict information about three-dimensional form.

The way in which I am using the term signification on the other hand replaces the relation between signifier and signified to one between signifier and signifier. That is to say, the relation is not between a signifier and something beyond and outside of its domain which we can access directly, a signified, because that which is signified can never be accessed except through signification, hence the signified is always a signifier. Thus when we speak of an effective representation we are not comparing a representational form with a true likeness which we can somehow approach outside of symbolic systems, our judgement is always already informed by symbolic systems.

An important question to ask therefore is when teaching and responding to observational drawing should we be instructing students to produce effective and unambiguous representational drawings which implies a didactic and sectarian pedagogy with an implicit hierarchy of achievement, or should we be concerned with encouraging students to respond to such drawing tasks by providing access to conventional drawing strategies but also respecting and legitimising more idiosyncratic productions and then trying to understand the ways in which they function as observational drawings for the student? The approach I will be taking is the latter. Whilst it is possible to argue that when used for specific purposes certain projection systems in drawing convey information more effectively than others, for example, an engineering drawing contains information for a specific purpose; a child or student's response to an observational task may take many forms depending upon how the child orients him or herself to the drawing practice. These individual orientations to drawing practice have to be considered carefully in relation to their graphic outcomes. Consequently when initiating drawing practices in schools we need to consider why we want students to draw, what will students achieve through drawing, what can we explore through drawing and how do we respond to the different strategies and outcomes of drawing practice? Here the notion of signification is, I believe, appropriate in that it provides a way of thinking about drawing practices in terms of their different signifying strategies. With these concerns in mind I will provide a brief introduction to semiotic theory and then show how it can help in our task of interpreting children's drawings.

SEMIOTICS

In various realms of social and cultural study today it is almost passé to acknowledge the view that perception and our understanding of reality is a semiotic construction through language or other sign systems including images. That is to say, there is no clear distinction between reality and its symbolisation and that therefore reality is a symbolic construction. However, in our everyday life contexts it is difficult to break the grip of simple communication models which suggest that language is a neutral medium that reflects or describes reality. Thus the suggestion that reality is a semiotic construction and that signs such as words or images shape our perception and understanding of experience and not the other way round, where we have experiences and then we find the right words to represent is sometimes difficult to accept.

But words or images are not labels that we attach to reveal prior ideas, events, experiences or perceptions, rather these semiotic orders actually create our conceptions of reality and therefore, the conceptual framework through which reality is made accessible. This suggests that conscious experience and thought is a construction built out of signs and that our lives are largely lived within and according to different sign systems that we inherit and develop. A further implication of this material production of reality through semiotic orders concerns our ideas about identity, of ourselves and of others. Again it is quite natural to think of our selves as unique individuals who possess an inner core of self, a distinct personality or identity and that language allows us to access this unique psychological sphere (Walkerdine and Blackman 2001, p. 17). We do not in contrast normally consider our selves as fragmented, partial or incomplete. However, if we accept the shaping of meaning by linguistic or visual signs it is possible to acknowledge that this unified conception of self is a consequence of words such as 'I', 'me', 'myself', 'you', or 'yourself', which appear to designate a unified individual.

The Saussurian legacy

The study of semiotics today constitutes an important field of enquiry in social and cultural studies. There are numerous texts that describe historical and theoretical developments (see for example: Bignell 1997; Hawkes 1977; Kress and Hodge 1991; Barthes 1973, 1977; Saussure 1959; Eco 1976; Sebeok 1969; Kristeva 1986). It is generally agreed that Charles Saunders Peirce and Ferdinand de Saussure were the founding figures. Saussure's division of the sign into its constituent parts of signifier and signified formed the basis of later work by Levi-Strauss (1966), Barthes (1973) and many others. Saussure's division does not articulate the relation between a sign and a referent in the world, it exists purely within the realm of signification. If we take the verbal sign *house* the signifier consists of the verbal sound whilst the signified is the concept, and together they constitute the verbal sign. In visual terms a picture of a house can be understood similarly so that the signifier consists of the visual marks whilst the signified is the visual image and together they constitute the visual sign. Barthes (1973) developed Saussure's sign division onto a second level of meaning which he termed myth or ideology, so that the sign on the first level of meaning becomes a signifier on a second level. We can grasp these two semiotic levels by considering a well known consumer brand name such as *Calvin Klein*. On the first semiotic level the letters (signifier) simply denote a name (signified). However on the second level the name *Calvin Klein* signifies a world of designer fashion and it becomes a fashion statement that circulates within the wider textual semiotics (visual and verbal) of contemporary fashion design.

We can think of the first level as the level of denotation in that on this level we can study the surface level relations of signifier and signified which form the sign. We can think of the second level as the level of connotation where the sign links with wider systems of meaning which introduce ideological issues such as, for example, class, race, gender or sexuality. If we return to the visual sign of a house, we can treat it simply as signifying a house on the denotative level but on the connotative level the visual sign relates to wider systems of meaning, which may relate to housing conditions in affluent suburbia or inner-city slums that then relate to further issues of wealth, poverty and equality. It is possible to see here Barthes's concern with intertextuality and the point that on the connotational level signs exist and inter-relate within a complex semiotic universe. Intertextuality thus refers to complex processes of semiosis in which sign systems inter-relate. Barthes was keen to explore this connotational level of meaning and how its ideological or mythic aspect comes to appear natural. Hawkes (1977) writes about the level of myth, which for Barthes constitutes the level of signification:

> With signification we have of course encountered an extremely powerful, because covert, producer of meaning at a level where an impression of 'god-given' or 'natural' reality prevails, largely because we are not normally able to perceive the processes by which it has been manufactured. Barthes's analysis of semiosis (the semiotic process), in moving via Saussure on to this level, begins to take us 'behind the scenes' as it were of our own construction of the world (p. 133, my brackets)

It is the naturalising of the level of myth that is the crucial point to bear in mind. We can use Barthes's two levels to consider children's and students' art work. For example, an observational drawing of a plant or a person can be considered on the first semiotic level of denotation as simply an observational drawing, a series of drawn marks which we can analyse according to the formal constituents of the drawing. But on the second level when placed within a framework of school assessment the drawing signifies the ability of the student which then becomes naturalised. In other words the drawing as sign relates to wider systems of meaning relating to cultural understandings of representation and practice, which are valued and normalised, and through this process of normalisation the ability of the student appears natural. On the level of myth therefore the drawing functions as a signifier for a teacher within specific socio-cultural codes of representation in which it is given a value. On the second (mythic) level meaning is constituted within an ideological space (which appears natural) of institutional assessment where it seems perfectly reasonable to speak in terms of a student's 'natural ability'. In this brief illustration it is possible to see that signs establish and confirm particular meanings and processes of identification and in doing so they create ideas of normality and, by implication, abnormality. It is then possible to ask which identities are sanctioned and legitimated within pedagogic practices and discourses.

Barthes's work on myth and ideology encourages us to recognise the contingent and ideological aspects of meaning and identity that I will develop in Chapters 5 and 6. However in order to gain more insight into children's and students' art practices I want to turn to the work of Peirce. His work on semiotics predates Saussure by several decades and his triadic articulation of sign functioning is I believe more pertinent to my investigation into how drawings function locally as signs for children and older students and how they are interpreted as signs by teachers.

The Peirceian legacy

In 1868 Charles Peirce published papers in the *Journal of Speculative Philosophy*, later published in a series of volumes of collected papers (1931–35). Peirce pioneered the development of semiotics which was to become a major field of enquiry in the following century. In a remarkable series of statements that pre-date the work of Saussure by nearly fifty years Peirce (1966) writes:

The only thought, then, which can possibly be cognised is thought in signs. But thought which cannot be cognised does not exist. All thought, therefore, must necessarily be in signs. From the proposition that every thought is a sign, it follows that every thought must address itself to some other, must determine some other, since that is the essence of a sign.
    . . . every thought must be interpreted in another, . . . all thought is in signs.
(Questions Concerning Certain Faculties p. 34)

This quote will be important to bear in mind when I discuss the orders of metaphor and metonymy in the formation of meaning in children's drawing practices and our interpretation of them. The idea that signs relate to each other, rather than to some external referent to constitute meaning is also a radical suggestion for its time. Saussure echoes this idea when he discusses the idea that meaning is a consequence of difference in sign relations and it is also developed by Derrida in his idea of iteration, which suggests that meaning is never final because other readings and interpretations can always be made in the endless signifying chains of language.

In a second paper Peirce (1966) makes an even more radical suggestion for his day, echoing post-structuralist non-essentialist ideas of subjectivity a hundred years later.

For, as the fact that every thought is a sign, taken in conjunction with the fact that life is a train of thought, proves that man (woman) is a sign . . . (Some Consequences of Four Incapacities p. 71, my brackets)

In these early writings on semiotics we are presented with ideas on meaning and identity that are ahead of their time but which are current today. Heidegger (1977), for example, argued that, "Man acts as though he were the shaper and master of language, while in fact language remains the master of man (p. 324)." Coward and Ellis (1977) suggest:

Because all the practices that make up a social totality take place in language, it becomes possible to consider language as the place in which the social individual is constructed. In other words, man (woman) can be seen as *language*, as the intersection of the social, historical and individual (p. 1 my bracket).

The key difference between Saussure's sign relation and that of Peirce lies
in the contrast between Saussure's signifier-signified relation and Peirce's sign
(interpretant)-object-ground relation. For Peirce, "A sign is something which
stands to somebody in some respect or capacity" (Vol. 2, p. 228). Hawkes
provides a useful breakdown of Peirce's definition of a sign:

A sign thus *stands for* something (its *object*); it stands for something *to* somebody (its
interpretant); and finally it stands for something to somebody *in some respect* (this respect is
called its *ground*). These terms, *sign, object, interpretant* and *ground* can thus be seen to refer
to the means by which the sign signifies; the relationship between them determines the precise
nature of the process of *semiosis* (p. 127. my emphasis).

The relation between sign and interpretant is important in that it designates the phenomenological dimension of interpretation, that is to say, it
concerns how the sign-object relation is interpreted (through the interpretant) in consciousness. Again the simple relation between a sign and an external
referent is denied because the latter always exists in the form of an interpretant, which in turn is informed by contextual forces suggested by the phrase,
'in some respect.'

It is Peirce's concern with the phenomenological grounding of semiosis, the
semiotic process, that I find helpful for approaching the semiotics of children's
and student's drawings. A key term in this process is *ground*, that is to say,
that respect or capacity in which a sign stands for something to somebody.
Ground can therefore refer to the local context of sign functioning which
includes the specific way in which a sign is functioning as a representation
for somebody, a teacher or a student. When we examine the drawings below
made by children and students it is important to bear in mind the local nature
of semiosis for the child who makes a drawing and for the teacher who has
to interpret.

The triadic nature of semiosis, of sign, interpretant and ground, is theorised in great depth by Peirce who identified over sixty classes of signs but
the sign categories which have received most attention are those which concern
ground and functioning. A sign can stand for something to somebody in some
respect by functioning as either an *icon, index* or *symbol*. An *icon* functions
as a sign "by means of features of itself which resemble its object." An *index*
is a sign "which functions as a sign by virtue of some factual or causal
connection with its object." A *symbol* is a sign "which functions as a sign
because of some 'rule' of conventional or habitual association between itself
and its object (Hawkes 1977, p. 127)."

Peirce is in fact describing different interpretational relationships between
a sign and its object through the interpretant for a person within a particular
socio-cultural context. It is important to understand that the sign categories
of *icon, index* and *symbol* are not mutually exclusive but that they co-exist
(Hawkes 1977, p. 129); they identify three different kinds of relationship
between a sign and its object for somebody where one sign relationship may
have dominance over the other two, depending upon the context of its func-

tioning. For example, a child's drawing which depicts mainly the enduring or canonical shapes of objects, consists of iconic signs.

The drawing in Figure 2 contains iconic signs for circular shapes of the table surface and the ashtray and the side-on view of the shape of the drinking glass, that is to say each drawing sign signifies the enduring or canonical shape of the objects. However the sign relation is symbolic when we consider the marks that represent the liquid inside the glass and the surface of the liquid in that these marks relate to what might be termed graphic conventions. The refracted line of the table rim as viewed through the glass on the other hand could constitute an indexical sign relation within the drawing, indicating a causal connection. Considered in this way this drawing consists of a series of different semiotic relations as it is produced and functions as a drawing for the child.

Although my analysis of this drawing establishes inter-related semiotic relations it does not indicate how these relations arise and evolve as the drawing unfolds for the child.

If we consider the amazing range of graphic forms which appear in observational drawings made by students as signs which, for the student signify,

Figure 2.

in some respect or capacity, a particular idea or experiential relation with the subject matter, this allows us to avoid reading drawings purely in terms of view representations. The relation between vision and representation will be discussed in greater depth in a later chapter but for now I only want to contrast the idea of visual representation as a mimesis of visual perception with the idea of representation as signification. If the representational efficacy of student's observational drawings is assessed according to how closely the drawing resembles visual experience (which is in fact not the case, as I will show in a later chapter, but which is often thought to be so) then, according to our understanding of visual experience, some drawings are considered effective representations whilst others are not. This was, I believe, the position I adopted in my early years of teaching. However if the representational efficacy of an observational drawing is assessed according to how a student manipulates and orchestrates mark configurations as signs in his or her particular way in order to capture or express information which is not only concerned with views then the notion of a visual correspondence between a drawing and its referent in the world as seen from a particular viewpoint is no longer an adequate criterion of judgement. What we need to do in this case is to find out how the student is using his or her graphic constructions as representational or expressive signs and to consider what kind of sign relations are functioning for the student in the semiotic process of the drawing. This entails a shift of emphasis from an understanding of representational images as reproductive to embracing art practice as a semiotic activity which is productive.

Understanding observational drawings as signs that involve different sign relations, which students form, manipulate and develop according to their own graphic logic presents a more complex practice of representation as signification than seeing this process as a mimesis of vision. It means that we need to put the emphasis upon trying to understand how drawings function for a particular student as semiotic material rather than judging a student's drawing according to a pre-established understanding of visual representation. Difficulties can arise of course if we interpret children's drawings within a particular understanding of representation that is not compatible with the semiotic strategies that are employed by the student. Moore (1999, pp. 88–97) describes an incident in an art lesson which typifies this semiotic 'mis-match'. The incident concerns a class in which there are bi-lingual students. The teacher asks her class to produce a drawing of one of three ornamental figures. They are sitting around a central table on which the figures are placed. The assumption by the teacher is that the students will produce a drawing from their fixed viewpoint. However one boy, Nozrul, leaves his chair to walk about the room in order to examine his chosen figure from a variety of viewpoints. On completing his drawing he takes it to the teacher for approval. Moore describes the drawing:

It is a drawing that is unlike that of any other child in the class: the figure's arms emerge from its jaws, there is a gap between head and hat, its legs have no discernible feet and the decoration on the figure's back (not visible from where Nozrul has been sitting) appears on the front. As such it is reminiscent of drawings of much younger children (p. 88).

Reflecting upon the drawing and its unusual appearance for a student of Nozrul's age Moore deliberates whether the drawing should be understood as deficient in motor-coordination or hand-eye coordination skills or even perception, or as a drawing practice that is rooted within a different cultural tradition of visual signification. As it turns out the drawing is treated by the teacher as inadequate, for her:

. . . the simple line drawing, with its apparent anatomical errors and physical naivety, means only one thing: Nozrul has a 'learning difficulty' (p. 90).

The importance of this incident, as Moore suggests (p. 91), is that the teacher sees the child as having a psychological problem that needs to be corrected rather than in terms of a semiotic difference which, if understood more sympathetically, could be addressed. This has real implications for the construction of the child's ability, his pedagogised identity, as a learner in the eyes of his teacher. Equally it is also significant for the perpetuation of the teacher's pedagogised identity. Moore traces the teacher's explanation for the form of Nozrul's drawing to the narratives of developmental psychology:

It is not difficult to understand the diagnosis made by Mrs Green, or her reasons for making it. It is a diagnosis prompted by a dominant psychological discourse of development, based on universals and patterns of conformity rather than on variability and idiosyncrasy. . . (p. 92).

He is of course referring to the influential developmental discourse of 'stages of development' in which children are described as proceeding through incremental stages of development, in which each stage is characterised by particular graphic structures. In this psychological model development is viewed as a progression from early scribble drawings to the accomplishment of linear perspective, although only a minority will attain this end-point.

Another clash of semiotic practice is described by Taber (1978, 1981) when, as a teacher, she reflects upon different cultural traditions of representation in relation to her Asian students:

One needs to think more carefully about what is taken to be 'realistic' representation of a three-dimensional world. Our standard method of drawing objects from a fixed point of observation (more or less the procedure of photography) produces a picture that totally distorts certain aspects of reality . . . I began to realise that I was judging my students' work by the standards of a procedure that they had not attempted to use. The drawings had an element of truth and power that projective representation cannot achieve as it involves technical problems that mar visual clarity. . . . The projective method is only a 'realistic' style when defined by current 'Western' ideas. (Taber 1981, pp. 61–62)

The importance of this statement for me is that it embraces semiotic difference in art practice as something which is cultural and social. By refusing to view 'odd' or 'mysterious' drawings as indicating cognitive or perceptual or even technical deficiencies, and in the process marginalizing the student's sociocultural experiences and background, this statement foregrounds the life-world of the student and legitimises his or her semiotic activity. This paves the way for a pedagogy of inclusion which, in the domain of art in education, must adopt a more expansive understanding of the semiotics of visual production.

Metonymy and metaphor in drawing practices

Jakobson's (1956) work on the structure of language, in which he distinguishes between metonymy and metaphor, can be used to understand the local formation of semiotic strategies in drawing practices. Essentially we can say that drawing practice consists of an arrangement of marks (signifiers) that are produced in relation to each other on the drawing surface. This constitutes a combinatory relation. In a representational drawing the marks also constitute, for the student, a representational relation with the referent of the drawing. Jakobson termed the combinatory relation *metonymy* and the representational relation *metaphor*. We can consider drawing as an evolutionary process in which students produce marks or graphic forms which they organise and combine on the drawing surface. Drawing thus extends along a metonymic axis and refers to the internal relations or graphic syntax of mark configurations (Atkinson 1987 p. 224; 1993). In the drawings of young children it is possible to observe the early development of metonymic relations in drawing. The work of John Matthews (1994, 1999), which I will be discussing in more depth, shows quite clearly how young children begin to develop a repertoire of marks: horizontal and vertical arcs, radial forms, angular attachments, crucifix forms, and so on, which they combine to form a complex graphic syntax. Such metonymic relations provide the child's drawing practice with order and structure.

Metaphorical relations are those that constitute the semiotic power of a drawing for the child or student. They are concerned with the signifying potential of the drawing for the student. To summarise then, the metonymy of a drawing concerns the syntactical structure whilst the metaphoric dimension is concerned with signification and meaning. In the flow of a drawing practice a dialectical interaction may occur between metonymy and metaphor, between syntax and meaning. Observing both young children and older students in school art rooms it is possible to notice this dialectic. When drawing objects or people for instance, a student finds that her emerging drawing form is unsatisfactory, it fails as an effective representation and so the metaphoric axis of the drawing is fractured. Exclamations such as, "I can't get this right," indicate such moments. Subsequently the metaphoric axis is suppressed in order to work at the graphic syntax, the mark configurations which now fail to function as effective representations. New metonymic relations (a more developed syntax) need to emerge in order for the student to develop, in his or her eyes, a more acceptable signifying form.

Perhaps the task for the teacher is to try to understand how children and older students construct their drawings along the metonymic axis to create a graphic syntax and then how this syntax is employed on the metaphoric axis to create representational significance. And this is where a form of representational 'mis-match', such as that described above by Moore, can occur, because the teacher's response to student's drawings is also structured by metonymic and metaphoric axes. Let me explain. If we are confronted with a student's drawing which we find incomprehensible or strange, as is the case in many drawings produced by very young children, but also by older students, it is probably because we fail to accommodate the drawings within our codes of recognition which are formed according to our understanding of representation. Our incomprehension may arise because we fail to appreciate the syntactical (metonymic) relations of the drawing and thus how they provide the drawing with signifying (metaphoric) power for the student. Our codes of recognition include syntactical (metonymic) and semantic (metaphoric) relations which may not be commensurate with those of the student. For example, if we employ linear perspective as a criterion to assess the representational efficacy of a student's drawing, the syntactical and semantic relations of perspective may be incommensurate with those of the student's drawing which, for the student, form a legitimate representation.

The importance of viewing observational drawing as a semiotic practice, which disrupts a mimetic link between representation and reality, is that we can move away from seeing such drawing as a reproductive activity and understand it as a process of production. Consequently we can try to understand how these drawings as sign relations function for the student in the local ground of his or her drawing practice. The pedagogical consequence therefore is not to assess or judge the variety of student's representational forms according to a dominant or *correct* representational system, but to establish a hermeneutical relation in which the legitimacy and power of the child's or student's drawing as a semiotic activity can be acknowledged and developed. I am not arguing therefore that we simply accept what children and students produce in their drawing practices without question or critical evaluation, it is vital that the pedagogic function attaches importance to such ideas as progression, self-evaluation and refinement but they need to be located within local routes of practice and understanding.

This brings me to the next stage of this chapter, which is to consider the relationship between semiotic practices such as drawing and how we interpret them. I have indicated briefly how we can consider drawing practices as signifying systems, now I want to consider different interpretational frameworks in which drawings can be comprehended. This has already been hinted at in my reference to Moore's description of Nozrul's drawing. In this incident we can see that the child's interpretational process involved in making the drawing was quite different to the teacher's interpretation of the drawing. Here we have a good illustration of contrasting interpretational structures that frame the drawing differently for child and teacher.

HERMENEUTICS AND THE PROBLEM OF INTERPRETATION

My brief discussion of semiotics emphasised the point that meaning is a process of material construction within sign systems such as language or image. We can now move onto a consideration of how semiotic material is interpreted and also how one kind of semiotic material, language, interprets another kind, visual images. This is of great importance in art educational contexts where teachers need to discuss, evaluate and assess their students' visual productions. It is difficult to be fully conscious of the slippage of semiosis in which visual productions, such as paintings, sculptures and drawings, are inevitably conflated with verbal representation. The recognition that there are two distinct semiotic processes at work here, but which are inextricably fused, can be easily obscured in the search for meaning. In this section I will provide a brief description of contrasting hermeneutic strategies, some of which are developed more fully in later chapters, and indicate briefly how drawing practices are conceived differently within them.

Hermeneutics, a Greek word meaning interpretation, was initially a form of enquiry concerned with the study of ancient texts, which sought to unearth original meaning. In the nineteenth century Dilthey (1976) sought to establish hermeneutics as the key methodology for social science enquiry in contrast to scientific method used in natural science. His purpose was to show that through the use of correct interpretational procedures a true or accurate understanding of social and cultural phenomena could be achieved. Throughout the twentieth century, particularly in the work of Heidegger (1962, 1977), Gadamer (1989) Habermas (1972) and Ricoeur (1976, 1981), the emphasis of contemporary hermeneutics shifted from the search for original meaning to an investigation of the conditions of interpretation through which meaning is formed. Contemporary hermeneutic enquiry therefore considers the factors that allow interpretation and meaning to take place and how meaning is made possible. An obvious focus is language. The conditions of interpretation also invoke phenomenological, social and cultural contexts of action and interpretation which introduce issues of race, gender, class, sexuality, age or disability. A central task of contemporary hermeneutics therefore is trying to understand how meaning is formed within such complex social sites and to acknowledge that meaning is always conditioned by media such as language and image within specific social and cultural settings. It is also conditioned and affected by relations of power. The meaning of an art work produced by a student for a teacher who needs to respond to it is dependent upon the socio-cultural life-world contexts in which the art work as semiotic material functions. There may easily be a conflict of interpretations between the meaning of the art work for the student and for the teacher which depends upon the phenomenological and socio-cultural ground of each person. This is made clear in the previous description of Nozrul's drawing practice, where his teacher failed to appreciate the cultural basis of his practice. Here we can see the effect of a particular interpretational stance taken by the teacher and also detect

the way in which relations of power determine the outcome of this particular pedagogical engagement.

A key concern of hermeneutics for teaching and learning is that understanding of the world is created within the specific orientation of the individual
and that socio-cultural processes in turn inform this orientation. All understanding is filtered through previous understanding socially and culturally
formed. As new understanding develops both individual and world are changed.

Phenomenology and hermeneutics

Phenomenological hermeneutics developed by Ricoeur (1981) builds upon
Husserl's work in phenomenology, a form of enquiry where the emphasis is
placed upon how objects (real or imagined) are presented to consciousness,
that is to say phenomenology is not concerned with the meaning of objects-
in-themselves but with the meaning they have for an individual. Phenomenology does not deny the existence of an external material world but it is
concerned with how this world is presented to consciousness. The translator's
introduction to Ricoeur's book *Freedom and Nature: The Voluntary and the
Involuntary* (1966 pp. xiii–xiv) states:

There is no consciousness unless it is consciousness of an object – and conversely, an object
presents itself as an object only for consciousness . . . but imposing the phenomenological brackets
we transform the contents of experience from a physical world of objects into a world of
phenomena, that is objects as meanings presenting themselves to a consciousness.

The material world is therefore not knowable 'in itself' but in terms of conscious experience. This infers that in processes of understanding the very
idea of the existence of material objects already presupposes a prior process
of classification. A further implication therefore is that the idea of objectivity has to be seen as a socio-cultural construct. My ability to distinguish
shapes, colours and objects, for example, is culturally and socially conditioned.
Phenomenology is therefore concerned with how the world is experienced in
consciousness and given meaning by individuals. Coupled with hermeneutics it attempts to locate how meaning is formed by individuals in their relations
of being-in-the-world, it attempts to explore how these relations of being are
given representational form. If we relate these ideas to art practice then in
attempting to grasp the phenomenology of a child's art practice we are trying
to understand something of the child's conscious experiences of art practice
and how these are given form in the art work. Phenomenology provides an
ontological grounding for practice and interpretational strategy that is
consistent with Pierce's idea of the ground of semiosis. However it could be
argued that phenomenology fails to take sufficient account of social and cultural
factors that construct conscious experience and the ground of practice, or
even to acknowledge the idea, to be discussed in Chapter 9, of the denial of
any direct access to conscious experience because of the necessary involvement of mediating processes such as language or image.

Hermeneutic circle

The linguistic framing of our experience arises as a consequence of acting in the world and being able to employ a series of linguistic categories in which we are able to categorise and thereby understand our actions and other phenomena in the world. We approach and act in the world according to a series of assumptions about it, we act 'as-if'. A particular framing process functions effectively, for example, until its specific forms of categorisation no longer appear to agree with the outcomes of our actions, until they meet resistances in action. The outcome of such resistances is likely to be a re-ordering of our linguistic framing in which ourselves and the world which we suppose are changed. Such framing is therefore a dynamic temporal process. Similarly a visual framing of experience in the form of a drawing, painting or 3D construction, arises as a consequence of acting in the world and being able to employ a series of visual signs with which we can frame and so express our actions and other phenomena in time. A particular visual framing process functions until it no longer suffices to express or signify our experiences. This suggests a continuous process of negotiation between experience and a form of linguistic or visual (semiotic) framing in which we represent and comprehend experience. In hermeneutics the term *hermeneutic circle* attempts to describe the dynamical interaction between experience of the world and the linguistic (or visual) framing of our comprehension of experience. In other words this circle refers to the confirmation of experience through the interpretations which we construct in respect of it.

This theoretical device indicates that the formation of meaning is dependent upon assimilated meaning structures that are historically and socio-culturally located and according to which experience is framed and can thereby be understood. There are echoes of this device in Piaget's triad: accommodation, assimilation and equilibration (see Piaget 1950, pp. 1–50). The key idea here is that the frameworks through which we understand and act in the world in the very process of framing constitute a temporal closure. Ricoeur (1981, pp. 145–164) describes the hermeneutic circle as consisting of a circular movement between explanation and understanding. By understanding the world through the process of categorising it, I can make constructions in language which explain it, but such explanations are never permanent, they are always contingent and temporal. Thus future experiences in the world I suppose may meet resistance; I may find my explanations no longer make sense, something mysterious arises. This gives rise to new forms of understanding and a modified series of explanations, which in turn affect the way I act in the world.

Caputo (1987), after Gadamer, describes the nature of hermeneutic enquiry:

We stand already (implicitly) in a sphere which we are not (explicitly) cognizant. And it is the task of thinking to take stock of that implicit sphere which is to be understood no longer as an implicit horizon but as that of which the horizon is itself a certain construction or closing off (p. 101).

The task of hermeneutic enquiry therefore is to attempt to make perspicuous those framings of the world which constitute the-world-as-presupposed and thus to be able to understand our actions in respect of it. In a variety of modes, which I shall describe shortly, contemporary hermeneutics attempts to explore such framings in order to view their closure effects and thus provide the possibility of proceeding to explore new frameworks for understanding, which of course inevitably produce new closures. Gallagher (pp. 100–110 and 156) gives a diagrammatic formulation for the hermeneutic circle that according to him consists of a sequence of inter-relations between tradition, interpreter and object. The object of interpretation (a drawing) becomes a meaningful object through its location in the traditions of knowledge that we inherit and which form our understanding. Thus we explain the drawing through such traditions until they no longer seem to provide adequate explanations. This hermeneutic process indicates that our identities as interpreters, our subjectivities, are not fixed entities but contingent upon the forming and re-forming in time of interpretational discourses.

The interpretational relation between interpreter and object may subsequently affect prior knowledge structures and cause a readjustment or it may simply confirm prior structures of understanding. The prefix of the word 'recognition' illustrates this circular process; in order to recognise something, someone or some idea we require prior frameworks of comprehension or experience. Difficulties of interpretation arise when we are confronted with events or things that we do not understand and that appear mysterious. We treat such situations in a variety of ways: by finding ways to assimilate them within existing forms of understanding, by admitting defeat, by consigning them to a category of non-sense, or explaining them as a 'one-off'. Alternatively we may be encouraged to extend our frameworks of understanding in order to accommodate what was initially incomprehensible and establish new meaning. How this arises in practice is a complex process and rather difficult to describe. This can occur if the mystery which confronts us creates a disturbance large enough to cause us to reflect critically upon our assimilated forms of understanding, to evaluate what Caputo describes above as 'our implicit horizons', which we can then modify. Perhaps if we think for a moment about children's art work and the hermeneutic frameworks in which we interpret their paintings and drawings and about our experience of what happens when we are confronted by work that we find difficult to comprehend. What are the traditions of comprehension relating to visual representation, for example, in which we form our understanding and how do such traditions affect and inform our interpretations? I shall elaborate on these questions when I discuss children's and student's drawing practices.

The action of teaching can also be considered in terms of hermeneutic structures. A personal illustration of specific hermeneutic relations operating in a particular practice of my teaching comes to mind. I remember teaching a lesson in which students were making small paintings of the landscape surrounding the school. A student asked me to show her how to 'create a sense of distance' in the sky. We talked about the problem and then I proceeded to

demonstrate a simple wash technique on a scrap of paper. Other students
were interested and so I demonstrated the technique to them. Of course when
I put their work on display at the end of the lesson I saw twenty-five paintings that looked more or less the same! The shock of realising what I had
done remained for some time and it made me think critically about my teaching
method and about how I could operate in a way that did not lead to students
producing the same work. This disturbance affected me I believe in retrospect because I saw little benefit in students producing similar paintings.
They were individuals and should therefore be encouraged to respond
accordingly, to give a personal response, not one guided and over-influenced
by me their teacher.

To summarise then, hermeneutics is concerned with exposing and exploring
socio-cultural frameworks and forces that effect and give shape to the
formation of meaning and understanding in the various contexts in which
we act and comprehend. Linguistic practice is the chief focus of hermeneutic
enquiry because it is through such practice that meaning is formed and sus-
tained within different social contexts. But in education we can extend the
focus of hermeneutics to consider the circularity of pedagogic actions as well
as pedagogic discourses. Whilst early hermeneutic strategies sought to discover
the original or the intended meaning of texts, contemporary forms of
hermeneutic enquiry promoted by Gadamer and Ricoeur seek to show that
interpretation is always a production of meaning mediated through language
which is informed by socio-historical processes.

HERMENEUTIC STRATEGIES

In *Hermeneutics and Education*, Gallagher (pp. 9–11) presents four hermeneutical frameworks, *conservative hermeneutics*, *moderate hermeneutics*, *radical
hermeneutics* and *critical hermeneutics*, which are then applied to the field
of education. Each framework is illustrated through the theoretical writings
of major figures in their respective fields of enquiry. I will take my lead
from Gallagher's hermeneutic frameworks but I will replace them with what
I term hermeneutic strategies and extrapolate these strategies to the context
of art in education. My purpose here is to present a brief reading of different
approaches to hermeneutic enquiry and to see how these might offer a productive engagement with art in education. Some of the more radical approaches
taken by Foucault and Derrida, which I term post-structural hermeneutics,
would not be considered as belonging to the field of hermeneutics but I believe
that their analysis of linguistic practices and the social construction of meaning
although different does have affinity with the hermeneutic approaches of
Gadamer, Ricoeur and Habermas. Although I distinguish different hermeneutic
strategies in order to describe their particular concerns, the issues that they
confront, such as meaning, power and subjectivity, are always interwoven in
contexts of social practice.

Hermeneutics of reproduction

The idea of hermeneutics as a process of reproduction stems from the work of Dilthey (1976) during the nineteenth century, he sought to establish hermeneutics as the methodology for the human sciences. Briefly, armed with the correct methodology the interpreter is able to transcend their historical situation in order to reach the intentions of an author or artist. According to Dilthey this is the central aim of interpretation so that by attaining the intended meaning of a work it can be disseminated through time and context. In many ways this hermeneutical approach can be described as being concerned with cultural reproduction. Gallagher (pp. 213–220) cites the work of E.D. Hirsch (1987) in the USA as a keen proponent of this hermeneutic strategy. In the context of art history the series of television programmes entitled, *Civilization*, produced by the BBC and written by Kenneth Clarke, is a clear illustration of this interpretational strategy at work whereby specific meanings and values are attributed to key works of art in the west. The title of this series also had the unfortunate effect of associating western art with the idea of civilisation and, by implication, non-western art as outside or other. Gombrich's book (1984) *The Story of Art*, might be associated with this hermeneutic strategy, in his description the developmental of Western art, though his teleological sequence does not quite correspond to the idea of reproduction.

More recently the writings of Cunliffe (1999, p. 118) and Pascall (1992) advocate teaching and learning strategies that seem to fit this hermeneutic strategy. Cunliffe advocates a form of cultural relativism which does not reject learning about traditions of art practice in other cultures but feels that:

For students from Western Europe, there are learning advantages in selecting contexts from the European tradition, because such works and styles are embedded in our form of life, making the cycle of learning much easier in that the cognitive maps can relate more readily to the surrounding cultural territory (p. 118).

Cunliffe states further that in other cultures such as Japan students should study their indigenous art and its more direct influence from Chinese or other Asian cultures. This approach to teaching and learning in art education thus presupposes a rather essentialist notion of culture and tradition as steady-state systems which we might wish to question, particularly in relation to the plural socio-cultural constitution of social contexts today. Pascall, writing in 1992 about the content of the National Curriculum for Art in England, argues that although we live in a multicultural society, "this does not mean that we live in a society which has no dominant culture (p. 5)." He suggests therefore that it is important, "to construct a curriculum which is designed to transmit that heritage to the young whilst also providing opportunities to experience the rich cultural diversity of Britain today (p. 6)."

In the field of critical studies in art education this hermeneutic strategy can be seen clearly in that approach which draws upon an artistic canon, that is to say, upon particular works of art and particular artists deemed to be of great value. In such work particular values and meanings are widely accepted as being immanent and enduring, a residue of artistic intention and genius. It is the task of the art educator therefore to instruct students in these enduring values and their artistic worth. It will be not be surprising to mention that up until very few years ago in England this canon still consisted of the Impressionists and Post-Impressionists (particularly Monet and Van Gogh), a smattering of Renaissance art, Cubism, Surrealism and Pop Art. Art from other cultures or art produced by women until recent years was given little acknowledgement or status. Richard Wollheim (1987) also advocates a strategy of reproduction when interpreting paintings in his book, *Painting as an Art*, he writes:

To the experience, to the experience hard won of the painting, I then recruited the findings of psychology, and in particular the hypotheses of psychoanalysis, in order to grasp the intention of the artist as the picture revealed it (p. 8).

The source of meaning in a painting is therefore the artists intentions, the painting is a trace of such intentions and the experience which prompted them. It is the spectator's task to make a close and careful reading in order to extract the meaning of the painting put there by the artist. In her analysis of Wollheim's views on artistic intention and meaning, Pollock (1995) states:

What is seen when looking at a painting is, then, the trace which takes us back to that definable and cogent subjectivity for which the painting's visual form is only a sign (p. 39).

This hermeneutic strategy thus perpetuates a particular kind of interpreting subject who is able to discover the intentions of the artistic subject, irrespective of social and historical positioning, and this is due to an idea of universal human nature which is expressed by the artist in the art work. Related to the ideas of the artistic trace and reproduction when interpreting art work is the concept of *self-expression* which is still used by many within art in education as a justification for art practice. Central to this concept is the idea of intentionality, the idea that the self is expressed through the art process and in the artefact.

The idea of reproduction also underpins what Bryson in, *Vision and Painting: The Logic of the Gaze* (1983, pp. 10–12), terms the *natural attitude* to representation. This attitude holds that the practice of representational painting or drawing involves a direct unmediated feedback loop between object and the perceiving body, so that with the necessary technical skill the contents of perception, can be reproduced on the drawing or painting surface. This relies on the idea that information of objects contained in rays of light from the exterior world passes through the retinal membrane and is interpreted directly 'as it is'. Practices of observational drawing and painting that take place in many schools are frequently assessed and evaluated according to this natural attitude to representation. This hermeneutic strategy thus presupposes the idea of a transcendent and autonomous individual as well as the idea of knowledge as separate and universal, which can be transmitted through the neutral media of language or image. Any error in transmission is put down to errors of perception, cognition or technical ability.

In teaching contexts art practice is understood inevitably according to established traditions. For example, if we consider practices such as painting, drawing, printmaking and ceramics, specific skills and understandings are taught in such as way as to confirm valued traditions of practice, as manifested in the work of celebrated artists, which are taken to be essential for student's to acquire. The important point about this hermeneutical relation to practice and understanding is that in valuing particular traditions of practice it attempts to reproduce them and thus perpetuate a particular cultural hegemony towards practice and understanding in art education. The difficulty for pedagogy within this hermeneutic strategy is how to embrace new or more contemporary forms of practice and ways of understanding practice. The development of contemporary art practice provides an ongoing challenge to established traditions in which the artist, practice and the art work are all conceived within a different epistemological paradigm. Similarly contemporary critical theory presents a radical challenge to the interpretation of art works based upon reproducing the artist's intentions and the idea that meaning is contained in the art work. This book provides a critical engagement with educational practices and pedagogy that are grounded within this hermeneutic strategy.

Hermeneutics of dialogue and tradition

In contrast to the idea of reproduction of tradition through valuing a particular heritage of works and practices, Gadamer (1989) advocates an ongoing dialogue with tradition in which both interpreter and tradition are changed. He denies any transcendent or superior interpretational position because interpretation is always *prejudiced* by our history, which is embedded in language and the conversation with tradition that we are. According to Gadamer, in the process of interpretation we enter a "dialogical conversation," a "fusion of horizons, a creative communication between reader and text" (Gallagher 1992, p. 9). We never achieve a state of complete interpretation, which is the aim of a hermeneutics of reproduction, because we are constrained by our historical and linguistic contexts. In contrast to the idea of cultural reproduction, Gadamer's hermeneutics implies a creative dimension to interpretation whereby the individual participates in the production of meaning according to his or her historical situation. The relevance of this hermeneutical strategy for art in education is that although the idea of tradition persists there is always a possibility for creative expansion, for tradition to be reinterpreted in order to establish new horizons, new possibilities for and understanding of practice. In order to avoid essentialist overtones tradition is viewed as fluid and 'in process' and the practice of interpretation changes both the one who interprets and the tradition in which interpretation occurs. Individuals are therefore positioned within particular traditions of practice and understanding with which they are able to form a creative dialogue. Thus the idea of tradition is dynamic and dialectical. In this hermeneutical relation when students interpret the work of artists they do not retrieve the artist's original meaning or intention but they are involved in the production of new meaning, which emerges from their historical, social and cultural positioning in relation to the work. Similarly in the realm of art practice, students do not reproduce valued and accepted skills and techniques, rather they are engaged in a creative dialogue and extension of such skills and techniques within their local making contexts. Implicit to this hermeneutic strategy therefore is the notion of a socialised and historicized individual and the idea of knowledge as a process of production, (not reproduction) within local socio-cultural contexts. This strategy also advocates the idea that interpretations of past events or historical objects such as artefacts can only be constructions in the present. If we return to Pollock's critical review of Wollheim's reproductive approach to interpreting paintings and take on board the idea of a creative dialogue, we can appreciate the point that the act of looking at a painting is not a neutral or ahistorical process but one in which the spectator is socially and culturally located. The act of interpretation is therefore not concerned with revealing a prior trace of intention deposited in the painting by the artist but with how the painting is read by the spectator within his or her specific socio-cultural location which will be formed by factors relating, for example, to gender, race, class and sexuality.

Phenomenological hermeneutics: narrative and textuality

Ricoeur's detailed studies of textual interpretation and narrative form an important contribution to hermeneutics. Their particular emphasis is to provide the practice of interpretation with an ontological/phenomenological grounding. In his early work on interpretation theory Ricoeur showed that an author's intention and the meaning of a text cease to coincide and that therefore the author's original meaning cannot be used as the criterion for interpretation. In *Interpretation Theory* (1976), Ricoeur writes:

With written discourse . . . the author's intention and the meaning of the text cease to coincide . . . Inscription becomes synonymous with the semantic autonomy of the text which results from the disconnection of the mental intention of the author from the verbal meaning of the text, of what the author meant and what the text means. The text's career escapes the finite horizon lived by its author. What the text means now matters more than what the author meant when he wrote it (pp. 29–30).

The reading of a text by another constitutes a reconfiguration of meaning in the life-world of the reader. This leads to the possibility of an endless dialectic between configuration and reconfiguration, to the idea of a polysemy of texts and a rejection of absolute meaning. The idea of polysemy has important implications for the interpretation of children's and student's art practices and also for teaching critical studies in art education.

The concept of *appropriation* is used by Ricoeur (1981, pp. 182–193) to elaborate his point that interpretation is not concerned with revealing the original meaning of a text placed there by the author, but, on the contrary with the reader's production of meaning within the intersection of the text and the life-world of the reader. Ricoeur argues (1981, pp. 190–193) that appropriation is not concerned therefore with a) *psychologism*, that is to say, the recovery of the author's intended meaning; b) *historicism*, that is to say, the attempt to coincide with the original audience and to identify with them; or c) *subjectivism*, that is to say, the assimilation of the text into the present capacities for understanding of the reader. Appropriation is not concerned with a recovery and taking possession of meaning but with a process of meaning production. Valdez (1991) writes:

The final act of appropriation is less the projection of the reader's prejudices into the text than the fusion of horizons that occurs when the world of the text and the world of the reader merge into each other (p. 38).

What we must be careful to bear in mind is that Ricoeur does not anticipate a unified self in this fusion of horizons but a self that is produced in narratives and discourse. Interpretation is therefore a grounded experience where the text is open to the dialectic of appropriation, which consists of the ontological positioning of the reader to the world of the text; there is therefore no absolute and definitive interpretation.

In order to refute psychologism therefore Ricoeur, drawing on Gadamer, views interpretation as a fusion of horizons that results in new semantic production. We have to remember here that the fusion does not refer to the fusion of two minds but a fusion of discourses that form the narratives of self and text. Historicism is rejected because of the point that a text is open to anyone who at any time can interpret and form a meaning. Subjectivism is rejected because an encounter with a text involves a refiguration and a production of new meaning, no matter how minute.

I shall say that appropriation is the process by which the revelation of new modes of being – or, if you prefer Wittgenstein to Heidegger, new 'forms of life' – gives the subject new capacities for knowing himself (herself). If the reference of the text is the projection of a world, then it is not, in the first instance, the reader who projects himself (herself). The reader is rather broadened in his (her) capacity to project himself by receiving a new mode of being (form of life) from the text itself (1981, p. 192, my brackets).

Ricoeur's work indicates the importance of thinking carefully about how we interpret the art work of children and students, as well as how we interpret the work of artists with children and students. If we can view visual productions as texts then the idea of appropriation raises some difficult issues about the meaning of an art work for each child or student who produces it and the meaning it has for a teacher who needs to interpret. The difficulties are made more complex when we acknowledge that the visual production of an art work is a different semiotic material to a verbal interpretation of it either by the maker or the 'reader'.

We tend to think of art practice as involving a movement from life experiences (e.g. perception or imagination) into the art work, for example when we ask students to make observational drawings or to make paintings of their choice. However when we are concerned with interpreting art practice, hermeneutics (apart from reproductive strategies), and post-structural theory abandon the search for an artist's intended meaning and place emphasis upon the interpreter's configuration of the 'text,' and the polysemy of the 'text.' We are therefore involved with a narrative production of the student's identity as a learner and a primary aim of post-structural hermeneutics is, according to Ricoeur, to "recover the narrative identity that constitutes us" (p. 436 in Valdez).

Hermeneutics of emancipation

The work of Habermas (1972, 1984, 1987), who is associated with the later developments of the Frankfurt school of social and cultural theory, is concerned with developing enquiry that searches out ideological distortions of linguistic practice created, for example, by political forces, for the specific purpose of developing emancipated forms of communication. He is often viewed as extending the Enlightenment project for social emancipation through the development of rational subjects. There is an implicit teleology to his project, which aims to do away with those social and cultural structures and discourses that proliferate bias in respect of culture, class, race, gender, age or disability. Habermas is therefore concerned with exposing extra-linguistic forces such as power relations and hegemonies within which positions of dominance and dominated perpetuate specific forms of injustice, victimisation or discrimination. If we consider art in education we might want to reflect upon the kinds of practices that are valued and the ways in which they are assessed as involving specific power relations that establish forms of discrimination. For example, do the practices of teaching and assessment that we initiate produce ways of learning that are gendered or culturally and racially biased? Habermas's project therefore concerns developing a state of emancipated communication and practice through critical enquiry. His project is often contrasted to Gadamer's project of conversation in that the latter rejects the idea of an emancipated and ideology-free form of communication. For Gadamer even critical enquiry itself is rooted within ideological frameworks and therefore all that we can hope to achieve are negotiated states of agreement that are implied by a fusion of horizons. Thus whereas Habermas's project can be considered teleological, Gadamer's project is rooted much more in the 'here and now' of negotiated action and comprehension. If we transpose the different projects of Habermas and Gadamer onto the field of educational practice we could argue that a Habermasian critique would involve exposing ideological frameworks and hegemonic relations in which teachers and students are constructed, whereas a Gadamerian critique would work towards forming negotiated agreements between teacher and students in order for both to develop and extend their comprehensions of practices of teaching and learning.

Earlier in relation to critical studies in art education, I mentioned Wollheim's reproductive interpretational strategies which involved the spectator being able to uncover the artist's intentions in the art work. According to Pollock this is made possible by the assumption of a universal idea of human nature that can be encoded in the image by the artist and deciphered by the spectator. However Pollock argues against this universal assumption and puts forward a reading strategy in which the production of art and its interpretation needs to be "radically historicized". Thus art work has to be read "under the mark of difference, not fictions of sameness, (p. 29)" in the form of an appeal to a universal human nature, which she believes is a pretext for domination and exclusion. Pollock is using the notion of difference to refer to the articulation of different viewing positions which, for example, involve gender, race or class. She writes forcefully:

The issue is a matter of politics. Wollheim indulges in fantasies of a universal human nature, an ideology of sameness which is only possible because of an uncritical acceptance of the authority of masculinity, whiteness and Europeaness when the most urgent struggles of our time involve throwing off their burden. Under the imperialising claims which Western notions of humanity have cloaked, the humanity of many of the world's peoples, genders and religions have been denied with varying degrees of violence. Race, gender and class are the theoretical terms by which the very basis of Wollheim's and Western Art History's assurances are being challenged worldwide. The question now is who is looking at what, at whom with what effects in terms of power (p. 40).

Pollock is attempting to establish a politics of looking and how social and cultural positionings determine or affect this process. She is eager to deconstruct the hegemony of Wolheim's reproductive hermeneutics in order to take into account different viewing positions, in other words to consider the historical and social contexts of looking and to provide these with a sense of legitimacy. This also involves a form of looking at art works in which notions of absence become important, for example, in relation to gender or race. When black students visit the National Gallery in London how do they read the representation of black people (or lack of representation) in European paintings? Pollock's project is close to Habermas in that she is concerned with the emancipation of looking from the hegemony of particular Western traditions of interpretation. But she is also close to the work of Foucault, which I will discuss shortly and in Chapter 5, and his analysis of power and subjectivity.

Pollock's critique of interpretation in Habermasian terms has important implications for critical studies in art education. For example, who decides which artists and art works should be studied and how they should be studied? How are students taught to look at paintings? Is a particular interpretation of art work privileged? Does this looking reinforce a particular way of interpreting art work? Does this looking reinforce particular stereotypical attitudes to ability in art practice? When teaching students in school how much attention do we give to thinking with them about how they are constructed ideologically as viewers by art works and other visual productions? Such questions raise the

issue of a politics of looking and suggest a critical engagement in the
Habermasian sense of exposing ideological factors which play a strong part
in forming students as critical subjects.

Gadamer, Habermas and Ricoeur:
A summary of implications for art in education

What do the above outlines and discussion of hermeneutic strategies imply
for an interrogation of knowledge and practice in art in education? Gadamer's
position is rooted in the idea of an ongoing dialogue with tradition which is
'reinterpreted and reinvented in terms of its implications in the here and now
(Ricouer 1981, p. 82)'. For him all experience is linguistic that is to say it is
mediated by forms of language. Even scientific discourses are subject to
hermeneutic processes because they are dependent upon human discussions
and perspectives for their implementation and interpretation. Equally any
discussion about art practice has to take place in language, any assessment
of art practice in schools is a linguistic practice. For Gadamer it is important to expose, through dialogue, those prejudices or forms of pre-understanding
that operate in traditions in order to renegotiate and reconstitute them. Seen
in terms of this hermeneutic of tradition and dialogue, art in education would
appear to be a process of continual renegotiation with traditions of art practice
and understanding within current socio-cultural contexts. Questions arise therefore in relation to the nature of such traditions and their relevance to an
increasingly plural social context. How can we renegotiate, reinvent or establish a dialogue with traditions of practice within a social context in which
so many different cultures and their traditions exist, coalesce and at times
clash?

For Habermas the key issue would be to interrogate particular traditions
of practice and understanding in order to move towards a state of emancipation from their ideological effects. He seems to be offering a meta-
hermeneutical position from which to expose ideological interests and forces
that are embedded within institutions and their discourses, such as education. Thus for Habermas institutional language is infected with processes of
domination and power which distort communicative action in such contexts
and it is the task of a critical hermeneutics to expose this 'systematically
distorted communication' in order to move towards a more emancipated state
of communicative practice. Taking up Habermas's critical position in relation
to art in education we might wish to ask questions about the approach to
pedagogy that is promoted by a particular art curriculum or about the nature
of assessment practices in order to reveal their ideological or political underpinnings.

There seems to be an implication in the critical attitude of Habermas of
the ability of linguistic signifiers to identify already constituted signifieds, that
is to say those distorting influences. Gadamer on the other hand would remain
within the signifier, that is to say, he would argue that there is no way in which

we can escape language and so, for him, Habermas's distortions are always constituted by language and that any attempt at revelation would itself also involve ideological distortion. Ricoeur seems to position himself somewhere between these two positions. His description of the hermeneutic circle which relates a continual shifting between explanation and understanding suggests a dynamical process in which the world is always a world-as-conceived-in-language, (close to Gadamer's notion of tradition) by the individual, but that it is a world which can be (for a time) objectified in explanation (Habermas's critical position).

In relation to learning it would seem that for Gadamer learning is a creative enterprise involving processes of self-reflexion through hermeneutic processes in which both individual and world-as-conceived evolve in time through a dialogic relation with traditions of practice. Understanding is not a process which develops in the mind according to pre-linguistic structures of logic as intimated by Piagetian learning theory (see Gruber and Voneche 1977, p. 507; Brown 2001, p. 51), it is a process which is formed within social practices of language or other signifying forms such as visual signifiers in which meaning is negotiated. For Habermas the process of learning is more of a transformative process relating to emancipatory practices which enable the individual to free herself from ideological and political forces such as class, gender and race.

Both Gadamer and Habermas, in their respective hermeneutic positions present some questions about the relationship of current to future educational practice. It seems that Gadamer's concern with an ongoing dialogue with tradition is rooted within a past-present time frame oriented towards a future, whereas Habermas's critical practice is being determined from a future state of emancipation. If we consider educational practices as providing students with those forms of knowledge and practice evolved within socio-cultural contexts then we can see how Gadamer's dialogue within tradition leading to renegotiated practices and Habermas's critique of tradition leading towards a more emancipatory state might be applied. Both approaches seem to presume either a world we know and renegotiate or an idealised world for which we can aim. However if we think about education as also preparing students for a world we will never know because the rate of environmental and social change is so rapid then both positions present difficulties for educational practices. How can we conceive art in education in a context of rapid socio-cultural changes which problematises any notion of tradition and, alternatively, how can we be sure that any critical stance towards such a world is not rooted in a way of thinking which is incommensurable with an emerging world? The theoretical position of post-structuralism may offer a framework within which we might be able to find some way of theorising this dilemma.

POST-STRUCTURAL HERMENEUTICS

One way of differentiating between the hermeneutics of Gadamer, Habermas and Ricoeur and the work of Derrida and Foucault is that whilst the former authors suggest in different ways some idea of location, either in tradition, a state of emancipation or a notion of a more appropriate interpretation, and also a notional idea of reality behind language but always mediated by language, the latter authors focus their attention on language itself as the place where meaning and reality are produced. In post-structural theory therefore it is not possible to access any essence of tradition or to achieve a state of ideological emancipation because these are always ongoing constructions in discourse whose ontological underpinnings cannot be accessed.

Surveillance, regulation and power

Foucault's seminal work on power and discourse provides the opportunity to consider the art curriculum as a particular *discursive practice*, a construction of practice in which students (and teachers) are positioned and regulated. This will be discussed in detail in Chapter 5. Along with Bourdieu's (1992, 1993) and Bourdieu and Passeron's (1977), investigation of relations of power and legitimacy in cultural and social processes, Foucault's work allows us to consider how specific curriculum discourses and practices lead to a normalisation of practice whereby particular forms of practice and representation are valued and legitimised whilst others are viewed as defective or pathologised. Bourdieu, constructing a discourse upon economic metaphors, argues that accepted and valued forms of practice and knowledge can be considered as *cultural capital* which, when acquired, constitutes *symbolic capital* allowing access to restricted social fields such as higher education. Practical manifestations of power, cultural and symbolic capital in the context of art in education can be seen in the perpetuation of those art practices which are valued through tradition and in assessment of student's work. The valuing of particular skills, techniques and forms of representation over others establishes a form of cultural capital for which students should aim and in gaining them through examination success they acquire symbolic capital which allows access to higher education. Those students who are not able to acquire cultural capital, in the form of valued practice, are therefore denied access to symbolic capital. We can see here the operation of power that informs and regulates both teachers and students in their practice and understanding. It is within such regulatory process and the valuing of particular forms of art practice that both teachers and students acquire and develop what I call *pedagogised identities*, that is to say, their specific identities as teachers and learners. Such identities are formed according to processes of normalisation and regulation that are perpetuated in practices of teaching and learning. For now it will suffice to mention that relations of power and cultural capital can be exposed in art education when we consider the fact that accepted and valued systems of representation and practice are brought to bear upon student's work in the form of assessment criteria. The consequence is that some student's work, according to the criteria, is valued whilst the work of other students is not. The assessment criteria create a regulatory discourse in which students are made visible as particular kinds of learners.

The value of this particular hermeneutic strategy is to reveal the contingent character of such criteria, to show that they are not inviolable but that they are cultural constructions that establish a particular conception of practice and ability. Here the idea of ability seen as natural talent is rejected and viewed instead as contingent upon social and historical traditions of value and practice. When the cultural and historical contingency of practice and ability is exposed we open up the possibility to accommodate other conceptions and forms of practice. The purpose of this hermeneutic strategy therefore is to lay bare conceptions of practice and their respective discourses, which exert particular hegemonic forces and power relations, in order to promote a more inclusive understanding of practice. Implied here is a need for constant vigilance of the effects of power and regulation in education. In this hermeneutic strategy the individual is not seen as a natural entity but is viewed as a product of particular discourses and practices in which he or she is constructed as a subject. Here we are concerned with how one is *written* as a particular kind of subject and how one is *allowed to write oneself* as a subject within the discourses and practices of art in education. Knowledge is viewed as power in that the acquisition of particular forms of knowledge and practice equip individuals with cultural and symbolic capital. If we are able to examine how students and teachers are formed within the knowledges and practices of art in education it may be possible to consider how such knowledges and practices construct subjectivities not only in relation to ability but also in relation to class, race and gender.

The natural attitude to representation previously discussed can be contrasted with frameworks of interpretation that foreground the historical and sociocultural shaping of interpretation and understanding. For instance, we can consider visual perception as a cultural process formed within particular technologies and processes of vision that inform and construct the observer's perceptual experience of the world. Visual perception is comprehended therefore as a historical and material practice as opposed to a purely natural process. In a recent edition of *Omnibus* (BBC 11.6.2000) David Hockney discusses the use of the camera lucida, suggesting how this optical device appeared to enable a more natural or accurate depiction of the human portrait. In his book, *Hidden Knowledge* (2002), he also shows how artists relied upon lenses and other optical devices to create what appears to be the depiction of natural perception but which in fact is a highly constructed form of visuality. His central argument, echoed by Crary (1996) in, *Techniques of the Observer*, is that such representations of visual experience are optical productions made possible by specific technologies which organise a particular kind of vision and which in turn produce particular kinds of observers.

Here the idea of "a self-present beholder to whom a world is transparently evident" (Crary, p. 6) is rejected and replaced by the idea of an observer and a world which are both constructed within specific material practices and technologies of vision.

Dissemination, deconstruction and differance

Jacques Derrida (1976, 1987) provides an even more radical approach to language and meaning in his work where he argues that it is not possible to attain original meanings, intentions, essences or states of presence. This is because any attempt to do this is mediated by representation, that is to say forms of language, and such mediation always defers any attempt to attain origins. There is therefore no final interpretation because we can always make further interpretations and this is possible because of the endless play of linguistic signifiers. This idea of endless deferral is suggested in his neologism *differance*, which is a combination of the verbs, to differ and to defer. According to Saussure, meaning is possible not because of the signifier's direct relation to a referent but because of the difference between linguistic signifiers which can be combined in the process of signification to form meaning. Derrida drew on this idea but also combined it with the idea of deferral, that is to say, with the idea that meaning is never final. The implications of these ideas are radical for art in education if we apply them to those practices in which we interpret the art work of students and children and make statements about their ability. Lacan, whose work I will discuss in Chapter 6, also places emphasis upon the signifier, arguing that the signifier is more potent and stable than the thing to which it refers. The holding form of the signifier affects the way in which we respond to that which is signified. Our imaginary identifications (signifier) of particular students and their practice inform our responses to them (signified).

Derrida is also well known in post-structural theory for his term *deconstruction*. A key concern of deconstruction is to examine the conceptual classifications and categorisations through which understanding is formed and to unearth their contingent and metaphysical qualities. For example, the dualistic categories that we use frequently to describe or theorise experience: masculine-feminine, objective-subjective, right-wrong, able-disabled, inside-outside, culture-nature, rational-irrational, are interrogated (deconstructed) in order show that what we take to be quite natural categorisations are in fact cultural constructions, in which the first term in each paring often achieves dominance. Such dualisms constitute the production of a particular metaphysical framework that shapes our comprehension. The relevance of this hermeneutical strategy for art in education is that it can be employed to deconstruct the conceptual structure within which our understanding of art practice is formed. The importance of this deconstructive move is that it provides an opportunity to challenge traditional values and practices that are 'taken for granted' or regarded as 'fundamental' or 'natural' and thus consider the legitimacy of alternative practices. In Chapter 9 I will describe how Derrida's deconstruction of the idea of 'presence', which underlies our everyday use of terms such as 'experience' or 'perception', provides the opportunity to deconstruct naturalistic, psychological or biological discourses of ability in art practice in order to expose their non-essentialism and con-structed character.

Summary

The post-structural hermeneutic strategies I have described will be devel-oped in more detail in subsequent chapters as they relate to various aspects of understanding identity and practice in art in education. These will offer contrasting epistemological and ontological frameworks of understanding and practice but all follow the post-structural precept that linguistic framing and categorisation bring phenomena into existence. This precept has major impli-cations for understanding educational phenomena such as practices of teaching and learning in that it suggests that these are socio-linguistic constructs and not natural entities or processes.

In general Gadamer, Habermas, Ricoeur, Derrida, Foucault and Bourdieu all challenge in different ways ideas of cultural reproduction, cultural bias and the retrieval of original meaning and intention that are central to a hermeneutics of reproduction. In many ways this challenge can be equated with the challenge I shall make in relation to art in education where I believe ideas of representation, practice, ability, cultural bias and value persist within a reproductive model which underpins some aspects of practice and the art curriculum in England. Indeed it might be argued that educational processes in general are by and large conservative and slow to change.

Whilst Gadamer's hermeneutics of a dialogue with tradition and Ricoeur's phenomenological hermeneutics might suggest that some interpretations are more appropriate than others, Derrida dismisses any phenomenological or ontological link. Habermas is eager to unearth institutional hegemonies and power relations with a view towards emancipated states of communication and practice. But again Derrida and other post-structuralists focus upon more deceptive and cunning aspects of communication that is the metaphysical framework in which all understanding is framed and from which it is impos-sible to escape. Foucault's work on discourse, surveillance and power locates the constitution and framing of the human subject within cultural and histor-ical discourses so that, as Walkerdine (1984, 1990) has argued, the meaning of concepts such as *the child*, *development* and *the teacher*, do not refer to natural entities or processes but that they are constructions within specific discourses that appear natural. They are *fictions-functioning-in-truth*, (Walkerdine and Blackman 2001, p. 103). Such discourses establish ideas of normalisation according to which particular behaviours and ways of under-standing are expected and regulated. For art in education an important task is to consider where and how such processes of normalisation affect the production and regulation of both teachers and students to the extent that conformity ossifies teaching and ignores the diversity of student responses.

Hermeneutics therefore provides a variety of theoretical tools and interpretational strategies that we can employ to interrogate the epistemological grounds of understanding and practice in the field of art in education. It allows us, for example, to consider why we understand visual representation in the way we do and why we adopt a particular approach to assessing and evaluating children's and student's art practices. It also allows us to interrogate why we teach art in the way we do and thus to expose, for example, the cultural basis of art practice and understanding. In doing this hermeneutics exposes the limitations and constraints of our understanding and invites the possibility of expanded frameworks of comprehension and meaning. By interrogating those linguistic and visual practices in which understanding is framed our enquiry can proceed on different levels: we may be concerned with examining curriculum content and policy for art in education in order to expose its ideological underpinnings; we may be interested to understand teachers' attitudes towards representation or assessing students' abilities; or we may be curious to understand the representational strategies and content of children's or student's art work, which at times can be quite mysterious. In the next Chapter I will apply semiotic and hermeneutic strategies to students observational drawing practices in order to consider how their identities may be shaped by the way in which these practices are interpreted.

SEMIOTICS, HERMENEUTICS AND OBSERVATIONAL DRAWINGS

If we acknowledge that responding to students' and children's drawings is a process of interpretation then we are, I would suggest, acknowledging that this process is constituted within hermeneutic relations. It is how these relations are constituted that is so important for the pedagogical outcome. When I began teaching in secondary schools I often used collections of objects as a starting point for a drawing activity. During the lesson I would try to *correct* those drawings that appeared to deviate too much from the family of projection systems known in the West as perspectival projection, assuming, wrongly, that this should be the form of representation which students should aim for and try to achieve. If I came across a drawing which appeared strange or incomprehensible one my responses I remember vividly was to insist that the student 'looked more carefully', thereby assuming that this was not happening. Another tactic I adopted for explaining drawings that I read as weak or mysterious representations was to believe that the student *lacked* drawing ability. In those days my pedagogical approach took little account of what kind of information a student might be attempting to encode in his or her drawing form and the semiotic logic he or she employed. I was in fact guilty of ignoring the possibility that a student's drawing form was legitimate for its semiotic purpose. It seems then that in the context of teaching art I saw drawing as an activity concerned with developing accurate perception accompanied by competent hand-eye coordination to achieve a good representational image. Underpinning this conception of drawing practice are attendant ideas of the autonomous individual and the idea of universal vision. For as long as the eye received the necessary perceptual information and could translate this perception through technical competence into a drawing there should be no problem, and if there were problems they were the result of poor perception or lack of technical skill.

My approach to student's drawings was predetermined by a particular representational expectation, that of linear perspective, which determined or influenced my judgement. This powerful representational technique was placed like a template upon student's drawings in order to evaluate the representational efficacy of a drawing. Historically perspective has occupied a privileged position in relation to representing views of the world, many people in the West still take it to be an 'accurate' representation of how we see objects in the world from a fixed viewpoint. The outcome of applying perspective as the main criterion for judging student's drawing practices is of course that those who are proficient in this drawing system are regarded as able drawers whilst those who do not are seen as lacking in drawing ability. My hermeneutical relation to student's drawings constituted therefore a form of cultural reproduction. That is to say I was interpreting my student's drawings through a particular representational tradition that I expected them to reproduce. I must make the point that my early teaching practice may or may not have been typical of that of other teachers at the time, I can only recount that from conversations with other teachers about assessment my views and practices were not uncommon.

It took some time for me to realise that not being able to employ perspectival projection in an observational drawing does not necessarily equate with a lack in drawing ability or faulty perception. Drawings produced by children and older students often manifest what appears to be a complex amalgam of drawing systems (Dubery and Willats 1972), which we can separate out into orthographic projection, oblique projection or naïve perspective, for example. Such drawings can appear as muddled or confused if we expect to see a perspectival drawing. But if we try to consider a drawing from the student's position of interest and try to understand what semiotic information he or she is attempting to encode, we may begin to realise that the use of different drawing systems or mark configurations within a drawing may allude to fluctuating interests and the encoding of different kinds or qualities of information which are quite different from view-specific information. Thus a drawing from observation may not be concerned only with representing objects from a specific viewpoint, but other kinds of information may be included.

If we examine Figure 3, a drawing produced by a year nine student (13–14 years) in secondary school in the UK, this drawing seems to indicate a variety

Figure 3.

of interpretational interests. The way in which the glass is depicted through the use of a naïve perspectival drawing system may indicate an interest in representing a view of its three-dimensional form in space. When we consider the depiction of the plate however on which the glass is placed and also the table mat on which the plate stands a different drawing system, orthographic projection, is employed which may indicate a different semiotic interest, perhaps a desire to signify the enduring or canonical shapes of these objects. When we consider the depiction of occlusion in the drawing there are some interesting semiotic strategies. The glass containing dark liquid occludes the rear portion of the plate and the edge of the table through an implied horizontal plane. However, there are also 'on-top-of' relations which are depicted – the crisps layered on the plate, the plate on top of the table mat – which involve occlusion through an implied vertical plane. The fusion of different semiotic interests facilitated through the use of different drawing systems and mark configurations give this drawing a fascinating spatial semiotics.

In general terms the drawing could be said to manifest a mixture of viewer-centred and object-centred representational interests (Atkinson 1993; Matthews 1999). These interests seem to demand different syntactic rules for their respective semantic structures. The syntax of a drawing can be said to constitute the graphic elements and the rules by which the drawing is constructed for the student. It is the metonymic logic by which the lines and marks constitute the drawing and relate to each other. The difficulty with such an analysis of the drawing is that it fragments and abstracts what in effect is an organic and evolutionary process that unfolds as the drawing practice proceeds through time. Such evolution can be seen as an holistic and dynamical semiotic sequence, a process of semiosis, which involves a layering of different experiential interests which, in turn, demand an orchestration of different drawing repertoires (Atkinson 1993; Wolf and Perry 1988).

If we only employ perspective, for example, as a criterion to assess the efficacy of this representational drawing we may overlook different perceptual and cognitive experiences and semiotic interests that led to its production. But there is also a further difficulty with the deeper analysis I have provided. Teasing out the use of different drawing systems, oblique projection, orthographic projection, and so on, may be helpful for making more effective responses to student's drawing practices, but in the duration of the drawing practice the mark configurations which form the drawing systems we abstract may constitute responses to different experiential interests in the objects *as well as* to the unfolding syntactical (metonymic) structure of the drawing (Atkinson 1993). In other words, the student's own drawing practice may constitute a developing semiotic language, a process of semiosis that is functioning reflexively on both semantic and syntactic levels. Put more simply a drawing practice may consist of two dialogues, one which involves the student functioning reflexively upon the quality and potential of his or her mark making, and another which involves functioning reflexively upon the efficacy of the drawing as a signification in relation to its referent, imagined or real.

The drawing practice can thus be understood as a complex dialectic between forming and responding to graphic structures as well as responding to the drawing as a representational sign. This dialectic is manifested in the inter-relation of the metonymic and metaphoric dimensions of drawing practice which I have discussed earlier. The student's response to what is infolding on the drawing surface as the drawing proceeds may thus be important to the development of future drawing strategies. This does not necessarily depend entirely upon a prior conceptual or perceptual assimilation, but also upon the contemporaneous nature of the drawing practice in which a relation with the unfolding drawing intersects with a relation with the subject of the drawing. The student's development of different representational repertoires can thus be seen partly as a consequence of a response to evolving forms as they emerge on the drawing surface and not simply as a response to a developing percep-tual and cognitive awareness of the world. Described in this way drawing practices become complex hermeneutic processes in which the student fuses different semiotic concerns and layers of meaning that are held by the graphic signifiers.

The difficulty for any art teacher is to try to interpret the student's graphic configurations in order to comprehend the semiotics of the drawing and thus its representational/signifying purpose for the student. Put another way the teacher's hermeneutic task is to try to understand the drawing from the ground of the student's practice. Lowenfeld and Brittain (1970) state,

There is no subject matter in art, only different ways of portraying the artist's relationship to object, people, feelings and emotions about the world around him (her) p. 36. (My emphasis and addition.)

This relationship will operate on many levels of experience that will be manifested in innumerable semiotic strategies for signification and meaning and it will also, as suggested, involve a relationship with the unfolding graphic structure of the drawing. The need for the teacher to 'come alongside' the representational semiotics of a student's or child's drawing in order to under-stand their significance for the student or child is not an easy task and it is one in which, as a teacher, I failed frequently.

When faced with the task of assessing student's drawings from observa-tion do we assess the drawing and thus the student's drawing ability by comparing the drawing to a particular view of the subject matter? Or do we assess the efficacy of an observational drawing and student's ability by guaging the drawing to a particular representational system which is used as a yard-stick? Or, do we attempt to enquire into the student's experiential relation with the subject of a drawing and consider how this relation is articulated by the student through the semiotics of the drawing? The latter seems to me a more effective approach and it demands a different hermeneutical strategy than the one I occupied in my early years of teaching. A different hermeneutic approach would place the emphasis upon interpreting the student's visual semiotic strategies, it places emphasis upon the *experiencing other* who engages in a dialectical process of drawing as described above and which constitutes his or her drawing practice. Such a hermeneutical relation with the student's drawing practice changes the way in which what the student produces is accepted as meaningful and legitimate by the teacher. If we return to the hermeneutic strategies I have already described perhaps we can see this approach to interpreting student's drawings as commensurate with a hermeneutics of Gadamer in which the individual is engaged in a dialogue with traditions of practice. This strategy suggests a 'fusion of horizons', an attempt by the teacher to seek out how the drawing functions as a representational sign for the student. In contrast to the notion of cultural reproduction where the purpose of drawing practice would be to acquire and repeat the skills and techniques of valued traditions of practice, this hermeneutic framework is concerned with production, with the evolution of a creative dialogue within tradition according to the historical place-time of the student.

The limitations and problems of using a particular drawing system, such as perspective, to evaluate and assess the representational efficacy of a drawing and, by implication, the ability of a student are hinted at by Habermas (1972),

The problem of the universal and particular is that singular experiences have to be brought into agreement with abstract general categories. For hermeneutic understanding the problem is reversed. It grasps individual life experience in its entire breadth but has to adapt a set of intentions centred around an individual ego to the general categories of language. Here the problem of the relation of the universal and particular does not arise owing to the inability of a concrete world of experience to meet the logic of general statements but rather because of the inadequacy of this logic to life experience (p. 162).

Students' and childrens' drawing practices are located within different experiential interests on different semantic and syntactic levels, and the struggle for the teacher is to gain some understanding of how the semiotics of the drawing form function in relation to the student's or child's experience. This is not easy in that teachers will tend to approach these individual productions through the established categories of art practice which they have assimilated and with which they will read the student's practice. Here we can perhaps see the power of the signifying abstract category which *writes* the student's drawing practice for the teacher.

Consider another drawing in Figure 4 made by a girl aged 11 years. It is a drawing of objects on a round table. If we consider the image of the glass we can see that she has drawn an elliptical form for the base, which could indicate an interest in the three-dimensional form of the glass. However there is no attempt to produce an ellipse to signify the mouth of the glass, rather she describes the contour of the glass from a side on position as well as the contents of the glass. She is also interested in depicting the glass occluding part of the table edge as seen from her viewpoint. Further, she also signifies her experience of refraction as the line of the table rim passes through the glass filled with liquid. The table top is presented in its canonical form, a circular form and not an ellipse, which indicates that she is not interested in depicting a view of the table from her position (although she has done this with the

Figure 4.

base of the glass). Similarly the ashtray is depicted entirely by a plan elevation which indicates that she does not wish to present a view of the object from
her viewing position, but that she is interested in its enduring shapes, the
inner and outer contours of the ash tray rim and the parallel grooves for cig-
arettes. The girl's treatment of the book is also interesting; she seems concerned
to capture information about the flat rectangular shape of the book but also
to describe its three-dimensional 'thickness'. Here she is using what Willats
(1997, pp. 49–52) identifies as a vertical-oblique drawing system. Read in
this way the hermeneutics of the girl's drawing practice thus includes a complex
semiotic arrangement that requires a compatible hermeneutic sensitivity by the
interpreter.

Students of all ages sometimes produce observational drawings that appear
strange or mysterious, and it is tempting to dismiss such work as defective,
weak or confused, particularly if we occupy a hermeneutical relation in which
Bryson's description of the natural attitude to representation dominates. And
even if we occupy a hermeneutical relation which foregrounds the child's or
students' idiosyncratic semiotic arrangements the mystery may still remain.
Consider the drawing in Figure 5 made by a student aged 14 years.

It is taken from the same set of drawings as the drawing in Figure 3 dis-

Figure 5.

cussed earlier. Whilst I may be receptive to the general outline form of the glass, the use of an elliptical form to represent the mouth of the glass and the dark areas to signify the liquid inside the glass, the semiotics of the separation of the dark areas representing the liquid and the two parallel undulating lines between them are difficult to interpret. What do they signify for the student? I might guess that the student is struggling to describe the transparent quality of the glass and the phenomenon of refraction. Thus some of the semiotics of the drawing forms – the contour of the glass and the ellipse – fit within my understanding but others do not. I can discuss the drawing with the student and this may reveal the significance for the student of the parts of the drawing that I find incomprehensible, but sometimes even this approach proves unsuccessful. Furthermore, and this is too big an issue to tackle here, the articulation of the meaning of an art work in words does not duplicate the art work but it creates a different text.

It is important to acknowledge that what I may perceive as a mysterious, or even defective or confused drawing is **not** inherent to the drawing. The mystery or sense of confusion is the consequence of my informing ground, my hermeneutical relation with the drawing, as I attempt to understand it. The constraints of time make it difficult for teachers who work with between twenty and thirty students in an hour to make close readings of their drawing practices. But a semiotic approach does seem to offer the opportunity to embrace the high variety and often-ingenious representational semiotics which children and students develop in their drawing practices. The drawings presented in Figures 6–8 illustrate the variety of representational semiotics existing within one class of twenty-five students. The teacher asked them to make a

Figure 6.

Figure 7.

drawing of a group of objects placed on a table and to concentrate upon the relative positions of objects, their shapes and surface details. As I watched the group at work and considered their finished drawings I was struck by the different ways in which each student found different graphic strategies for presenting the objects and their spatial relations. The drawing in Figure 6 is concerned with depicting the entire arrangement, with the depth of objects in space and their relative positions on the table as seen from the student's viewpoint. The description of tone across the drawing, of elliptical forms to represent the mouths of the two vases, of occlusion and oblique angles (particularly in the presentation of the paintbrush) all suggest this concern. The

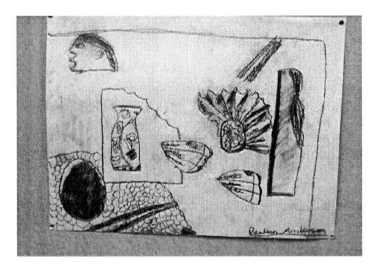

Figure 8.

drawing of the table indicates that the student is interested in describing the depth of the table as seen from his viewpoint. In order to do this however the student employs what might be termed inverted perspective, which might be considered as a representational error if we choose to use perspectival projection as a criterion of judgement. On the other hand we might speculate that the use of inverted lines to represent the side of the table that run away from the student is a consequence of sitting close to the table surface, so that the edges appear to diverge rather than converge.

The drawing in Figure 7 zooms in to describe the arrangement of five objects as viewed from the student's drawing position. When we consider the depiction of objects in this drawing the major drawing system is orthographic projection except for the elliptical presentation of the mouths of the vase; but even these can be interpreted as employing a vertical-oblique drawing system which is essentially orthographic (see Willats 1997). The use of this drawing system depicts the objects in space rather like a series of stage-flats that partially occlude each other. In comparison with the drawing in Figure 6 this drawing does not employ oblique lines to connote the depth of objects in space.

My immediate response to the drawing in Figure 8 was one of incomprehension. I recognised the outline shapes of various objects but I was puzzled by the semiotics of the overall composition. If this drawing was interpreted through the discourse of linear perspective then it could well be considered as a poor representation. However, if we consider the drawing from another interpretational relation we can detect that the student is attempting to depict objects in space according to their local relations, (consider the combination of orthographic projection and occlusion particularly in the bottom left quarter), as well as attempting to depict objects in space in the overall arrangement of objects on the table. There is no evidence of the representation of the depth of each object in space but there appears to be a desire to signify the co-ordinate arrangement of objects, to fix their location on the table surface. In other words this drawing is rather like a map that conveys the co-ordinate positions of each object on the table. Understood in this way this drawing presents a very different representational semiotics of objects and their spatial arrangement to the previous two drawings.

The hermeneutical strategies we adopt when responding to student's observational drawing practices are crucial if we are to provide effective pedagogical support. The complexity of this task cannot be underestimated because with each child or student we could be faced with a series of different semiotic strategies for visual representation which are meaningful and legitimate for the student. The value of adopting a Gadamerian hermeneutical strategy to understanding the semiotics of student's drawing practices is that it recognises that there is no essential truth, in this case to visual representation, against which the drawing can be assessed and that therefore each student's drawing practice can be seen as an ongoing dialogue between traditions of practice and each student's context of experience and practice. Each student has the potential to develop representational strategies and their respective semiotic relations that, for her, are legitimate and meaningful.

Other hermeneutic strategies discussed in the previous chapter would raise other issues relating to the practice of observational drawing. For example critical hermeneutics might wish to question the value of such practices in relation to their determination of drawing ability. A Foucaultian analysis might wish to trace the historical emergence of such practices, how they came about and how subjects of practice were formed and regulated by them. Such questioning would also involve asking why these art practices are perceived as important fpr students to engage with at the beginning of the twenty first century. A Derridean critique would problematise the relation between the drawing as signifier and the idea of an accurate or truthful representation since no such representational form is possible in the sense of representing perceptual experience as-it-was. Consequently this raises some difficult issues for the practice of assessment of such art practices because it illustrates the contingent nature of assessment and value. The Derridean critique also problematises the relation between image and language, so that in educational contexts where art practices and productions have to be evaluated and assessed in language, the discursive signifier, the linguistic categories we employ to discuss visual practice supersede the visual. In the next chapter I will continue to explore drawing practices of young children in order to describe them as semiotic constructions.

CHAPTER THREE

THE SEMIOTICS OF CHILDREN'S DRAWING PRACTICES

The analysis of student's observational drawings in the previous chapter explored a number of semiotic strategies that students may employ when making drawings from observation. I introduced the ideas of syntax and meaning in relation to the terms metonymy and metaphor in order to consider how each drawing might function as a legitimate semiotic production for the student rather than reading or assessing a drawing as a view-centred production which demanded the use of a particular representational system such as linear perspective. In this chapter I want to consider drawings produced by much younger children in order to show that even in very early drawings we can detect the emergence of a graphic syntax, a local semiotics, that the child develops to produce representational images. There is a wealth of study on the development of children's drawing practices (see for example: Goodnow 1977; Luquet 1927; Lowenfeld and Brittain 1970; Piaget and Inhelder 1956; Cox 1998) and ample reviews of this literature already exist (see for example: Thomas and Silk 1990) which is easily accessed. I do not intend to provide a detailed analysis or review of this work but I shall refer to the research and publications of John Matthews (1994, 1999) who I believe has made considerable headway in helping us to understand the complexity and sophistication of children's early drawing as visual semiotic practice.

In many studies of young children's drawings (see for example Lowenfeld and Brittain 1970) there is a tendency to view their early mark-making as random and meaningless. Such drawings are often referred to as *scribble* drawings, an interesting word with pejorative undertones. In terms of the development of visual representation, scribble drawings are viewed as the first stage along a hierarchical route that leads to the development of recognisable visual forms. The end point of this route is usually taken to be the ability to employ the drawing system we know in the West as linear perspective. It has to be said immediately that such ideas on development are underpinned by a representational paradigm which is eurocentric, and that in other cultures children use different graphic forms for symbolic and representational purposes. Cox (1992) argues that children need to be given training in particular representational techniques like perspective drawing so that they can acquire drawing skills to produce 'realistic' pictures, in a similar sense to them acquiring correct grammar and spelling in their learning of Standard English. This argument assumes a particular understanding of the purpose of visual representation, which is to produce drawings in which the three-dimensional forms of objects seen from a particular viewpoint are depicted and easily recognised in the two-dimensional forms of the drawing; and the most effective way of achieving this is through the use of linear perspective. In many

ways this representational system is given the status of being able to represent visual perception, in other words it appears to depict optical truth.
Development in visual representation therefore consists of a developmental
continuum from the random chaos of scribble to the order and authority of
projection systems such as perspective.

However in a body of research spanning over twenty years Matthews proves
quite conclusively that scribble drawings are not random or chaotic but
organised and meaningful. In his book, *The Art of Childhood and Adolescence*,
he describes the origins of what I have termed visual syntax and syntactical
relations and how these function for the child to encode both conceptual and
expressive concerns. Matthews describes three *generational structures* of marks
(pp. 19–27) which children produce and by combining these simple marks they
begin to explore objects people and events within the phenomenology of
their experience:

> Some early paintings and drawings are not pictures of things, but they are representations in a
> fuller sense, in that they record the child's process of attention to objects and events. Far from
> being meaningless, the early paintings and drawings are products of a complex or family of
> representational and expressive modes (pp. 20–21).

Matthews shows with abundant evidence of hundreds of drawings and paintings that very young children are capable of employing the simple syntax of
the three generational structures for complex representational purposes. For
example, by using a series of 'push-pull' and 'horizontal arcs' (first generation) a child of two years represents an aeroplane as an object; and then in a
series of elliptical rotations an aeroplane in flight (see p. 34). Each drawing
has therefore a different semiotic purpose, the first to represent the configuration of an object, the second to represent a dynamic movement. Second
generation structures include continuous rotations, moving points and demar-
cated line endings (pp. 25–27). Third generation structures include core and
radial forms, the use of parallel lines, right-angular structures and U shapes
on baselines (pp. 27–28).

Throughout this book Matthews provides a highly detailed study of how
children devise and explore simple syntactical structures and semiotic relations
in their early mark-making and drawing to represent all kinds of experiences
including; objects, people, movement of objects, time sequences, narratives,
action sequences, sound and play. In other words Matthews is describing the
beginning of semiotic activity and early processes of semiosis in young
children's drawing practices. The drawing of objects from a fixed viewpoint,
the major criterion framing many studies of the development of representation,
is not of central concern to young children as they draw.

In my own studies (Atkinson 1991) of young children's paintings and
drawings a similar picture emerges in relation to syntax and representation.
Simply scanning their drawings for recognisable features may fail to appreciate the different ways in which drawings function as representations. Consider
the drawing in Figure 9, made by a 6 year old boy, Captain America, the

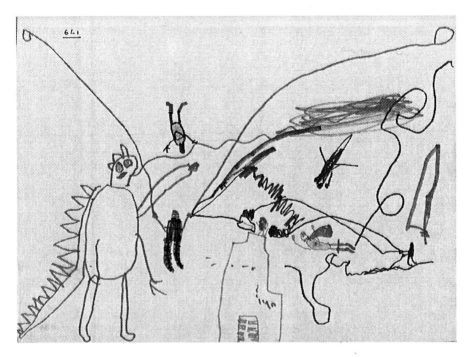

Figure 9.

horizontal flying figure right of centre, is placed at the end of a spiralling line, deliberately constructed to represent his acrobatic flight path. Spiderman, the vertical figure left of centre and to the immediate right of the monster figure, is depicted with lines projecting from both hands to the left and right top corners of the drawing surface where the lines form a loop. These lines signify Spiderman's anchor ropes and the loops signify the anchor points that allow him to escape the monster's clutches. They also signify the 'firing' of these ropes and their 'anchoring' around their respective anchor points. The lines emerging from the small figure, bottom right, depict a missile or laser trajectory and their end-points suggest explosive impacts. Similarly the line from the monster's mouth ends in a series of elliptical rotations suggesting that the lines represent explosion and fire. Thus these linear forms are employed by the child to represent the actions of flight, laser-fire, flame trajectories and rope trajectories, in other word they can be read as both time and action representations. But when we inspect the child's depiction of the various figures in the drawing we find that similar lines are used for quite different representational (semiotic) purposes. Captain America's outstretched arms are depicted by a single line with a circular blob on the end. The line is used to depict the linear extension of an arm in space. However, both legs are depicted by a line that depicts the contour of each limb, as are the legs of the monster. These lines depict therefore both the volume and extension of each limb. In other words, according to Willats (1997) these lines have different denotational values which represent different formal aspects of solids in space.

A further analysis of this drawing as a visual narrative suggests that whilst making the drawing the child is able to occupy different narrative positions as the drawing develops. He is able to relate these positions to each other whilst simultaneously orchestrating the entire sequence of actions. So as well as employing a simple syntactical structure for a variety of representational (semiotic) purposes concerned with action sequences, time sequences, and different object depictions, the child orchestrates a complex narrative plot. This plot constitutes the temporality of the semiosis of the drawing and the semiosis of the drawing constitutes its temporality. When interpreted in this way perhaps we can begin to appreciate the complexity of this drawing practice and how it is functioning for the child on different syntactic (metonymic) and semantic (metaphoric) levels as a representational practice. Put another way the child orchestrates a sophisticated semiotic web that constitutes a complex hermeneutic practice; a hermeneutics of time, space and object relations.

In Figure 10 a simple syntactical structure constitutes the form of diving figures but here the emphasis again is upon narrative. The figures depict the 'same' diver running out of air and as a consequence he heads downward towards a certain death. This drawing also raises issues relating to the production of temporality in the narrative function of the drawing and thus how the drawing as narrative produces a particular structure of time. Notice that the sequencing of action is mapped along a right-to-left horizontal axis.

The drawings in Figures 11 and 12 were produced within the time frame of a few weeks by a child aged 9 years. They contain quite different representational strategies to depict the child's different interests in soccer. In Figure 11 a carefully composed time and action sequence is articulated as the child plots the series of passes made by the figures leading up to a goal. The representational schema used to depict each player is quite minimal, consisting mainly of what we might refer to as 'match-stick' figures. A series of single looping lines depict the flight path of the ball as it moves from player to player.

Figure 10.

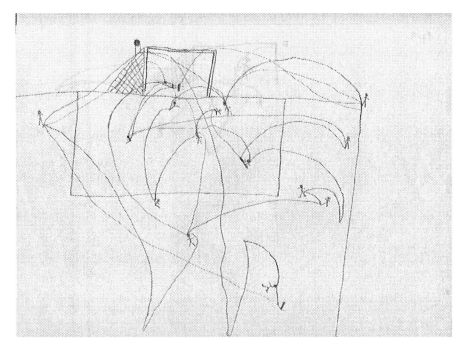

Figure 11.

The drawing involves a series of what might be termed narrative positions, which are coordinated by the child as the game is played out in the drawing practice. Thus the drawing is functioning for the child on different semantic levels concerned with the representation of the participants of the game, the time and action sequences of the game and the overall coordination of the game narrative. In relation to temporality this drawing as a narrative produces a complex temporal structure that is difficult for an observer to comprehend.

The next drawing in Figure 12 made by the same boy only a week or two after the former drawing reveals quite different representational (semiotic) concerns and their appropriate signifying strategies as well as a different temporal structure. The syntactical structure and relations of this drawing are quite different. A goal is about to be scored but now the emphasis seems to be upon the footballers themselves and the detail of football regalia. Players are depicted from front, rear and side views. Foreshortening and occlusion occur in the depiction of the boots worn by 'Pele' and the right upper leg of the player at the bottom right is also occluded. Occlusion is also to be found as the goalkeeper, the ball and the right goal post obscure parts of the goal net. The treatment of the depth of the goalmouth is interesting in that the child is employing a horizontal-oblique drawing system (see Willats 1997). The interesting point about the relation of these two drawings is the nearness in time in which they were produced. The child can employ quite sophisticated figure schemata, as in Figure 12, but can also select much simpler schemata,

Figure 12.

as in Figure 11, when this is desired. Each drawing constitutes a different football narrative in which different plots that produce different temporal structures structure each drawing. Again if we consider the two drawings in relation to metonymy and metaphor, each drawing has a different metonymic chain of signifiers as they constitute the drawing on this level of signification, and each metonymic chain establishes a different metaphorical production. This metonymic-metaphoric difference involves contrasting constructions and coordination of temporality by the child.

LANGUAGE GAMES, DRAWING GAMES

Wittgenstein's (1953, p. 43) aphorism, 'The meaning of a word is its use in the language,' has relevance for me when I consider the child's facility for employing different graphic schemata for their respective semiotic purposes. From the common currency of language we are able in our local contexts of action to generate local discourses and meaning. Wittgenstein gave us the notion of 'language games' to remind us that when we use language we do so from within different 'forms of life', and so for him a language game is a form of life. Difficulties relating to ambiguity and misunderstanding are always possible when people from different contexts of experience use the 'same' terms. Perhaps we can apply these ideas from Wittgenstein to children's drawing practices so that we could argue that the meaning of a mark or mark configuration, is its use in the drawing. Further, we might argue that a drawing viewed in analogical terms as a visual discourse represents a particular 'form of life'. This allows us to consider a child's eclectic use of drawing practices as the production of different drawing discourses which accord with the child's changing and developing interests and experiences. Although the child may employ similar syntactical structures in drawings, the semantic dimensions may be quite different according to how the drawing functions as a semiotic production for the child.

The next series of drawings of trees were produced by a small group of children age 6 years (see Atkinson 1995, 1998a, 1998b). They were working in the school playground with their teacher who asked them to look at the trees. A brief discussion followed in which the children were asked to consider the structural aspects of the trees. For example, they talked about how the trunk supported the main boughs and how these in turn supported the smaller branches to which the leaves were attached, and so on. Then the children were invited to choose one tree and make a drawing that would describe its structure. I have selected five drawings to consider. The drawings in Figures 13–17 all exhibit idiosyncratic features but they all seem to fit into a proto-typical semiotic format to which I could respond. I am able to relate to them iconically as tree drawings perhaps because for me they describe an essen-

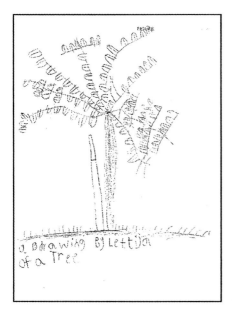

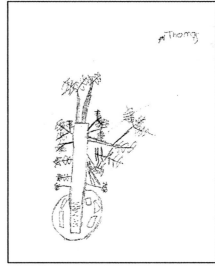

Figure 13.   Figure 14.

tial gestalt, an assimilated structural form. This might suggest that their exists
a metonymic link between my own symbolic coding of tree representations
and the formal properties of these drawings.

The graphic syntax of these drawings used to represent structural aspects
of trees can be elaborated through Matthews's generational structures. For
example, in Figure 13 if we consider the depiction of leaves, the child has
employed the use of what Matthews (1999, p. 27) terms an upturned U shape
on a baseline, a third generation structure. The main boughs are represented
by a series of single lines which radiate out from a central core placed at
the very top of the trunk, and the grass by a series of parallel lines.

The drawing in Figure 14 foregrounds a different graphic syntax, the use
of right angular attachments to depict the projection of the boughs from the
trunk. The child decides to represent the trunk by depicting its contour shape
and describes the circle of soil from which it emerges in its canonical form,
but notice the use of occlusion as the circle passes behind the trunk.

In Figure 15 the drawing seems to be foregrounding the solidity of the trunk
and boughs by employing the drawing tool to describe mass and area. The
drawing in Figure 16 employs a similar graphic syntax to the drawing in
Figure 13, boughs radiating from a central core which is placed at the top of
the trunk. When I was confronted with the drawing in Figure 17 I was quite
puzzled because this drawing is so different from those already discussed. I
struggled to make sense of this drawing as a tree representation. Although
we can recognise the syntactical elements such as upturned U shapes, single
lines and contour lines, the meaning of the drawing as a representation of

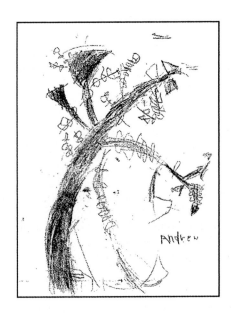

Figure 15.   Figure 16.

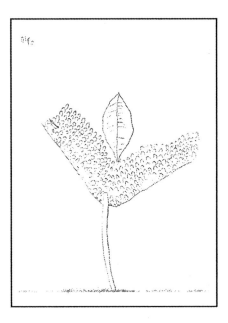

Figure 17.

tree structure is difficult to conceive. I spoke to the boy who made the drawing but he was quite shy and said little. I am still unsure as to how this drawing functioned for the child as a semiotic production. One interpretation could be to argue that he was not 'looking carefully' and therefore to view it as a weak representation but then this assumes, of course, that this drawing is the result of an attempt to depict a particular view. I am not convinced by such interpretations. If we return to the two inter-connected notions of metonymy and metaphor previously discussed, another interpretation is possible. I have already spoken of the metonymy of the graphic syntax of a drawing; the way in which the child employs different graphic structures to constitute the internal logic of a drawing. The important point to consider about this drawing is its metaphoric axis. The child is attempting to represent the structure of a tree, and whilst the other drawings attempt to depict tree structure from a more view-centred orientation, it is possible to argue that this drawing does not. Yet if we look at it carefully it is a drawing about tree structure. If the drawing is read as presenting a different kind of metaphor for structure, which is not view specific, then its representational significance for the child begins to emerge. The central contour shape can be interpreted as a representation of the tree trunk. The two lines which appear to depict the main boughs can be understood as arm-like projections which hold and support the lines of leaves. The large leaf form hovering emblematically over the serried ranks of leaves signifies the structure of each leaf. Thus as a representation of tree structure it is possible to argue that this drawing constitutes a different metaphorical axis to those drawings already described. It is a drawing which is the outcome of the child's experience of and positioning within a specific discourse and visualisation of tree structure. Could it be that the significant difference of the visual structure of this drawing from the others is a consequence of the children positioning themselves differently within the teacher's discourse?

DRAWINGS FROM AUSTRALIA

A few years ago I watched a television documentary (BBC 1996) entitled, *Windows of the Mind*, made by Rosemary Hill. The film is a brief study of the development of young children's drawing practices and it contrasts the drawings made by children in the west with drawings made by children of the Warlpiri people at Yuendumu, Australia (see also Cox 1997). Because the Warlpiri people have embraced or are familiar with western visual (representational) codes as well as their indigenous symbolic visual codes, the Warlpiri children have developed the versatility to function in two quite different semiotic registers in order to produce representational pictures.

In their drawings these children are able to produce representations of objects and people which are similar to the representational schemata used by children in the west. Such schemata for representing a car, a house, a chair and so on, are constructed by using orthographic, vertical oblique and oblique drawings systems. In the same drawings however these children also include representations of people and objects by using the semiotics of traditional symbols from their indigenous culture. For example, the aboriginal symbol for a person is a U-shaped region, and when one girl is asked to make a picture of herself she draws herself sitting on a chair. The chair is depicted by an oblique projection but she depicts herself by a U shaped region on the seat of the chair. Matthews (1999, p. 156) argues that both western schemata and indigenous Australian symbols are constructed by a similar graphic syntax, for example the use of zigzag lines and enclosed shapes. This may indicate that the syntactical structure is a universal. The interesting issue for me is not to argue that these children's drawings indicate cultural variation in drawing development but that by employing different syntactical relations corresponding to two distinct semiotic codes in the same drawing practice two very different metonymic and metaphoric graphic logics are integrated to constitute the child's semiotic production. In a crude analogy it is rather like someone alternating between the syntax of two languages to produce an integrated grammar. Many of the Warlpiri children's drawings described in the film consist of visual narratives, something which is also common in western children's drawings. In relation to the fusion of western and indigenous Australian visual codes in the Warlpiri drawings it is interesting to consider how this fusion constructs the temporality of the drawing for the child. Do these drawings combine western and Australian aboriginal conceptions of time and space which are quite different? If so do these drawings combine different ontological orientations that relate to contrasting cultural categorisations of experience?

CHILDREN DRAWING OBJECTS

From 1994–97 I conducted a small piece of research in an Infants school in England that involved a group of twenty-four children working in groups of four to make drawings of an arrangement of objects on a table. The same children were asked to draw the same arrangement of objects once each year for three years. The arrangement, illustrated in Figure 18, consisted of a large transparent glass containing fruit juice and a drinking straw, the glass rested on the centre of a large circular plate on which were also a bread roll and a couple of rectangular shortbread biscuits. The plate sat on a large square table napkin underneath which lay a larger cotton towel. I have already discussed observational drawings made by secondary school students in order to explore their representational strategies what I wanted to do in this research was to find out what kind of representational interests and respective semiotic strategies young children would develop when faced with a similar drawing activity.

The arrangement was placed in the centre of a square table around which four children were seated. Each year I began by asking them to tell me what the objects were and what they could see from their viewing positions. From the very beginning, when the children were aged 5 years, they were generally quite vocal and were able to tell me in some detail the relative positions and shapes of each object as they saw them from their viewpoint. After our conversations I asked them to make a drawing of the objects. The outcomes of these drawings are interesting to consider not only in relation to the different semiotic strategies each child uses, but also in relation to the changing semiotic strategies each child employs over the three yearly drawings. If we are to interpret the drawings as representations of views then most drawings could be easily categorised as poor representations. Equally, if the semiotic strategies are assessed according to projective drawing systems such as oblique or perspectival projection then most drawings may be interpreted as weak or at least not very advanced. I have selected the drawings produced by five children over the three years in order to consider their semiotic strategies. I will take each child in turn and describe the drawings they produced over

Figure 18.

the three year period in order to compare the variety of semiotic interests and respective semiotic productions.

The drawing in Figure 19 made by Katie (5 years) seems totally disconnected with the arrangement of objects that she was observing. It consists of a series of mainly rectangular shapes with no apparent connection. When I spoke to her she told to me what each shape stood for i.e. the two horizontal rectangles 'are the biscuits' and the circular form to their right 'is the bread' and to its right lies 'the glass' with the drinking straw protruding from its mouth. The two square forms, one inside the other, represent the table napkin on top of the cotton towel. The plate is not represented. But what kind of drawing is this? It is certainly not a view representation, nor a plan, but it could be considered as a list or an inventory of the objects, excluding the plate. It could also be argued that each drawn shape has a topological correspondence with its object referent. A year later Katie (age 6 years) makes a drawing, Figure 20, which is quite different from her initial 'inventory' drawing. In this drawing she employs similar representational strategies to those used by the other children a year earlier. On-top-of relations are depicted for the plate, napkin and cloth whilst the plate contents are depicted as heavily shaded shapes. A year later Katie (age 7 years) Figure 21, produces a drawing which has significant differences from her two earlier drawings. Now there is a clear shape distinction between the plate, napkin and cloth and she has depicted the diamond orientation of the napkin against the cloth. The plate contains details of surface pattern and the spatial relations between objects are mapped from their relative positions to her viewpoint into spatial relations on a vertical plane. She employs 'X-ray' depictions in three cases where the inner rim of the plate can be seen through the objects.

In Jacqueline's (5 years) drawing, Figure 22, the large rectangular shape stands for the cotton towel and inside this shape lies another rectangular form with orthogonals which appear to converge, this represents the table napkin. Inside this shape is a circular form representing the plate. Inside the circle lie a series of shapes. The two large rectangles depict the shortbread

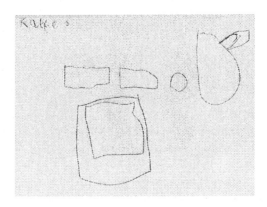

Figure 19.

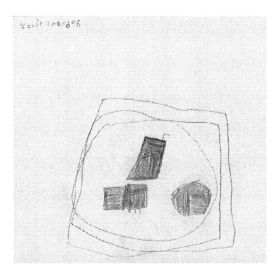

Figure 20.

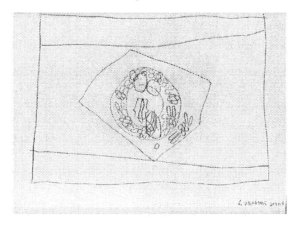

Figure 21.

biscuits and to their right the circular form identifies the bread roll. Above these three shapes the glass is depicted horizontally with the drinking straw inside. Notice that Jacqueline has drawn the line which indicates the surface of the liquid so that it is consistent with the planes of the top and bottom of the glass. The glass representation is the intriguing aspect of this drawing, why is it depicted horizontally? In this drawing on-top-of relations are combined with a series of shapes inside the circular plate that suggest an inventory. At 6 years Jacqueline Figure 23, now depicts the diamond shape of the napkin against the rectangle of the cloth. The plate representation now carries the pattern detail of the plate and the objects on the plate are also given more detail. It is also interesting to note that although the representation of the objects on the plate is not a view representation (they are given their canonical form),

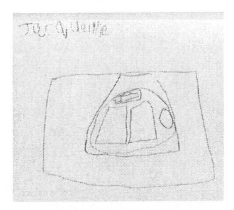

Figure 22.

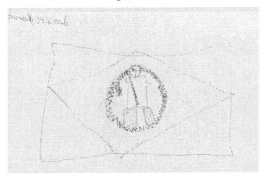

Figure 23.

she is placing them on the plate in their relative positions to her viewpoint so that the biscuits lie in front of the glass and the bread roll behind. In order to depict this spatial relation she draws the objects on a vertical plane whereby bottom is near and top is further away. At 7 years Jacqueline produces a drawing, Figure 24, quite similar to her previous drawing, except this time she is seated in a different viewing position. The level of liquid inside the glass is marked and there is an attempt to depict the ellipse around the mouth of the glass

The drawing made by Bethan (age 5 years) Figure 25, is a very interesting combination of different representational interests. She has depicted the table from a side elevation using a single line to draw the top and two legs. On the horizontal line which indicates the table top she has constructed an elongated undulating shape to signify the cotton towel and then a heavy dark horizontal mark to represent the table napkin. In the centre of the table surface stands a circular shape representing the plate upended as though it is standing on the lower part of its rim. Inside this shape we can clearly see two rectangular blocks representing the biscuits, then above them a circle, the circumference is clearly defined and a darker interior and heavy line spanning its diameter vertically represents, respectively, the glass, liquid and drinking straw.

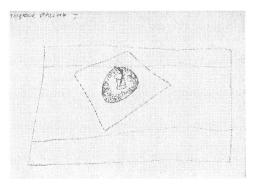

Figure 24.

Figure 25.

Above the glass representation, touching its upper rim, a circle depicts the bread roll. The squiggles to the right and left of these small shapes signify the patterns on the plate surface. This is a complex drawing which seems to combine a side elevation (table) with a plan elevation (plate and contents) thus it functions semiotically for the child on different representational planes. Bethan's second drawing, Figure 26, seems to abandon the representational complexity of her first attempt where she employed side and plan elevations. Now she produces a drawing of a series of on-top-of relations for the table-cloth, napkin and plate, whilst the objects on the plate are given a similar representational treatment as in her first drawing.

Lee (age 5 years), Figure 27, draws the table on which the arrangement is placed but his drawing depicts the table legs in a splayed out fashion projecting from the four corners of the rectangle representing the table surface. Inside this rectangle he attempts to show that the table napkin is placed on top of the cotton towel so as to form a diamond shape against the rectangular form of the towel. The circular shape standing for the plate is easily discerned as are the objects sitting on the plate surface, which are depicted by their canonical or most easily recognisable forms. However, an interesting aspect of the plate representation is that the circular pattern lying under the glass in the centre of the plate is depicted as a squiggly series of lines which

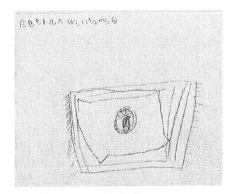

Figure 26.

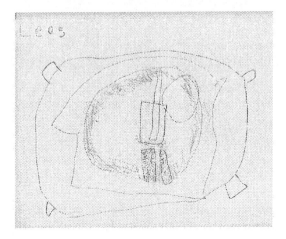

Figure 27.

echo the horizontal depiction of the glass bottom. Is this a view representation or simply showing that the glass 'sits' on top of the pattern, because Lee is quite able to represent the circular pattern around the rim of the plate?

At 6 years Lee produces a second drawing, Figure 28, in which he is really struggling to depict the diamond shape of the napkin against the rectangular shape of the cloth. This struggle was evident in his first drawing. The plate is depicted in its circular shape but now the glass and drinking straw are drawn as if from above. A year later Lee (7 years) produces a drawing, Figure 29 in which there is no attempt to represent the diamond shape of the napkin against the rectangular shape of the cloth but other interests are foregrounded. The plan depiction of the glass in his previous drawing is replaced by a side elevation in which he depicts the level of liquid and the phenomenon of refraction as he views the drinking straw above and below the surface of the liquid. He also represents the ellipse on the top of the glass. The glass representation occludes both the areas of the plate and the napkin which pass behind the glass from his viewing position, but there is no attempt to repre-

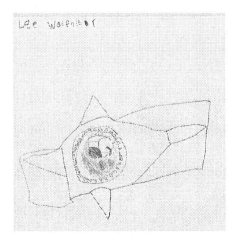

Figure 28.

sent these as they are seen 'through' the glass. The bottom right corner of the glass partly occludes the bread roll representation. This is a drawing therefore which combines view specific information with object specific information.

Leanne (age 5 years) produces a drawing, Figure 30, in which plate, napkin and towel are all represented by a series of concentric circular shapes, perhaps signifying the shapes of objects and their on-top-of relations. The glass is depicted by a simple circle suggesting a plan orientation but the drinking straw is depicted by a dark vertical elongated shape, suggesting the longtitudinal form of this object. Below the glass shape lie two small rectangular shapes depicting the biscuits and to their left a vertical rectangle which represents the bread roll. Leanne's second drawing a year later age 6 years, Figure 31, depicts similar on-top-of relations for the towel, napkin and plate but she is now also interested in surface pattern in her depictions of the biscuits. She

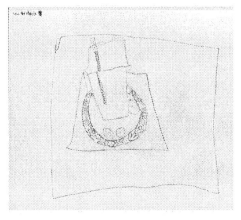

Figure 29.

represents the glass and drinking straw in their most recognisable shapes. The third drawing, Figure 32, produced a year later suggests quite different representational interests. The diamond shape of the napkin against the rectangle of the cloth is depicted and the objects on the plate are now depicted by a combination of view and object specific representations. The plate is drawn in its canonical shape, a circular form, but there is a curious combination of X-ray and part-occlusion representations.

Whereas the rim of the plate can be seen through the glass and the bread roll (placed behind the glass), the bottom of the glass is depicted as partly occluding the bread roll. The glass shape also partly occludes the edge of the napkin as it passes behind the glass from Leanne's viewing position. Leanne also attempts to indicate the top of the glass partly occluding the cotton towel. Thus in this drawing objects are depicted in their canonical shapes (plate, napkin, towel, glass, for example) but also from Leanne's particular viewpoint.

In these drawings, produced at yearly intervals over three years, the most common drawing system is orthographic. There is no indication of oblique or perspective drawing systems and yet within the paradigm of orthographic projection it is possible to argue that these children are able to use drawing

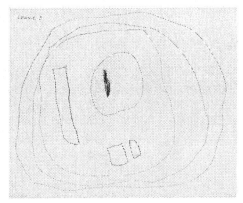

Figure 30.

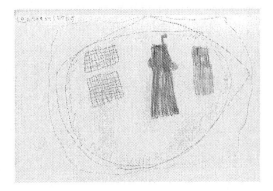

Figure 31.

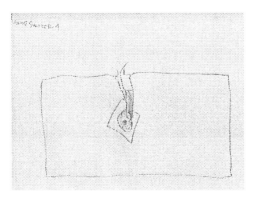

Figure 32.

as a semiotic practice to depict a variety of different representational interests and strategies which convey conceptual as well as figural understanding.
All of these children told me what the shapes in their drawings represented,
'the plate', 'the towel', 'the straw through the glass', and so on, but it is
difficult to prove, for example, that Katie's first drawing (Figure 19) is intended
as an 'inventory drawing'. Equally it is difficult to decipher the graphic logic
in the representation of objects on the plate in Leanne's final drawing
(Figure 32) or in Lee's second drawing (Figure 28). However if we try to
foreground the child's hermeneutical relation within the drawing practice and
attempt to read the different semiotic relations therein, we may be able to
gain a deeper understanding of both representational interests and semiotic
strategies. The value of Peirce's notion of the interpretant is important here.
Such drawings are not representations of objects but they are in some way
related to each child's idea or imaginary construction of their experiential
relation with the objects.

If in our hermeneutical relation to these drawings we foreground a particular representational paradigm and its respective drawing systems, we may
be tempted to view them as naïve or poor representations. The difficulty, always
present, is that my interpretations of the representational significance of these
drawings for the children who produced them, can never be 'total', I am not
party to their imaginary. Neither can I reveal the 'true meaning' of the drawings
because there is always the possibility of further interpretation. But by
recognising the need to adopt a compatible hermeneutic stance and thereby
attempting to consider different representational possibilities and their respective semiotic strategies, that is to say, by extending the discourses in which
I reflect upon the semiotics of representation, I can operate in language to
hint at how the phenomenology of a child's drawing practice and its local
process of semiosis is given visible structure and meaning. Semiotic theory
based upon Peirce's description of sign functioning suggests the possibility
a variety of local signifying (representational) strategies whereas hermeneutic
theory indicates the importance of establishing compatible interpretational
stances.

MYSTERY

There are drawings as well as other kinds of art work which students and children produce that are difficult to understand, for example, the drawings in Figures 5 and 17 above. What happens to us when we experience such art work and how we respond, can be considered as a hermeneutical process. The dynamics of this process can be quite complex depending upon the level of our response. W.M. Brookes in *Philosophy and Action in Education* (1976) explores this process by describing possible scenarios which our responses might take. Writing about those occasions when in teaching we are confounded by the response a child makes in a particular activity, Brookes uses the term 'disturbance' to indicate our initial experiential state. For example, the tree drawing in Figure 17, reminds me of my state of incomprehension and the subsequent state of not knowing how to respond or to proceed. In other words this drawing was a mystery to me. Brookes suggests that when confronted with mystery one way to proceed is to explain it away. I could, for example, treat the drawing as a failed representation and so smooth over my initial distur-bance. There are many ways in which we can do this in order to dissolve the initial disturbance and regain stability. Brookes is keen to point out however that the mystery is not the 'disturbance-thing', that is to say, our state of mystery stems not from that which disturbs but from the limitations of our interpretational frameworks. If the disturbance is severe enough we may be unable to explain it away quickly and then one possibility is to consider our frameworks of interpretation and meaning. This requires a secondary kind of action, which some refer to as reflexive action, in which the frameworks through which we understand children's and student's art work are interro-gated. The consequence of this secondary action, or what we might call philosophising in the Wittgensteinian sense of 'untying knots in our under-standing' (see Wittgenstein Philosophical Investigations paras: 123–126) can lead to a new interpretational state, that is to say a new hermeneutic relation, into which the work that caused the disturbance is placed.

This description of how we cope with mystery consists of two hermeneu-tical relations, the first involving the use of explanation to dissolve our state of incomprehension-in-action, the second precipitating a secondary action whereby that which causes disturbance is relocated within a restructured dis-course which facilitates interpretation and expanded action. By concentrating upon issues of practice to which we can relate in terms of our experiences of teaching and learning, Brookes comes close to providing a practical exemplification of Ricoeur's two theoretical poles of explanation and under-standing that constitute the hermeneutic arc (see Ricoeur 1982, p. 164). Brookes's treatment of local states of action provides a more complex under-standing of hermeneutical relations than Gallagher's description of the hermeneutic circle which I have already discussed. Although Gallagher insists that the interpretational process is dialectical, so that the interpreter, rooted in tradition, interprets the world and thereby gradually changes tradition and him or herself, he does not offer a description of the dynamics of local experiential states which result in conservation or change.

SUMMARY

In the above descriptions of children's drawings perhaps it is evident that the kind of hermeneutical relation, which is necessary for developing an empathetic understanding of their visual semiotic strategies is that proposed by Gadamer. His notion of agreement achieved through dialogue and fusion of horizons, for interpreting children's and student's art work is important. "To be in a conversation, however, means to be beyond oneself, to think with the other and to come back to oneself as if to another (Gallagher 1992, p. 49)." This suggests that as educators we try to form some understanding of the ways in which visual signs are used by children and students and this may often involve a self-examination of our 'prejudices' and traditions of understanding representation and art practice; to try to recognise that our interpretations function, 'behind our backs' and also out ahead of us (Gallagher 1992, p. 91). Such recognition leads into further more complex issues, for example, what kind of power relations function in our interpretations and how do these relations impact upon our identities as teachers and learners. I will discuss this particular question in chapters 5 and 6 when I look more closely at the work of Foucault and Lacan. We can also enquire into what kind of traditions of practice dominate our interpretations and what kind of discourses of practice do we use to make our interpretations of children's and student's art work.

We tend to think about development in relation to children's learning and behaviour as an expansive and evolutionary process. This is understandable and it would be foolish to deny, children do acquire and develop skills in a variety of ways. As they grow their physical capabilities increase alongside their cognitive powers. They develop social skills within particular cultural contexts, their interests expand as they meet new people and new experiences, and so on. But it is also possible to consider development as a funnelling process so that as children enter social practices and institutions, such as schools and particular forms of knowledge and practice, development becomes regulated and controlled. In describing and interpreting children's drawing practices my purpose is to show that, given the opportunity and support, children use drawing and other practices such as painting or constructing, for a rich variety of expressive and representational purposes. Children use such art activities to construct narratives, to depict time sequences, to play games, to represent actions, to describe objects, to describe object and spatial relations, and much more. In these activities children are developing semiotic strategies as well as conceptual understanding. However in my experiences of teaching in England, by the time many children reach late primary or early secondary education the phrase, "I can't draw", is a common expression. By this time they have acquired a much narrower view of the purpose of drawing, which is to produce realistic pictures, and a firm understanding of what makes a good drawing, that it looks 'real'. This funnelling process from earlier eclectic uses of drawing as a tool for enquiry, play, expression and representation, to a specific representational use is not a natural and inevitable process, but one which is formed within specific practices, attitudes and values. In other words it is a process that could be reversed if, for example, we develop pedagogies in art education that acknowledge, celebrate and extend the early eclecticism of practice through primary and secondary education. The recognition that children's drawing practices involve the production of complex semiotic structures which require careful consideration is important and when we discuss their art work a sensitive hermeneutic approach is required.

This brings me back to Ricoeur's work on hermeneutics and in particular to his notion of appropriation discussed earlier. Drawing on Gadamer, Ricoeur views interpretation as a fusion of horizons, which in the case of interpreting children's drawings, consists of a fusion between the teacher's discourse and sedimented understanding with the child's drawing and his or her words of description. The drawing becomes a production as a consequence of which both child and teacher extend their understanding. To quote Ricoeur again:

> I shall say that appropriation is the process by which the revelation of new modes of being – or, if you prefer Wittgenstein to Heidegger, new 'forms of life' – gives the subject new capacities for knowing himself (herself). If the reference of the text (drawing) is the projection of a world, then it is not, in the first instance, the reader (teacher) who projects himself (herself). The reader (teacher) is rather broadened in his (her) capacity to project himself (herself) by receiving a new mode of being (form of life) from the text (drawing) itself (1982, p. 192, my brackets).

Thus if we apply this argument to the drawing practices I have discussed it would seem that the teacher's task is to try to appropriate the form of life which is produced through the child's drawing practice and in doing so she extends her capacity to function effectively as a teacher. The idea of drawing as a production or presentation in contrast to a reproduction or representation, introduces the notion of world-making which I will discuss in Chapter 9. It is a notion that places emphasis upon an ontological understanding of practice. Such understanding concerns different life-world contexts and different uses and purposes of drawing practice and the value of this for art education is, I believe, to develop approaches to drawing practice that build on the eclecticism of children's drawing practices by extending this eclecticism into secondary education. This entails an approach to educating through drawing (and other art practices), which is not over-reliant upon observation but uses drawing to explore other forms of experience. In the next chapter I want to extend my discussion of children's drawings in order to consider the notion of visuality and how this term offers the possibility for reflecting upon children's drawings as visual structures embedded and embodied within local socio-cultural domains.

CHAPTER FOUR

EXPERIENCE AND THE HERMENEUTICS
AND SEMIOTICS OF VISUALITY

This chapter aims to extend the previous chapter's description and discussion of the semiotics practices in children's and student's art work. I shall consider visual representation and expression as constituting or constructing particular structures of the visible that manifest different visualities. I am using this term in line with Evans and Hall (1999, p. 4) who define visuality as "the visual register in which the image and visual meaning operate." However there are complications here because the functioning of image and meaning (visual register) can be different for the child or student who produces it and the teacher who interprets.

This means that we can conceive the production of drawings, paintings and other visual productions by children and students, as visible structures that may accord with traditional visualities and their respective visual registers, but also the possibility that others forms of visual production (see Figure 5 for example) may not. Rather than marginalize the latter however it is important to try to comprehend their semiotic coherence for the child or student. The notion of visuality has been employed to interrogate images and the way they are viewed and interpreted in many areas of visual culture such as film, television, advertising and photography (see Foster 1988; Bryson, Holly and Moxey 1991, 1994; Mitchell 1995; Hall and Evans 1999), but for the purpose of this book I will limit my use of the term to the interpretation of children's and students' art practices.

Foster (1996, pp. 139–140) discusses visuality in terms of the "conventions of art, the schemata of representation, the codes of visual culture." It is important to distinguish between vision understood as a purely optical process in contrast to socio-cultural constructions of visuality that are formed within specific technologies and codes of representation that precipitate particular 'ways of seeing' (see Berger 1972) and visual meaning. I have already mentioned the work of Jonathan Cray (1996) who describes in his book, *Techniques of the Observer*, how particular technologies of vision such as the *camera lucida* and the *camera obscura* produced particular visualities, particular structures of the visible, which constructed particular ways of seeing. Hockney (2002) also illustrates how artists have used mirrors and lenses to make representational paintings which create a constructed visual field which in turn produces a particular kind of viewer.

It is possible therefore, using the term visuality, to consider visual productions from different cultural contexts in order to explore how visual meaning is constructed. For example, a medieval altar painting, a renaissance perspective painting, an Indian *Ragamala* minature, an Australian Aborignal painting, a Minoan vase motif, a cubist painting, a nineteenth century Osaka print from

Japan, an Egyptian tomb painting, an American Navaho sand painting, all present different structures of the visible, different visualities which produce different semiotic structures of meaning. These structures function according to their respective visual registers on both structural and ideological planes. For example, linear perspective as described by Alberti in Italy, creates a specific visuality in which the world is organised and represented for a specific representational purpose and for a specific kind of viewer. As Rogoff (2000) states:

Linear perspective as thematised by Alberti was not just the process of binding the picture to vision and visual perception but also the definition of what he chose to term a picture; it was not just a surface but a plane serving as a window that assumed a human observer whose eye level and distance from that plane were the essential factors in determining its rendition (p. 95).

As we shall see shortly this particular visual structure established a specific ideological framework involving a transcendent powerful subject who is able to gaze upon an objective world.

Visuality can be understood therefore as the production of specific visual structures and the production of particular viewers within specific socio-cultural settings. For my purposes there is a need to distinguish between conventional systems of visuality and their respective semiotic codes which have common currency within a culture, such as the drawing and painting practices with which we are familiar, and more local or idiosyncratic visualities constructed by many children and students, which may not accord with the gaze established by such conventional systems. This is important because what I want to argue is that traditional forms of visuality frequently hold sway over idiosyncratic forms which many children and students are able to produce, not because the former are more correct, more accurate or appropriate, (although this appears to be the case) but because through convention they have become valued and naturalised. Dominant or traditional visualities, such as linear perspective, are socially and culturally constructed and can be understood as generating a series of desires that dictate how we interpret visual practices such as painting and drawing. My purpose is to roll back the hegemony of conventional visualities, that is to say, those frameworks of visual representation which have acquired in Bourdieu's (1993) terminology, *cultural capital*, in order to explore structures of the visible within which many children and students form and develop a semiotics of visual practice. My purpose described in another way is to explore and extend a hermeneutics of the visual in children's and student's local art practices. Irit Rogoff (2000) in her book, *terra infirma: geography's visual culture*, describes her desire to formulate an alternative viewing position to the consensus attitude of value and quality in relation to art work and she emerges with the idea of 'the curious eye'.

Curiosity implies a certain unsettling, a notion of things outside the realm of the known, of things not yet quite understood or articulated, the pleasures of the forbidden or the hidden or the unthought, the optimism of finding out something one had not known or been able to conceive of before (p. 33).

It is in this spirit of the curious eye that my work is located but tempered with the knowledge that curiosity will always be affected, influenced or modified by assimilated positionings and understandings. It is important to acknowledge that conventional visualities are infused with ideology and power, a point that I shall develop in Chapters 5 and 6 when I will suggest how students, and teachers' identities as learners and teachers are formed within traditional codes of representation and in the process how they become regulated, normalised and positioned respectively as learners and teachers.

The distinction between optical processes and the idea of visuality is important in relation to representation and meaning. The science of optics suggests that light carries unmediated information through the retinal membrane, and according to the *natural attitude* to representation, described by Bryson (1988), to which I will return shortly, the representational image conveys as effectively as it can to the viewer the artist's original perceptual experience. But, according to Bryson when I see I do so in terms of a socially constructed vision, through screens of signification.

When I see, what I see is formed by paths or networks laid down in advance of my seeing. It may be the case that I feel myself to inhabit some kind of centre in my speech, but what decentres me is the network of language. It may similarly be that I always feel myself to live at the centre of my vision – somewhere (where?) behind my eyes; but, again, that vision is decentred by the network of signifiers that come to me from the social milieu (pp. 93–94).

For Bryson seeing is always already ensconced within a world of visual signifiers and processes of semiosis. Processes of visuality are not concerned with the reception of information via light waves but with immersion in visual semiotic structures. The subject matter of vision is constructed therefore through traditional or developing local codes and schemas of signification that provide a semantic framework. It would be foolish to dispute the physicality of the optical process in that certain physical and biological conditions are necessary for vision to take place but this process does not occur within a socio-cultural vacuum. What and how we see is given meaning within established ways of seeing which are structured, not by physical laws, but by socio-cultural conditions and conventions. Looking and seeing are cultural and material practices. In recent feminist writings on visuality Rogoff (2000) argues that:

A division is made apparent between the subject, the bearer of the gaze and the object which is being looked upon. The structures through which this looking is done are dependent upon cultural narratives, projected desires and power relations, while the space in which the activity of looking takes place is animated with all the material and cultural complexities which represent the obstacles to the very idea of straightforward comprehension of what is being seen (p.11).

I am concentrating in this chapter upon the use of the term visuality to discuss the semiotics of representation and expression in children's art practices. In other words I am using the term visuality to refer to the different visual structures and their respective hermeneutic frameworks produced by children. But in Part 2 I will foreground the visual registers and discourses through which art work is interpreted and assessed by teachers. Such discourse consist of 'cultural narratives, projected desires and power relations' in which specific pedagogised identities are formed. It is important to recognise therefore that a particular form of visuality in which students are positioned, related and regulated in assessment practices is not a neutral or natural space, but one which is formed within particular social and cultural contexts: it is therefore an *ideological* space. In such spaces students are identified and regulated through particular representational and expressive orders (visualities) in which they themselves become visible as students.

Crary (1996, pp. 5–7) ponders the distinction between the terms "observer" and "spectator" and reveals that the etymological root of the former term does not mean "to look at" but, "to conform one's action, to comply with," as in observing rules, codes, regulations and practices. So an observer is therefore, "one who sees within a prescribed set of possibilities, one who is embedded in a system of conventions and limitations." He proceeds to argue that: "There never was or will be a self-present beholder to whom a world is transparently evident (p. 6)." Taking this into account it is possible to argue that an observer is not one who sees the world "as it is" but one whose viewing is formed within specific conventions and codes of visuality. An observer is a subject who acquires a particular subjectivity regarding vision, that is to say, someone who learns to see (observe) in a particular way and which is culturally embedded. As both Crary and Hockney argue in their historicizing accounts of visual perception, practices of visual representation produce particular kinds of gazes and viewers, in other words viewing practices are socially and culturally constructed. Drawing or painting from observation can be understood therefore as practices which involve specific techniques of visual representation that produce particular visual structures that in turn induce specific ways of seeing. These visual structures are interpreted within specific cultural codes or registers of visual representation (visualities), and not by physical laws of vision. Difficulties of interpretation arise for teachers when they are confronted by students' art work which does not 'fit' within assimilated codes of representation and expression.

The idea that observational drawing and painting is concerned with depicting the world as we see it, according to what Bryson (1983, pp. 10–12)) terms the *natural attitude* to representation, still persists in some discourses of art in education, as I intend to show when I consider assessment. In other words those practices aligned with the natural attitude to representation still constitute a significant form of visuality in art education in schools. Bryson provides five principles that for him constitute this attitude to visual representation. Drawing extensively on his text I will provide a summary of four of these.

1. *An absence of history.* The basic visual field is consistent across generations and corresponds to the fixed nature of the optical body. Visual experience is

thus universal and trans-historical and it is therefore possible to judge along a sliding scale how closely an image approximates the truth of perception. 2. *Dualism.* The retinal membrane separates the world of the mind from the world of extension. Outside lies a pre-existent reality flooded with light which is thus reflected inside by a passive specular consciousness. The self is not responsible for constructing the content of consciousness which is formed by the incoming stream of information from outside. 3. *The centrality of perception.* The natural attitude is unable to account for images which depart from universal visual experience except in negative terms: the painter has misperceived the optical truth or has been able through lack of skill to provide optical truth. 4. *Communication.* The representational image transports as perfectly as it can to the viewer the artist's original perceptual experience.

When assessing or evaluating drawings or paintings from observation, *the centrality of perception* frequently informs our judgements of students' and children's art work. Such judgements are based on an understanding of perception that involves the idea of a universal (ahistorical) visual experience and a directly accessible world. I think it also involves a direct association of a drawing with its referent in the world and not with its imagined interpretant. Thus drawings and paintings that depart from conventional understanding of representation are often regarded as the outcome of a lack of skill or a lack of concentration. My use of the term visuality disturbs the *natural attitude* to representation because it admits into our understanding historical, social and cultural contexts and, crucially, the effects of power, whereby a particular form of visuality hegemonises the field of visual production. Evans (1999, p. 18) referring to Derrida's critique of the idea of original presence (which I discuss in Chapter 9), an idea which is implicit the natural attitude to representation, describes this attitude as judging a visual representation, "in terms of its success or failure to reconstitute the missing presence thought to be the original source, the original content of the empirical form of the representation." She proceeds to argue that this attitude becomes redundant when we think of representation as a cultural construction, a material practice which does not reproduce a missing presence but actively constitutes a representational structure. A similar distinction between representation as reproduction, or representation as production is echoed in Gadamer's distinction between *vorstellung* and *darstellung* (see Davey 1999, p. 19 in Heywood and Sandywell 1999). *Vorstellung* refers to representation in the sense of a reproduction of a reality which is before or prior to the work, whereas *darstellung* refers to presentation in the sense that an art work does not reproduce a prior reality but instead it brings into being a reality, a world of meaning in the interpretational moment. If the material approach to representation embraced by *darstellung* is applied to children's and students' art practices then we can think of them in terms of local semiotic processes that present local visualities; local practices of meaning-making through visual structures.

One representational system used in painting and drawing that is often associated with the *natural attitude* to representation, in that it appears to represent the world as we view it, is linear perspective. If we abandon this attitude then this representational system has to be considered not as a representation of perceptual experience but as a visual semiotic production that has established a particular hegemony of vision in the material practices of painting and drawing in the West. It may be argued that this point is somewhat outdated because the ideological and cultural grounding of perspective have long been recognised and understood. Nevertheless, I have found that in the contexts of drawing and painting practices in schools the latent presence of perspective is still pervasive in both teaching and assessment practices; in those discourses that are employed to ascertain the efficacy or quality of an observational drawing.

PERSPECTIVE AND VISUAL REPRESENTATION

Perspectival projection is often an implicit criterion in assessment of secondary students' observational drawings. In Western cultures this system of visual representation developed an almost synonymous relation with vision, to replicate the way in which we see the world. In assessment of drawing practices an 'able' student is frequently, but not always, identified by the ability to employ perspective. Students who can employ this drawing system are often described as 'talented drawers' or 'students who possess a natural talent for drawing'. Those who are unable to use perspective in their drawings, and whose drawings manifest what appear to be less complex drawing systems, are often considered as producing less effective observational drawings. A similar attitude to drawing ability can be found in some developmental interpretations of children's representational drawing practices whereby drawing development is understood as a process from scribble through orthographic and oblique drawing systems towards the use of perspectival projection (see Barrett 1979; Atkinson 1991, 1993; Willats 1997; Gardner 1980).

Berger (1972, p. 16), Bryson (1983, pp. 1–12), Jay (1994, pp. 54–60), Panofsky (1991) and Pile and Thrift (1995, pp. 44–48) have all entered the debate on vision and representation, arguing that perspective developed during the Renaissance, does not faithfully represent vision, although it appears to do so, but that it is a particular (cultural) construction of vision. In other words, perspective establishes a particular form of visuality. Once this point is appreciated and the apparent naturalism attributed to perspectival projection is set aside, then it is possible to argue that students' drawing ability is not defined by the degree to which they can represent the way we see the world, but by their drawings' correspondence to a favoured representational system. Furthermore it is possible to argue that ability in drawing from observation is recognised and constructed within the discourse that is allied to this particular system of visual representation. In other words within this particular discourse of *visuality* drawing ability is made visible. Bryson suggests that:

For human beings collectively to orchestrate their visual experience together it is required that each submit his or her retinal experience to the socially agreed description(s) of an intelligible world (Bryson 1988, p. 91).

And further:

When I learn to see socially, that is, when I begin to articulate my retinal experience with the codes of recognition that come to me from my social milieu(s) I am inserted into systems of visual discourse that saw the world before I did. Thus I see in terms of a socially constructed vision . . . (Bryson 1988, p. 92)

Jay (1994) insists that the Renaissance development of perspective produced, "the technique for rendering three-dimensional space onto the two dimensions of the flat canvas'" and eventually this established a "naturalised visual culture" in the West. Within this representational paradigm the beholder's viewpoint becomes the privileged position from which objects in space are ordered "within a uniform system of linear coordinates" (p. 52).

Harvey (1990) describes how perspective homogenises both space and time to produce a totalising vision:

Which conceives of the world from the standpoint of the seeing eye of the individual. It emphasises the science of optics and the ability of the individual to represent what he or she sees as in some sense 'truthful' (p. 245).

Implicit to the visuality of perspective is a particular epistemology which separates a transcendent subject from a world of objects, a dualism whereby the subject occupies a space of control over the world he or she surveys. This dualism is clearly illustrated by the technology and apparatus of perspective whereby the omnipotent eye of the artist is fixed at a point from where he or she views the subject matter to be represented through a transparent grid which is repeated on the drawing surface. It is interesting to consider that just as the eye of the artist, through the use of the perspectival grid, fixes what is being observed, then similarly the technology of perspective ensure that when we gaze at a perspectival image then we are constructed as particular kinds or viewers. Rogoff refers to Panofsky's (1991) seminal text, *Perspective as Symbolic Form*, to make the point that he saw the historical development of linear perspective as, "the triumph of a sense of reality which is founded on a notion of objectivity and on the creation of a distance between the subject and object (Rogoff 2000, p. 95). The continual development of this visual system led to a particular categorisation of reality and the reinforcement of a particular categorising ego. According to Rogoff, the legacy of perspective as a visual system, "is the construction of a world view which is founded in notions of objectivity and rationality and the recognition of a central beholder who possesses these qualities and reconstructs the world according to their rationale (p. 96)." Within this visual system objects and space are colonised by a particular rationality that produces a specific kind of viewer.

Meleau-Ponty (1962) creates a distinction between 'geometric space' and 'anthropological space' which is relevant both to a critique of the universal and ahistorical eye of perspective and my concern with adopting a more expansive approach to visuality in art in education practices. As a system of visual representation perspective can be generally described as depicting the three dimensional form of objects and their spatial relations as seen from a specific viewpoint according to a strict mathematical formula. It is a tight administrative procedure in that it categorises, orders and manages visual perception. As a system of visual representation it is concerned with the production of geometric space. This space is therefore a reduction of our actual experience of perception which, in its fullness, is impossible to abstract. We have to ask if the fluctuating dynamics of our visual experience of the world can be captured by perspective's geometric space. In contrast to geometrical space therefore Merleau-Ponty (1962) provides a description of anthropological space as experienced in the everyday practice of walking around his flat:

When I walk around my flat the various aspects in which it presents itself to me could not possibly appear as views of one and the same thing if I did not know that each of them represents the flat seen from one spot or another, and if I were unaware of my movements, and my body as retaining its identity through the stages of those movements (p. 203).

It is the memories of who we are and our assimilated and embodied experiences which allow us to understand what and how we view the world. For Merleau-Ponty it is the primacy of the body that is the necessary condition for perception, not the detached omnipotent eye attributable to the geometric space of perspective. Bodily experience and memories of such experiences are necessary for us to comprehend visual experiences. There are important implications which flow from the idea of anthropological space and the primacy of the body in perceptual experience. For example, we can ask with whose body are we concerned and in which cultural or social context; who is looking and from which embodied position?

Developing these ideas from Merleau-Ponty, de Certeau (1984, p. 118) argues that, "there are as many spaces as there are distinct spatial experiences," it is important therefore to engage with 'ways of being' or forms of narrative (including visual productions) rather than 'states of being'. The logical extrapolation from this, as Buchanan (2000, p. 112) suggests, is that we concentrate upon 'ways of seeing' as opposed to 'what is seen'. This idea of 'ways of seeing' takes us back to Wittgenstein's 'forms of life' and I believe this has great significance for working with and responding to the visual productions of children and students in the contexts of art in education.

VISUALITIES OF DIFFERENCE

I suggested above that in my experience one of the great difficulties for teachers who need to respond to, evaluate or assess student's art work arises when they are confronted with work which does not fit within traditional codes of practice and recognition. Alternatively the problem can be put the other way in the sense of the need to dissolve the hegemonies of traditional visual codes. How therefore can we develop a hermeneutics of vision in which we can extend our understanding of student's and children's visualities? If ever there was a question grounded in contradiction this seems to be one, for how can we break out of our ways of understanding, how can we begin to accommodate that which lies beyond our frameworks of recognition? Merleau-Ponty's notion of anthropological space, in contrast to geometrical space, seems to offer a way of conceiving a phenomenological approach to visuality.

In *The order of Things*, Foucault (1970, p. xv) refers to a passage from a short story by Borges which describes a Chinese encylopaedia in which it is written,

That animals are divided into: (a) belonging to the Emperor, (b) embalmed, (c) tame, (d) sucking pigs, (e) sirens, (f) fabulous, (g) stray dogs, (h) included in the present classification, (i) frenzied, (j) innumerable, (k) drawn with a fine camelhair brush, (l) et cetera, (m) having just broken the water pitcher, (n) that from a long way off look like flies (p. xv).

In making reference to Borges, Foucault is foregrounding alternative epistemologies through which phenomena are ordered and known and in so doing he raises the issue of the limitations of our own epistemological frameworks. Foucault calls such strange epistemological systems *heterotopias*:

Heterotopias are disturbing, probably because they undermine language, because they make it impossible to name this and that, [. . .] because they destroy 'syntax' in advance, and not only the syntax with which we construct sentences but also that less apparent syntax which causes words and things [. . .] to 'hold together'. [. . .]; heterotopias desiccate speech, stop words in their tracks, contest the very possibility of grammar at its source; they dissolve our myths . . . . (p. xviii)

If I can be permitted a degree of flexibility in my interpretation I believe that Foucault's description of heterotopias, combined with Merleau Ponty's phenomenological notion of anthropological space can be useful for reflecting upon those art practices which do not fit our codes of recognition; for conceiving those mysterious art practices with which teachers are confronted. It could be argued that such art work presents visual heterotopias. It is a term that helps me to theorise art practices which foregrounds experience and local forms of representation and expression. We only need consider the practices involved when children draw and paint to realise that we are often confronted with graphic forms that disturb the conventions of syntax and grammar through which we understand art work. Yet we know through a growing amount of research into this area of art practice (see Taber 1981; Matthews 1998; Atkinson 1991, 1995, 1998a; Moore 1999), that children and older students often produce art work which may appear defective or mysterious to teachers and other interested parties, but which are composed according to local ontologies of practice that involve sophisticated and diverse forms of semiotic production. Thus the concepts of visual heterotopias and anthropological space provide theoretical devices that alert us in such cases to try to adopt a more receptive approach to difference in students' and children's art practices. In other words the mystery of heterotopias and their

anthropological spaces can force us to confront the limits of our ways of understanding.

If we consider the following drawings produced by a group of year 5 (9
years old) children perhaps we can begin to see the value of what might be
called heterotopic-anthropological sensitivity, that is to say an awareness that
art practices, such as drawings and paintings, frequently involve logics of
composition, narrative and representation which lie beyond our assimilated
understanding. In other words a heterotopic-anthropological sensitivity can
be said to be concerned with an awareness of the possibility of narratives or
visualities of difference. The children were asked to make a drawing to describe
how they ate their evening meal at home. Rather like Meleau Ponty's embodied
perceptions of his flat, these children's drawings could be said to involve
the idea of embodiment leading to the presentation of anthropological space.
The diversity of response is immediately striking and it would be difficult,
for example, to place these drawings in any hierarchical order of representational efficacy. The drawings do employ common semiotic conventions or
stereotypical forms, such as in the depiction of figures or the representation
of objects, but as entire drawings they present us with a series of different
visualities, each one structured by local semiotics of composition, each one
grounded within specific life-world contexts and meaning. There are 16
drawings in total but I only have space to comment upon five.

Notice the depiction of chairs and people in Figure 33, a drawing by Drahim,
as though on a fairground Ferris wheel. The same schematic form depicts
each figure, more or less front-on, whilst their chairs take the form of a side

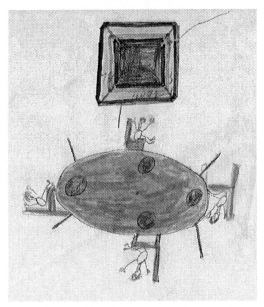

Figure 33.

on depiction. The table however is not drawn as a side-on depiction but as from above with the legs splayed out at right angles. Each of these depictions could be said to be stereotypical or canonical, that is to say each object is depicted in its most easily recognisable form. But the arrangement of these forms, the graphic logic by which the drawing is organised, is not stereotypical, it is highly idiosyncratic. The drawing in Figure 34, by Inan presents a very different depiction of the dining table and people eating, they are presented as though viewed from above. Again similar schema are used to depict the people but in a way which ignores the convention of occlusion. We are slightly disorientated by the child's use of what might be loosely termed aerial perspective and the x-ray depiction of the people eating.

The drawing in Figure 35 by Amie also appears to be an aerial depiction

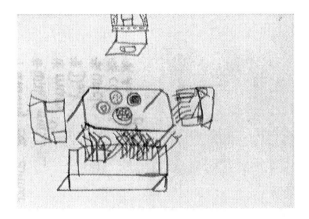

Figure 34.

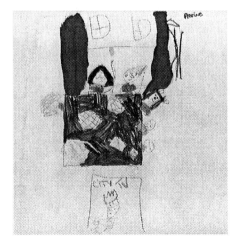

Figure 35.

Figure 36.

Figure 37.

of the dinning table, but we could say it is organised according to a representational logic which Willats (1997) has termed vertical oblique projection.
That is to say, near to far relations such as the front and back of the table,
and top to bottom relations, such as the top and bottom of the curtains, are
all depicted in a vertical plane. The people in this drawing are depicted by
slightly different schemata, mouths for example are represented by a single
curving line or by a contour shape. Similarly, noses are represented by a
single line or a contour shape. The positioning of the people around the table
is quite different from the drawings by Drahim and Inan.

The drawing in Figure 36 by Rebecca presents a horizontal arrangement
of the dinning table and people eating. Again this drawing provides a quite
different spatial organisation to the other drawings. Remarkably similar
schemas are employed to represent the women and their facial features whilst
a different schematic form depicts the child's father. Sonia's drawing in
Figure 37 provides another quite different visuality. The table far right middle

is placed away from Sonia's sister, bottom right foreground, and her grand-mother, the small seated figure above Sonia depicted far left. Again Sonia employs the same schema for representing herself and her sister, noticeably lacking arms and very different from the figure schemas contained in the other drawings.

I have only commented upon the different spatial organisations and orientations of the contents of each drawing, on the different viewing angles and the different schema employed to depict people in each drawing. We could make a more detailed analysis of the *denotational* property (see Willats 1997; Matthews 1999) of each line and the representation of three-dimensional form. I have said nothing about the meaning of these drawings for each child because I have no access to the different domestic experiences and the respective phenomenologies on which they are based. But each drawing could be said to present a different visuality, a different series of rules of formation, or graphic logics, according to which the whole drawing is organised and acquires meaning for the child. These drawings are grounded within local experiential and temporal contexts that are given visual form by each child. I would argue that it would be difficult to classify these drawings according to a normative description of representational practice if we respect and acknowledge their different visualities. The 'whole' drawing practice will include not only the production and arrangement of visual schemata and other visual configurations but also those embodied aspects of the practice which involve family rituals, relations and discursive practices which constitute for the child the domestic context. Included here will be not only the child's conscious reflexive production of the drawing but also the child's fantasising practices of and within the domestic economy.

The focus of Part One has been to consider art practice as a semiotic practice through which children and students produce meaning in visual form. An important pedagogic task for the teacher is to interpret the art practices of children and students and this can involve adopting a variety of hermeneutic strategies. One strategy is concerned with trying to understand the semiotic logic of a drawing; this entails trying to understand how visual signifiers signify meaning for the child. Another is concerned with teachers developing a reflexive awareness of their own interpretational frameworks. A third is concerned with dissolving the hegemonic power of dominant forms of visual representation, which may be incommensurable as criteria to assess and evaluate children's and students' drawings. The key aspect of Part 1 therefore has been to discuss the relationship of the subject to the signifier, the relationship of the student to his or her drawing and similarly the relationship of the teacher to these drawings. If Part One concerns the relationship of the subject to the signifier Part Two will attempt to show that it is through the signifier that the subject becomes a subject of a particular kind.

IDENTITY AND PRACTICE

Part One is concerned mainly with the interpretation of children's and student's drawing practices. I employed hermeneutic and semiotic theory in order to reflect upon semiotic strategies which students and children employ in their art work. The value of hermeneutics and semiotics for my enquiry is that they provide a framework of understanding within which differences of semiotic practice can be legitimated, explored and responded to in the educational context of art in education. I have aligned myself with those hermeneutic strategies that insist that interpretation is not concerned with the production of definitive or essential meanings but with the idea that meaning is a construct of language. Language engages with and interprets practice but never produces a complete interpretation of practice. This means that meaning is always partial and that further interpretations are always possible. I considered how art practices can be understood as the production of local visualities or local visual structures constructed according to a local semiotics of production which I described as functioning on both metonymic and metaphoric axes. My chief focus therefore was upon how children and students construct meaningful visual structures in their art practices and how we might respond more effectively to them as teachers and educators.

In Part Two my emphasis will be upon the themes of identity and practice in art education and in particular how teachers' and students' identities are formed in this educational context. I call these identities *pedagogised identities* (see Atkinson 1999a, 1999b, 1999c, 2001) in that I am dealing specifically with processes of identification and practice arising in the educational fields of teaching and learning. My focus is therefore those discourses and practices, such as assessment, in which teacher and learner identities are constructed. By engaging with post-structural theory I leave aside conceptions of identity that are rooted in essentialist ideas of the self and the individual and move towards descriptions of identity and subjectivity that see them as processes of production and change that arise within specific discourses and practices relating to art in education. Foucault provides us with the notion of *discursive practices* in which subjects are formed, regulated, positioned and normalised according to specific practices and their respective discourses. Lacan provides a theorisation of subjectivity which is formed within the three orders of the imaginary, the symbolic and the Real. For Foucault the subject is created within specific discourses and practices whilst for Lacan the subject is formed according to processes of desire and lack and ultimately grounded in misrecognition that problematises the very idea of identification. These ideas of subject formation will be explored in relation to the formation of teacher and learner identities in practices in art education such as the assessment of students' art work.

In Chapter 5 I begin with a discussion of some Foucaultian perspectives on identity and subjectivity, which are extrapolated by reference to assessment discourses in art education. My claim is that it is within such discursive practices that teacher and student identities are formed (made visible) and develop. This will be followed in Chapter 6 by a description of Lacanian ideas on subjectivity and identity that are then applied to practices in art education specifically in order to consider how pedagogised identities in this field are formed and fetishised within this institutional site. Judith Butler's (1997) *rapprochement* of the discursive subject and the psychic subject is introduced to push the ideas on identification a little further in my attempt to grapple with the complex process of subject formation. In Chapter 6 Bourdieu's concepts of field and *habitus* are applied to art education in order to extend my description of the formation of pedagogised identities in art educational practices. This will include a discussion of practice and assessment outlined and advocated in curriculum documents, such as the National Curriculum for Art in England, and their construction of idealised pedagogised identities. I will also present and discuss a series of conversations with experienced art teachers in which they describe their approach to teaching and assessing students' art practices. I show in this discussion how, through different structurations and ideologies of practice, students' and teachers' identities in art education are constructed quite differently. The purpose here is to explore and suggest how, through these different forms of discursive practice, both teachers and students' identities are formed as pedagogised subjects.

CHAPTER FIVE

THE CONSTRUCTION OF IDENTITY
Theorising Subjectivity and Identity

THE TRUMAN SHOW

In Peter Weir's film *The Truman Show* we are given a graphic metaphor of the construction of social and cultural identifications. It is a parody of the socio-symbolic frameworks that structure our understanding and everyday practice. Unbeknown to Truman his entire life is the subject of a television drama-documentary; his world is that of a gigantic film set orchestrated by Christo, the director, who conceived the entire project. Thus all Truman's friends and the people he meets and works with on a daily basis are actors, even incredibly, his wife. We enter Truman's life at a time when particular events begin to disrupt his understanding; a giant spotlight crashes onto the road outside his house, an elevator door opens and reveals only a back room in which actors take a break. Such events trouble Truman but strategies are always found to explain them. Midway through the film we are introduced to Christo the director who explains how the show originated and how Truman's world is maintained on a twenty-four hour basis. He is asked why Truman has never suspected anything about his artificial existence, he replies: "We believe in the reality with which we are presented, it's as simple as that."

The importance of the film for the focus of this chapter is that it raises questions concerning how processes of identity and subjectivity are formed. The artifice of the film illustrates the 'real' ways in which, in Western communities, our lives can be seen as constructions which appear natural. The film illustrates how we live our lives according to detailed codes of behaviour and recognition and that when these are disrupted or violated their ideological 'attractors' (hegemony) soon return us to reality. On another level, because all the characters in Truman's world are not who they really are (except for Truman) we can also enquire 'who exactly is Truman?' What is Truman's identity? Such questions invoke complex issues concerning human subjectivity and identity, which are problematised in contemporary social and cultural theory. From Truman's perspective he is whole and rational, his world is ordered and normal, he is the centre of his world. Others however, acting as unbeknown post-structuralists, are clearly aware that Truman's identity is a production; he is formed as a person within a whole range of practices and discourses which regulate and position him, in school, at work, in friendships, at home in the family and in the community. In terms of post-structural theory his identity is decentred, a production of various practices and discourses in which he is constituted. This idea of identity lies in sharp contrast to the idea of a fully conscious and rational individual. For Truman then his world is real, natural and meaningful but for the audience and for the actors Truman's world is contrived, a panoply of signifiers and practices within which he is formed.

For me the film raises important issues concerning identity and subjectivity and how these are formed within the different socio-cultural contexts in which we live. Such issues concern, for example, identifications of gender, class, race and sexuality and how these are formed and understood within different practices in which we become subjects of a particular kind. My task here is much narrower, to consider how identities and subjectivities are formed within the specific contexts of art in education and how such identities lead to the formation of particular subjects of practice.

CHANGING THE SUBJECT

In exploring issues of subjectivity and identity I take my lead from a difficult but in-depth investigation into subjectivity and social regulation by a group of writers who collaborated on the book, *Changing the Subject* (Henriques, Holloway, Urwin, Venn and Walkerdine, 1984). Their focus was psychology and how as a discursive practice psychology can be viewed as a productive practice which:

... produces those regulative devices which form us as objects of child development, schooling, welfare agencies, medicine, multi-cultural education, personnel practices and so forth (p. 1).

My focus will be pedagogic discourses and practices in art education and how they invoke a particular production of teachers and students as they act and perceive themselves as actors through such practices and discourses. The general drift in social and cultural theory is away from essentialist notions of identity towards anti-essentialist notions. Essentialist ideas of identity take the human individual as a unified biological and rational individual whilst anti-essentialist theories from social, cultural and psychoanalytic perspectives treat the human subject as someone who is initiated, positioned and shaped within and by language and socio-cultural contexts. These contexts order, categorise and regulate people and, as Henriques et al. (p. 1) suggest, "produce those regulative devices which form us as objects of 'social enquiry', 'medicine', 'schooling', 'law', 'multi-culturalism'."

The humanist *individual* which assumes an autonomy prior to the social world is replaced by the materialist *subject* who is formed within already existing social and cultural processes. The implications of this shift from humanism to materialism are profound. The humanist subject of Piagetian developmental theory, for example, comes into the world equipped with mental and biological capacities prior to language, which facilitate development of the individual. In such theories of development the social is not denied but it is relegated to a minor role.

The humanist position sees the individual as the agent of all social phenomena and productions, including knowledge. The specific notion of the individual contained in this outlook is one of a unitary, essentially non-contradictory and above all rational entity (Henriques et al. 1984, p. 93).

In materialist theories of human development, such as the work of Vygotsky, it is the social and linguistic practices into which the child is born which condition this process. Henriques et al. (p. 95) ask an important question. "Is the subject constitutive or constituted?" My study will focus more upon the constituted approach to subjectivity and identity but I want to reject the notion of total determination by socio-cultural processes which therefore denies any sense of agency, and consider instead how we might theorise the redundancy of the split between the social and the subject. It is difficult to disagree with the suggestion that social and cultural forces largely condition and regulate existence but it is also difficult to ignore the point that some understanding of agency is required when considering action and change particularly in the field of art practice which, historically, is premised upon notions such as self-expression and individuality. Issues of agency will be explored in more depth in Chapter 6.

Before proceeding further I should distinguish between the notions of subjectivity and identity. The notion of subjectivity, particularly stemming from the work of Foucault, relates to the process of becoming a subject within specific social and cultural practices and it is in this process that the subject acquires a particular identity or, as Hall (1996, p. 2) would argue, a particular *identification*. Put simply, individuals are formed by regulatory forces within particular socio-cultural practices such as schooling, medical, legal and family frameworks. It is in such practices that individuals occupy particular positions and therefore acquire specific identities: teacher, student, parent, doctor, patient and so on. These positionings thus involve relations of power which activate or produce certain kinds of individuals or subjects. Judith Butler (1997) points to a particular paradox of subjectivation:

The term "subjectivation" carries the paradox in itself: *assujetissment* denotes both the becoming of the subject and the process of subjection – one inhabits the figure of autonomy only by becoming subjected to a power, a subjection which implies a radical dependency (p. 83)

Further she writes:

Subjection is, literally, the *making* of a subject, the principle of regulation according to which a subject is formulated or produced. Such subjection is a kind of power that not only unilaterally *acts on* a given individual as a form of domination, but also *activates* or forms the subject. Hence, subjection is neither simply the domination of a subject nor its production, but designates a certain kind of restriction *in* production (p. 84).

Extrapolating to the context of art in education perhaps we can see that curriculum and assessment practices invoke regulatory devices so that teachers and students occupy particular positions in relation to each other and in so doing they acquire specific identities as teachers and learners. In other words the apparatus of assessment can be viewed, in Butler's terminology, as a '*certain kind of restriction in production*' of pedagogised identities in art in education, in that certain practices, skills and techniques of practice are valued over others and lead to the production of particular kinds of pedagogised subjects.

ALTHUSSER

The French philosopher Althusser was interested in the way in which social practices position and regulate human beings. Using the notion of *interpellation* he describes how people are 'hailed' into subjective positions within institutional and other social contexts. According to him individuals (mis)recognise themselves from the positions they occupy in relation to others within specific contexts of practice. This can be understood in the relations that exist between doctors and patients or teachers and their students. Within the institutional dynamics of schooling, teachers and students position themselves in relation to each other respectively as, the 'subject supposed to know' and the 'subject seeking to know'. This is a relation of interpellation that is dependent upon a particular construction of knowledge, teaching and learning which are ideological rather than 'natural'.

For Althusser the idea of interpellation rests on the idea of subject *misrecognition*. What he means by this I think is that the ideological character of institutional formations, in which subjects relate to each other, goes largely unnoticed so that relations between subjects appear quite normal. The problem with the idea of *misrecognition* is that it seems to presuppose the something more fundamental, that the ideological identification covers over a prior, perhaps natural, reality. Ideology for Althusser is therefore a process of distortion that prevents the mind from gaining true understanding (see Henriques et al. 1984, p. 98). The implication of this idea of ideological distortion suggests that if we could reach behind the ideological fabrications of gender, class, race or sexuality, for example, we would be able to achieve an ideology-free existence. This sentiment is close to but not commensurate with the work of Habermas, discussed earlier, and his idea of an emancipated practice of communication. Althusser's essential point then is that it is not reality *in itself* which determines representation and meaning but the ideological processes of representation through which we understand social reality. But his use of the term *misrecognition* leaves open the possibility of theorising a prior ideology free state. Althusser's theory of interpellation is theoretically more far reaching than Habermas's notion of an ideal communicative state and in the next chapter I will show how Lacan and Zizek develop the idea of misrecognition in relation to subjectivity in a more radical direction.

FOUCAULT

The work of Michel Foucault has produced a strong and continuing impact upon social and cultural theory. His earlier work (1970, 1972) is concerned with charting the development of social institutions and forms of knowledge particularly those in the social sciences. By examining the growth of institutions, such as prisons, hospitals, asylums and schools, he describes how their respective changing practices form and then reform particular perceptions and conceptions of behaviour that create specific subjectivities and identifications. His work on madness (1967) describes how perceptions, practices and knowledges relating to the mentally ill have changed across centuries and, therefore, how perceptions of madness and mental illness change. This investigation leads to the idea that there is no essential truth about madness but that it is conceived differently within different historical practices and forms of knowledge. It is possible to conduct a similar examination of school practices and knowledges within which teachers and their students function. If we consider the content, structure and organisation of school practices over the last century it is possible to show how, within these practices, students and teachers have acquired specific pedagogised identities. The implicit materialism of this approach to understanding how subjectivities and identities are formed indicates that as pedagogical subjects both teachers and students are products of the specific historical discourses and practices in which they function. One of my tasks below is to show how teachers and students engaged in art activities achieve specific identities which are produced by certain discourses and practices and how, when these change, different identities and subjects of art education may emerge.

NORMALISATION

An important Foucauldian device for understanding how individuals and their particular identities are formed within institutional practices is the idea of *normalisation*. This concept relates to the point that within institutions and their forms of knowledge particular behaviours (skills, forms of understanding) are viewed as normal whilst others are regarded as odd, deviant or even pathological. In school examination and assessment practices the work of students is measured according to particular criteria that establish norms, which constitute desirable behaviour and practices. I shall discuss this in more detail shortly when I consider how student's art practices are assessed in schools. It is therefore according to the power of the norm that teachers and students as pedagogised subjects become regulated and their pedagogised identities formed. Norms of child development can be identified in conceptual frameworks such as 'stages of development' which were consolidated in developmental psychology as a consequence of Piaget's work on cognitive development. These stages describe the norms of behaviour, cognitions and perceptions which children are expected to evolve at different ages, as such they provide psychologists and teachers who ascribe to this particular understanding of development, (there are some who do not), with a pattern of normal development. What such norms do not question is the norm itself and how it is constituted within its specific focus of practice. In the context of art education the notion of stages of development has been applied to the development of children's drawings. These stages describe development in drawing as an incremental progression from so called scribble drawings towards linear perspective; although not everyone attains the latter. Lowenfeld and Brittain (1970, pp. 36–40) provide a clear description of these stages which they list as, the scribbling stage, the preschematic stage, the schematic stage, the stage of dawning realism and the pseudo-naturalistic stage. Barrett (1979) and Willats (1997, p. 292) also provide diagrammatic illustrations of developmental sequences in children's drawings. Both writers suggest that drawing development can be conceived as the employment of different drawing systems at particular ages. Each drawing system; non-projective systems, orthogonal projection, oblique projection, naÔve perspective and perspective, demands a more advanced understanding of drawing 'rules' that enable its production. Although these sequences can be observed in the drawing schemas produced by children at different ages they presuppose drawing development as the ability to depict views. Thus the idea of development in drawing is underpinned by a specific kind of representational practice and this tends to prohibit conceiving development as adopting other forms of visual production. The difficulty for me is the normalising effect of different drawing systems when they are used to identify a child's or student's level of drawing ability.

DISCOURSE

The formation and practice of discourse is an important focus of Foucault's work, and it is this practice which I believe provides the possibility of dissolving the dualism between the subject and the social, Henriques et al. (1984) state:

Foucault suggests that the social sciences are discourses and practices that positively help to construct the various apparatuses and institutions that together form 'society', or rather the 'social'. The social sciences, therefore, are actively imbricated in the practices and relations between people that constitute social existence. It is from that point of view that we regard the production of discourses and that of subjectivity and of sociality to be indissoluble (p. 106).

Foucault (1972) writing in purple prose states that he:

. . . Would like to show that 'discourses', in the form in which they can be heard or read, are not, as one might expect, a mere intersection of things and words: an obscure web of things, and a manifest, visible, coloured chain of words; I would like to show that discourse is not a slender surface of contact, or confrontation, between a reality and a language (. . .), the intrication of a lexicon and an appearance; I would like to show with precise examples that in analysing discourses themselves, one sees the loosening of the embrace, apparently so tight, of words and things, and the emergence of a group of rules proper to discursive practice. These rules define not the dumb existence of a reality, nor the canonical use of a vocabulary, but the ordering of objects. 'Words and things' is the entirely serious title of a problem; it is the ironic title of a work that modifies its own form, displaces its own data, and reveals, at the end of the day, a quite different task. A task that consists of not – of no longer – treating discourses as groups of signs (signifying elements referring to contents or representations) but as practices which systematically form the objects of which they speak (pp. 48–49 my emphasis).

In this passage from *The Archaeology of Knowledge*, Foucault leaves in abeyance the representational relation of words to things and begins to chart his project in which he investigates how discursive objects, such as, 'the child', 'the student', 'the teacher', 'the patient', 'the doctor', and so on, which appear natural, are formed within specific discursive practices such as education, medicine or psychology. Coward and Ellis (1977) state that:

Because all the practices that make up a social totality take place in language, it becomes possible to consider language as the place in which the social individual is constructed (p. 1).

The general picture to be drawn from much of the work on discourse therefore is that discourses as forms of language which function within particular sites of practice produce the objects of which they speak, rather than discovering them. Discursive objects such as *ability, standards, intelligence, learning* and *development* do not exist prior to discourse but are constructions made within specific practices and discourses. Discourses impart a controlling effect upon us because they structure our understanding and actions within our various sites of practice. Families, schools, political meetings, bars and playgroups all involve discursive practices that are particular to their contexts and which provide meaning to actions taken. Ball (1990) argues:

Discourses are . . . about what can be said, and thought, but also about who can speak, when, where and with what authority. Discourses embody meaning and social relationships, they constitute both subjectivity and power relations. . . . Thus discourses construct certain possibilities for thought (p. 17).

Because discourses structure understanding and meaning within contexts of practice they also construct specific subject identities. Teachers function within discursive practices constituted by bodies of knowledge and practice, in which they understand their actions as teachers and through which they read the actions and learning of their students. Further because discourses form the meaning matrices in which teacher's actions and students' learning are understood, such discourses are imbued with power. In schools therefore such discourses give substance to pedagogic authority. This imbuing of discursive power in relation to the formation of identity is described by Walkerdine (1990):

Modern apparatuses of social regulation, along with other social and cultural practices, produce knowledges which claim to 'identify' individuals. These knowledges create the possibility of multiple practices, multiple positions. To be a 'clever child' or a 'good mother' for example, makes sense only in terms given by pedagogic, welfare, medical, legal and other discourses and practices. These observe, sanction and correct how we act; they attempt to define who and what we are (p. 199, my emphasis).

Stuart Hall (1996) concludes:

Precisely because identities are structured within, not outside, discourse, we need to understand them as produced within specific historical and institutional sites within specific discursive formations and practices, by specific enunciative strategies (p. 4).

I will attempt to develop such understanding in relation to discourses of art in education.

DISCOURSES OF NORMALISATION AND IDENTIFICATION IN ART
EDUCATION (DISCIPLINARY KNOWLEDGE)

My concern is with the formation of pedagogised identities within the discursive practices which constitute art in education and which operate within
schools and curriculum policies. The way in which teachers perceive and understand their students as learners, and the way in which students perceive and
understand their learning, occurs through particular discourses which inform
and regulate teaching and learning. Such discourses operate through specific
enunciative strategies, such as assessment, which construct pedagogic meaning.
I can illustrate this point by reference to the text of a fairly recent publication in England by the School Curriculum and Assessment Authority
(SCAA 1996) concerning assessment of art practice at Key Stage 3 of the
National Curriculum for Art. The text, *Consistency in Teacher Assessment:
Exemplification of Standards*, contains a foreward from Sir Ron Dearing, the
chairperson of SCAA, to teachers which states:

By making assessments during the key stage you will build up your knowledge of individual
pupils' strengths and weaknesses, which will help you plan your teaching. By judging at the
end of the key stage the extent to which a pupil's performance relates to the end of key stage
descriptions set out in the National Curriculum Orders, you will provide important information
for pupils, their parents and your colleagues (p. i.).

It is my contention that the criteria that constitute the assessment discourse
are also constitutive of 'pupils' strengths and weaknesses' and the teachers'
'knowledge of individuals' produces students' pedagogised identities. An
illustration of this discursive identification process can be found at the
beginning of the SCAA document where an attempt is made to identify particular standards of art practice (in line with the current educational rhetoric
in England of standards in education), these standards, in Foucauldian terms,
establish norms of practice. Three paintings produced by students who are
engaged in a project on the local environment are used as exemplars to
represent three norms of practice. The discursive norms stated by SCAA are;
working towards, *achieving* and *working beyond* the expectation of practice,
which in this particular case is concerned with recording responses, through
observation of the natural and made environment. These three categories
establish a normative framework in which students' art practice is assessed,
positioned and regulated, but no definitions of what constitutes a particular
norm of *working towards*, *achieving* or *working beyond* are provided. But as
we read on and consider the assessment comments for each of the three painting
what the norm consists of becomes clearer.

The SCAA assessment comments focus upon the student's ability to record
what is seen, and, significantly, the term accurate is employed as a key
assessment criterion. The painting considered to be working towards the
expectation of practice at this key stage is described:

Information about the shapes of buildings and machinery which feature in the environment has been observed and recorded but greater analysis is needed in order to represent this accurately (p. 8).

The painting viewed as *achieving* the expected standard is described:

The shapes of building and other objects in the environment have been selected, analysed and represented with some accuracy, technical skill and attention to detail which indicates first-hand observation (p. 9).

The painting assessed as *working beyond* the expected standard is described:

There is detailed and accurate analysis of the buildings and their surroundings. The shapes of buildings and details of the setting have been selected, recorded and organised into a coherent form (p. 10).

The frequent use of the term *accuracy* and other terms, *observation* and *technical skill*, is telling and I believe that it is this deceptive word which constitutes the norm according to which the paintings are assessed. Further, it is according to this word *accuracy* that each student's pedagogised identity as a subject of art practice is produced. What does this term imply in the context of the student's art practice, which is concerned with recording observations of the natural and made environment? I suggest in the context of this specific drawing and painting activity it implies that drawing and painting as practices of observation and representation are concerned with the depiction of accurate views, (and that this is achievable). A further implication is that vision is assumed to be a universal process in which data from the external world is received unmediated and that the ability to render this unmediated information rests upon the individual student's skill. The term *accurate* implies, I suggest, that it is possible to produce a representation that directly corresponds to a particular view. Thus this term invokes what I have called earlier a particular discourse and practice of visuality in which each student's art work *becomes visible and regulated as art practice*. Variation in the standards (of accuracy) achieved by each student rests upon their varying ability as determined by this specific discourse and practice of visuality.

An interesting issue here is that it is well understood by many people that observational painting and drawing does not mirror reality, yet there is still a tendency, as the use of the words *accurate, technical skill* and *observation* demonstrate, to act as though that is its purpose. The term *accurate* establishes a conterminous relation between a visual representation and a prior observed reality and simultaneously a normative structure of representation within which the three paintings are positioned. Once we acknowledge that an *accurate visual representation* of perceptual experience is not possible, we might also begin to consider how the term *accuracy* is being used. I suspect that rather than invoking a prior reality which can be used as an assessment yardstick, it invokes an established and valued representational system. Thus the term *accuracy* is not concerned with the depiction of optical truth but with the ability to conform to a particular semiotic practice. Crucially then the term *accuracy* is a key discursive figure which designates a student's painting practice not simply and directly for other individuals such as other students and teachers, but primarily for the symbolic and normative order of a particular representational system in which the three paintings are inserted in order to achieve meaning.

Jenks (1995) warns us in relation to an uncritical acceptance of semiotic practices:

It is essential that we cast our critical gaze upon constellations of interests inherent in and protected by any social order of signs and images, or rather the consensus world view that they seek to promote – it is essential because we are now addressing the exercise of power (p. 15)!

The approach to assessment of students' art work I have just described can therefore be understood as a specific discursive practice in which particular norms of practice are established and according to which students' practices are positioned, regulated and understood. Such assessment practices are constituted by powerful codes of recognition through which student's art work is made visible. The immanence of power in such discursive practices is often difficult to detect because of our tendency to comprehend such practices as based upon natural capacities or facilities. But it is through the consecration of particular forms of art practice and the subsequent consecration of particular students of practice (often those seen to possess artistic talent) that relations of power in the pedagogic context constitute specific pedagogised identities in the field of art education.

POWER-KNOWLEDGE

Foucault employs the term *power-knowledge* to describe how knowledge is imbued with power in fields of practice. Manifestations of power-knowledge can be seen in the relations developed between teachers and students where particular forms of practice and knowledge are desired. Such relations can also be found in the construction and imposition of curriculum content and practices by government who then assess teachers' competence according to government standards. One view of knowledge and power is to regard them as separate entities whereby knowledge is viewed as a search for truth that is taken to exist in particular fields of practice. Power, on the other hand is often regarded as a kind of possession used to dominate others particularly in institutional contexts or organisations such as the state. Foucault's integration of power-knowledge invokes the idea that the acquisition, transmission or use of knowledge, (particularly disciplinary knowledge of pedagogic or curriculum discourses which constitute different teaching sites) implicate forms of power. According to Usher and Edwards (1994),

Power is manifested as relationships in a social network. . . . Power, through knowledge, brings forth active "subjects" who better "understand" their own subjectivity yet who in this very process subject themselves to forms of power (p. 89).

To understand this idea it is important to remember what was stated above regarding discourse and the idea that discourses constitute truths as opposed to revealing truths. The fact that a particular discourse of assessment in art education leads to the production of pedagogic identity means that the knowledge which constitutes this practice is imbued with power. I will describe a specific piece of practice and assessment in order to show how Foucault's conception of power-knowledge relations may be perceived in the teaching and learning nexus of art education.

Consider the drawing in Figure 38. It is the outcome of a homework assignment given to a Year 7 (11–12 years) student in an English secondary school. The students were asked by their teacher to, 'arrange a table setting for a meal'. They were to include a 'plate with food, knife and fork, cup and saucer, placemat, teapot, salt and pepper pots.' They were told to plan the composition carefully and to use tone to make their objects look three-dimensional. The assessment of this particular drawing was encouraging in relation to the student's use of tone, but then continued, "The angles of view and proportions are *incorrect*. Please try a similar drawing again after our discussion (my emphasis)."

The terms forming the assessment of the drawing, 'angles of view' and 'proportion', predicate a particular paradigm of representational drawing

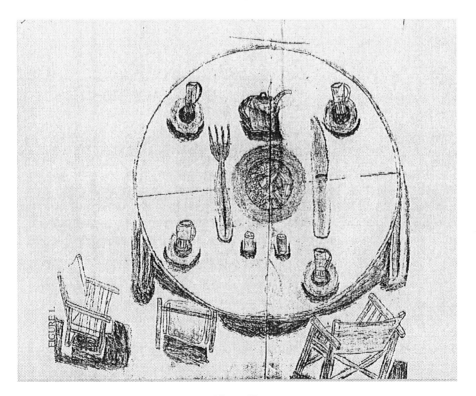

Figure 38.

practice often associated with drawing systems such as oblique projection or linear perspective. The predication of this representational paradigm in the assessment comments thus anticipates a particular drawing (representational) form and, by implication, a particular kind of drawer. It is this metonymic drawing-drawer relation in which the assessment discourse signifies the student's drawing where power functions and has productive implications for the perception and designation of the student's drawing ability. Put another way, it is in this discursive practice where the art practice of the student is made visible to both teacher and student.

If this drawing is assessed from within the practice and terminology of perspective, which involves drawing objects from a fixed viewpoint, then the assessment comment can be understood. This representational practice implies a specific drawing-drawer relation, in that a particular practice is invoked along with the expectation of a particular student of practice. Within this paradigm of representational practice therefore, a specific perception and positioning of the drawing is established as well as a specific construction of the student-as-drawer and teacher as assessor. Here the predication of a particular paradigm of representational practice exerts the Foucauldian power-knowledge relation in which students and their teachers understand their subjectivities as pedagogised individuals and who, in this process of identification subject themselves (unknowingly) to forms of power, which are somehow perceived as natural processes and propensities. However, assessing, positioning and regulating this drawing within the discursive practice aligned to a particular paradigm of visual representation, ignores the possibility of viewing the drawing in terms of other representational or signifying practices. I have already employed the terms visuality, metaphoric and metonymic relations of signification to discuss alternative semiotic practices that within the context of the student's practice, may constitute a legitimate and perhaps complex signifying logic.

Returning again to the ideas on discourse I have presented above. It is important to acknowledge that the assessment of this particular drawing is not an assessment of drawing ability *in* the student or *in* the drawing (although this appears to be the case) but that the assessment discourse constructs, regulates and confirms a particular kind of drawer within a specific pedagogic gaze. We are concerned therefore with contemplating how the signifier of ability brings the student and teacher as pedagogised subjects into being; how the subject becomes a subject through the agency of the signifier. A student's ability in drawing practice is not to be viewed therefore as an inherent capacity which can be liberated or discovered (even though we may think this to be the case), but as constituted in particular sites of practice and their corresponding discourses which, through their particular regimes of power-knowledge, constitute and regulate aspects of subjectivity, such as drawing ability and teacher assessment.

The power that is implicit to a particular discursive practice in the field of art education exerts inclusionary and exclusionary forces. In assessment practices students are subjected to the gaze of certain knowledge and practice discourses according to which their practices are measured and categorised. A powerful discourse in art education which in many ways is connected to the assessment statement relating to the drawing just discussed, concerns what might be referred to as the 'basic vocabulary of art.' This vocabulary is frequently highlighted in curriculum content discourses and designated programmes of study in the English National Curriculum for Art and Design. I refer to what are often called *basic elements* of art practice such as, line, tone, texture, pattern, colour and proportion, which constitute *visual literacy*. These elements and the notion of visual literacy constitute a specific discourse which identifies particular teachable aspects of art practice (see for example DfEE 1995). A good deal of art practice in secondary schools in England is still devoted to students acquiring and developing visual skills and techniques which relate to these basic elements. Within such a practico-discursive regime, students' identities as art practitioners are constituted in terms of their ability to develop skills in the basic elements. Thus it is within this particular discourse and practice (the basic elements of art) that students are perceived as powerful (able) or not (less able) and, as I have already stated, this categorisation appears to be based upon natural processes and propensities. Usher and Edwards (1994) point to the concealed and intrinsic aspects of power-knowledge discourses:

Power-knowledge formations operate through the practices which inscribe the person as a particular subject prior to entering an educational institution and those practices they are engaged in once within it; in becoming a 'subject' we learn to be a 'subject' of a particular sort. It is our assumptions about the nature of the 'subject' which then inform our practices as teachers and learners, yet the effect of power which gives rise to the particular positioning of subjects is effectively veiled (p. 96).

The basic elements of art provide a list of teachable skills and allow the teacher to assess ability in a particular aspect of art practice. Although it is not easy to identify an exact rubric for assessment in such assessment practices student's art work is often compared against a putative set of criteria relating, for instance, to proportion, tone, projection and composition, which are presumed but not made explicit. Such criteria establish a normalising discourse that separates, categorises and regulates individual ability. The students therefore *become* their abilities and similarly the teachers *become* their practices. The normalising criteria appear neutral, thus objective, and we believe that they are identifying natural processes and capacities. It is as though the discourse is identifying something in the student, something which is natural and inborn. My intention is not to dismiss the value of introducing students to those traditions of art practice associated with the basic elements but to illustrate the productive nature of such discourses and practices and how they produce particular kinds of subjects of practice. This may then open up possibilities for considering other forms of practice and recognising other subjects of practice.

In summary then, through such normalising discourses and practices students' abilities are classified, they become objectified in the eyes of their teachers as possessing particular levels of ability and, simultaneously, students learn the truth about their ability through assessment according to what appear to be neutral criteria. These criteria hide from scrutiny the specific cultural and ideological forces (power-knowledges) through which they have become established and, as Usher and Edwards indicate, appear to refer to natural capacities:

In effect they [the students] become their capacities and it is through these capacities, or the lack of them, that they become 'objects' of surveillance, examination and governance. The significance and power of normalisation is precisely that it appears to be neutral. In its objectivity it appears to be simply a neutral procedure for ascertaining inherent natural capacities (p. 103).

My reason for elaborating and applying Foucault's conception of power-knowledge formations is that I believe it can be helpful in ascertaining the hegemony of particular forms of practice and their associated discourses through which we understand and perceive student's art practices and, by implication teacher's practices. If we return to the assessment statement on the drawing in Figure 38, the word *incorrect* can be understood as a key term that invokes a particular discursive attitude to visual representation in which the drawing is perceived as weak or unsatisfactory. Further, this statement establishes in the mind of the student the idea that the drawing is not a successful visual representation. But it is possible to argue that the drawing is *incorrect* only if it is assumed that the task is to make an observational drawing from a fixed viewpoint, but this was not required according to the student's homework instructions. Another interpretation of this drawing which invokes a rather different metonymic drawing-drawer relation, can elicit a very different reading of drawing practice and subsequently the student's drawing ability. In contrast to comprehending this drawing as confused or incorrect it is possible to view it as a creative and inventive orchestration of visual semiotics. In the drawing, objects such as the table, plate, sauces, knife and fork are depicted in terms of their enduring shapes irrespective of viewpoint. Other objects, such as the cups and chairs are depicted as though seen from a particular viewing position. The relative sizes of the objects on the table, although not 'true to life', produce a compositional symmetry within the circle of the table and this arrangement may signify a symbolising hierarchy. It is as though in the process of drawing the student is responding to different semiotic interests some of which are not consistent with the depiction of views. If we look at the depiction of the chairs in this drawing we can perhaps recognise the student's struggle to deal with a different representational issue than that concerning his depiction of the table or the plates. Here we can see that the student is concerned with a series of different metonymic and metaphoric relations within the 'same' drawing practice.

The outcome of the drawing interpreted within this more expansive discourse is to view it as an elaborate medley of graphic forms that constitute an intricate and legitimate semiotic arrangement for the student (Atkinson 1993). In other words the drawing becomes a *different practice and product* when interpreted within this alternative discourse. It is essential to remember that the homework instructions did not insist upon or even mention that the drawing should be produced from a fixed viewpoint, but this seems to be implied in the assessment remarks. The assessment discourse predicates a specific form of visual production and thus a particular representational practice and a particular kind of drawer. In this sense the assessment discourse constitutes a power-knowledge discourse in which drawing ability makes sense only in the specific terms of the discourse (and its associated practice) for the student and teacher. Power is invoked through the use of the term *incorrect* in order to describe 'the angles of view.' This term may signify the incommensurability between the meaning relations that are intrinsic to the student's drawing practice and those of the assessment practice. However, when employed by the *authority* of the teacher this term positions and regulates both the drawing and the student-as-drawer within the teacher's drawing-drawer discourse.

Within such assessment practices therefore it is possible to see how students' pedagogised identities are constructed and also how teachers' identities are formed within the discourses and practices which they value or are expected to teach. It is within the specific meaning relations constituted within specific practices and discourses of art education that students' abilities are observed, sanctioned, corrected and positioned. My use of the dyad, drawing-drawer, is a theoretical device for reflecting upon the point that different discourses of interpreting drawing practices and drawing products will invoke different drawing-drawer relations. Consequently this enables the possibility of extending our understanding of drawing and other art practices and the different ways in which students are able to employ and orchestrate legitimate visual representations. It also allows educators to critically evaluate their understanding of art practice, visual production and visual literacy. Furthermore this dyad foregrounds the ontological orientation of students' different art practices and the important point that art practices, such as drawing and painting are the process and outcomes of locally grounded experiences and responses.

VIDEO SEQUENCE

A second illustration of the formation of pedagogised identities within discursive practices which form part of the field of art education can be seen in a video sequence in which a group of teachers are asked to assess two drawings of a chair produced by students aged 15–16 years. The video was produced by the Inner London Education Authority (ILEA) some years ago, in 1986, in order to disseminate key issues and the general framework of the General Certificate of Secondary Education (GCSE) Examination in Art and Design.

Although the GCSE Examination in Art and Design has passed through several changes since this video was released, the particular sequence to which I shall make reference contains comments made by teachers which I believe are still similar and not untypical of those used by teachers and educators today when discussing and assessing student's art work.

The GCSE examination was introduced in schools in England and Wales for students aged 15–16 years, and the examination places particular emphasis upon the art process as well as the final outcome. Preparatory studies in the form of sketchbook work or written notes and observations as well as the finished piece of art work are considered in the assessment process. Assessment must therefore try to incorporate and consider a student's intentions and the individual routes according to which the final piece of work is achieved. In the sequence I have chosen from the video a group of teachers of art and design in secondary schools in London are asked by the discussion leader to consider two pencil drawings of a chair. The leader asks the teachers if they are prepared to state which is the better drawing, even though they know nothing of the context in which each drawing was produced. The teachers all indicate that this is possible and together they proceed to describe the qualities of the more successful drawing:

Better composition . . . better structured . . . finer balance to it . . . more exciting . . . it moves you into the picture . . . it sits well on the paper . . . more awareness of texture . . . better perspective.

I have thought about this video sequence on many occasions and empathise with this group of teachers and their assessment remarks. I employed a similar discourse to assess student's art work when I taught art in secondary schools. For me the sequence raises important issues relating to how we interpret student's art practices and how, within such interpretations, the art work is made visible as art work. I want to stress the point that the teachers' comments actually *produce* the drawings as drawings of a particular kind within their specific discursive practice. In other words, it is in this particular set of terms that the drawings are conceived as drawings and further, that one drawing is viewed as more successful than the other. This point has significant bearing upon teachers' perceptions and understanding of all art work produced by their students and by implication upon student's perceptions of their own art practices.

As the teachers' discussion continues, directed by the discussion leader, they begin to consider the context in which student's art work is produced. They acknowledge the point that if a student believes the outcome of a particular art activity meets initial intentions then it would be improper to assess the work according to a set of prescribed formal criteria. In this case assessment, they agree, should be grounded in or be commensurate with the student's agenda for practice. The tricky issue here however is that whenever assessment of art practice occurs in relation to established art practices (e.g. Drawing or painting from observation) it is almost impossible *not* to allow prescribed formal expectations to influence assessment. Assessment discourses are themselves based upon consecrated art practices which establish specific discourses in which practice is acknowledged, understood and legitimated as practice. Such discourses, as I have stated, produce specific power-knowledge relations in which art practices are recognised and valued and, consequently, in which students' abilities are validated. Here perhaps we can see that when such discourses are employed they establish powerful forces of inclusion and exclusion that are accepted by both teachers and their students. The implication of such discursive practices, which constitute teaching and learning in art education, for responding to the difference of students' art practices is magnified when we contemplate the task of teaching and assessing art in an inter-cultural social context. Such implications will be developed in Chapter 9 where I look at issues for developing art education in contemporary socio-cultural contexts. However a more recent exemplar of assessment from the current GCSE (16+) examination in England raises similar issues.

In the Edexcel GCSE (2000–2002) examination in England assessment is described according to six assessment objectives according to which student's work should be considered:

AO1: record observations, experiences and ideas that are appropriate to intentions;
AO2: investigate visual and other sources of information;
AO3: explore and use a range of media for working in two and/or three dimensions;
AO4: review, refine and modify work as it progresses;
AO5: identify the distinctive characteristics of art, craft and design and relate them to the context in which the work was created, making connections with their own work;
AO5: make critical judgements about art, craft and design, using a specialist vocabulary.

Each of these assessment objectives are subdivided into five levels of ability, (limited, basic, competent, confident, fluent,), and the assessor's task is to plot each student's ability onto a particular level for each assessment objective. There is no clear indication of what constitutes the difference between the levels of ability, leaving those decisions to be made through the professional judgements of teachers. Leaving aside criticising this assessment discourse as a particularly mechanistic portrayal of art practice and learning through art, the way the assessment matrix is employed through different art teacher's anticipations and expectations, or to use a Gadamerian term, teachers' 'prejudices', of practice is interesting. In Chapter 8 I describe how one GCSE moderator had great difficulty assessing some of the work in one school because he felt it was, in his words, "too conceptual." He found great difficulty in placing this work within his expectations and understanding of practice as viewed through the assessment objectives of the assessment discourse.

I have concentrated upon the creation of pedagogised identities in art education by employing ideas from Foucault and others in order to describe the productive properties of discourse and the power-knowledge relations that are constituted within specific discursive practices that compose art in education. I want to extend this study of identity and subjectivity in the next chapter by drawing upon some psychoanalytic discourses, which I use to explore practices in art education.

CHAPTER SIX

IDENTITY AND PSYCHOANALYSIS

During the last three decades the study of identity in a variety of social and cultural fields has grown in almost exponential proportions, a growth rate which could be said to be correlative with the increasing diversity and plurality of social contexts in which people live. It is a concept of burgeoning complexity as is indicated by its study in the work of critical and cultural theorists, artists, film-makers, writers or musicians. According to post-structural theories of the decentred and fragmented self, the search for enduring stable identities and the idea of an essential self has to be abandoned. Any attempt to separate the individual from the social is problematic because they are interdependent and construct each other. It makes no sense therefore to speak of a unified and autonomous self who can be separated from the social, the self is always a social construction and this construction involves a series of intermeshing relations of power, ideology and practice.

The American artist Barbara Kruger examines and questions particular gendered identities in much of her work. In one untitled piece from 1985 two square red picture frames stand almost side-by-side; in the left hand frame is the text, 'HELP I'm locked inside this picture.' In the right hand frame there is a photographic image of a female face partly obscured by a framing device the woman appears to be holding. The piece raises several issues about the formation, or rather the framing, of gender. The physical structure of the frames are suggestive of other kinds of frames, such as language, discourse, ideology and practice, for example, in which identifications are formed. The frame also suggests an inside and an outside, an identity and an 'other' beyond the specific framing of identity. It could be argued therefore that although the frame appears to separate an identity from an outside 'other', that identity itself is dependent on this outside, this other. The work of Cindy Sherman also focuses on the construction of identities as she confronts us with contrived portrayals of women in film stills.

Stuart Hall (1996) writes:

It seems to be in the attempt to rearticulate the relationships between subjects and discursive practices that the question of identity recurs – or rather, if one prefers to stress the process of subjectification to discursive practices, and the politics of exclusion which all such subjectification appears to entail, the question of *identification* (p. 2).

The process of identification is highly complex. Much of Foucault's work investigates the formation of subjectivity in discursive and institutional practices and their implicit power relations. It could be argued however that, useful as Foucault's ideas on normalisation and disciplinary power are, they present an interpretation of the formation of subjectivity in which the individual is allowed little sense of agency or active performance. In his later work however Foucault (1987, p. 5) does suggest the idea of a more active subject when proposing "a hermeneutics of desire," in relation to a process whereby individuals investigate the methods through which they interpret themselves as subjects. For Hall (1996) this represents:

. . . a significant advance, since it addresses for the first time in Foucault's major work the existence of some interior landscape of the subject, some interior mechanisms of assent to the rule, as well as its objectively disciplining force, which saves the account from the 'behaviourism' and objectivism which threatens certain parts of *Discipline and Punish*.

It is the notion of 'interior landscape' that provides a way out of the behaviourist impasse often cited as a limitation of the 'discursive subject'. Zizek (1989, p. 2) discusses Foucault's later work on sexuality and draws our attention to the latter's concern with marginal lifestyles and the process of an aestheticization of the self, a production of the self through a particular art of living. However, for Zizek, this suggests a return to a humanist tradition close to the Renaissance ideal of making one's life a work of art. Although the notion of the subject possessing an essential core self has been disputed convincingly in post-structural theory we do need to understand how individuals *actively* engage with and take on or reject particular identifications rather than allow themselves to be passively determined by them. It is by reference to work in the field of psychoanalysis that we can begin to understand how such processes of active identification might arise and in this field the notions of *lack, desire* and the *other* and *fantasy* are key factors that must be considered.

LACAN, THE IMAGINARY, THE SYMBOLIC AND THE REAL

The work of Jacques Lacan offers a way of considering subjectivity and identity that moves beyond both essentialist, social constructivist and post-structural theorisations. Lacan theorises the processes of subjectivity and identification through three inter-connecting registers: the imaginary, the symbolic and the Real. His work is built of that of Freud, which argued that subjectivity cannot be understood in terms of the humanist, rational and conscious subject, but involves a split between unconscious, pre-conscious and conscious systems. It is this idea of a split subject that Lacan's work develops.

The imaginary

In a paper originally written in 1936 Lacan formulated his ideas about the mirror phase of development in early childhood. Buchanan (2000, p. 115) provides a helpful reminder that Lacan's paper was motivated by a brief footnote written by Freud (1984) in *Beyond the Pleasure Principle*. Freud describes the legendary *fort/da* game played by his grandson. In the game the young child is playing with a wooden reel tied to a piece of string, he throws the reel out of his cot so that it disappears to the exclamation 'o-o-o-o' (which sounded like a nascent *fort* the German word for gone). By pulling on the length of string the child retrieves the absent reel and this act is accompanied by the happy exclamation, *da*, meaning 'there'. The game is concerned with disappearance and return and the child's ability to control these processes. Freud argues that the game is a means by which the child is able to come to terms with the disappearance and return of the mother. The reel becomes a substitute, a representative of the mother and thus allows the child to cope with an unhappy situation by providing a source of pleasure in disappointment. This pleasure arises because it is the child who is actively engaged in transforming an unpleasant situation into one which is more pleasant. Freud (1984) describes a related game in a footnote where the child has found a way of making himself disappear.

He had discovered his reflection in a full-length mirror which did not quite reach to the ground, so that by crouching down he could make his mirror-image 'gone' (p. 284).

This act of recognition and its associated pleasure is a key factor in Lacan's description of the mirror phase as he describes the very young, uncoordinated child contemplating its unified image in a mirror. Lacan suggests that the child becomes seduced by and gains pleasure from this ideal image of itself because it provides the child with a sense of unity with which it identifies and desires. In other words the child's identification of itself is located in something (the mirror image) that it is not, something that is different from itself but which it desires. Identification of self is therefore formed according to an *ideal* 'other' of the mirror reflection. This imaginary process involves a fundamental splitting between the I which looks and the I that is seen, a splitting that is ameliorated by the possibility of coherence and unity provided by the mirror image. A coherence and unity that the child lacks but desires. Buchanan (p. 117) describes how in later life this imaginary process of identification with an ideal other can be detected in 'other mirrors', such as educational qualifications whereby we anticipate life after study. Here the qualification (GCSE, A Level, Degree), is that mirror towards which we strive, in which we perceive that other self 'without ever really knowing what it would entail to be that other self.' This is not a passive notion of contemplation but an active process involving the desire to assume a particular self, stemming from a perceived lack. The fascinating issue here is that although we are provided with an active idea of self through the process of desire, which thereby invokes a sense of agency, the self is a representation as it is formed in relation to 'an other;' we might in fact say that the self is 'other'. So the subject, by implication, is grounded in or constituted by a semiotic process and if we take this idea on board the self cannot therefore be conceived as a natural and unified entity but rather, as a constructed project.

The general purpose of the imaginary and the mirror phase is to describe early processes of (mis)recognition and identification with idealised images, signifiers, which prepare the child's access to Lacan's second domain, the complex world of the symbolic. It is not the case that the imaginary disappears on entry to the symbolic but that the symbolic comes to dominate understanding. In the symbolic orders of language and other forms of social and cultural practice the child's initial imaginary relation between self and other is developed into more complex identifications of self and others which arise, for example, in institutions such as schools. It is in such institutions that desires to develop and become particular kinds of individuals are engineered and regulated. The student's desire to become a particular kind of learner in the eyes of 'others' (her teacher, forms of knowledge, the examination) is therefore based upon a more fundamental relationship which includes the unconscious self of desire and the self (other) of signification. It is thus possible to argue that when we are assessing such things as ability in art practice our assessment is grounded in a relation of desire and signification whereby the student's or child's ability is identified not 'in-itself' but through and for the ideological signifiers that constitute the framework of assessment criteria. Ability is thus a signifier, it is not a substantial pre-existing signified which gives rise to a signifier. For Lacan the signifier provides the *illusion* of a pre-existing signified.

The symbolic

As the child becomes ensconced in the use and laws of language he or she becomes a subject-of-language. The subject thus becomes an effect of the power of the signifier. Easthope (2002, p. 5) quotes Lacan:

The definition of a signifier is that it represents a subject not for another subject but for another signifier. This is the only definition possible of the signifier as different from the sign. The sign is something that represents something for somebody, but the signifier is something that represents a subject for another signifier (Lacan 1972, p. 194).

Lacan prioritises the signifier over the signified in contrast to Saussure's more isomorphic relation. Saussure's definition of the sign relation between signifier and signified seems to suggest a representational relation of correspondence (see Stavrakakis 1999, pp. 23–24) in which the signified seems to precede the signifier. Lacan (1977, p. 149) erects a bar between signifier and signified placing emphasis upon the signifier and in doing this he disrupts the unity of the Sausurrean sign. For Lacan meaning is a consequence of relations between signifiers and not between signifier and signified, the signified is always slipping beneath the passage of the signifier. This does not mean that the signified is eliminated but, as Stavrakakis (pp. 24–25) claims, "Lacan understands the signified as an effect of transference." Further he writes, "If there is a signified it can only be a signifier to which we attribute a transferential signified function (p. 27)." This is to argue that the signifier creates the *illusion* of a substantial signified, thus the signifiers *ability* or *intelligence*, for example, create the illusion of an existing physical or psychological object. For Lacan therefore the key element of the symbolic is the signifier and it is relations between signifiers that effect meaning.

Lacan's term for the symbolic is the Other, however the terms 'other' and 'Other' can often seem confusing (see Evans 1997, pp. 132–133). In psychoanalysis, particularly in the writing of Lacan, the Other refers to culture; that is to say the symbolic orders of language, representation, ritual and other socio-cultural processes which form understanding. The Other therefore constitutes the symbolic frameworks, linguistic and visual, which form our understanding of art practice, and our identification of student's ability in art practice. There is a resonance here with the other of the mirror image in which the child identifies him or herself, but now the mirror is language or forms of visual representation that constitute examination and assessment systems in which the student is 'mirrored'. We might say that in the symbolic the gaze of the linguistic signifier replaces the gaze of the image in the imaginary. I will use the 'other' to refer to the other person or more specifically the other person as depicted by image or text, and the Other to refer to the symbolic order of language and culture. Confusion sets in however when we acknowledge that we can only speak about, write or picture the other person in the symbolic orders of culture, which is to say that the other is always a signifier, an imagined or symbolised other. Easthope (2002) writes further:

The other (lower case) is always my other, a point in the symbolic I imagine as my object, a signifier (or set of signifiers) with which I identify – 'his ego'. . . . For Lacan there can be no relation to the other except on the prior basis of the Other, no relation which is not an effect of the order of the signifier, so that any venturing forth toward the other – my other – is fundamentally narcissistic and replete with fantasy and misrecognition (pp. 145–146).

There are serious implications for teaching and learning if we take this statement on board, for it suggests that as teachers we can never know the student in him or her self, the student is always an *imagined other* who is constructed through the order of the signifier, the Lacanian Other. Similarly for the student, the teacher is never knowable in him or herself but is always an imagined other who is constructed through those signifying practices that constitute teaching and learning. In the light of this complex process of identification if we consider dialogues between teachers and students which relate to the latter's art practices perhaps it is important to consider the question, "Who is speaking and to whom?" The answer, I suggest, is not straightforward.

The Other is always lacking

Having made the point that we can only know the other person through the order of the symbolic, that is to say within practices of language, it is important to stress that for Lacan the symbolic order, the Other, is always lacking. When we enter the symbolic we lose something of our being, something of our pre-symbolic existence. Language can never quite capture what we want to express. The artist could be said to attempt that which is impossible, to express something of his or her being in the domain of the signifier. For Lacan (1977, p. 104) entry into the symbolic brings about a loss of being but at the same time the emergence of a desire for that which is lost. Thus for Lacan the lack in the Other by implication precipitates a lack in the subject which brings about the onset of desire. This means that the subject is always a barred subject; the subject can never know herself fully because there is no signifier to represent the subject-in-herself, but this sense of fullness and identity is what the subject continues eternally to desire. The subject manages to cover over this sense of lack through fantasy, through a series of imaginary and symbolic processes that provide, temporarily, a sense (transferential illusion) of identification and fullness. A feeling of identity is gained therefore through identification with a signifier but this identification is never total.

Within education the Other relates to those curriculum discourses and practices within which teachers and students are formed, those signifiers relating to practice and assessment which provide a sense of identification. The student is constantly addressing herself to the demands of the Other in the form of the teacher by asking what does the teacher (the Other) want? Whilst the teacher on the other hand addresses the demands of the Other in the form of the student by asking what does she need? Both questions are filtered through 'the defiles of the signifier' (Lacan 1977, p. 264; Easthope 2002, p. 5), that construct the other for the subject within the discourses that constitute educational practice. This interaction therefore involves a complex hermeneutic process and is by no means as straightforward as it might appear.

The Other and marginalized identifications

The implications of Easthope's statement above for inter-cultural education, where teachers work with and need to respond effectively to students from a variety of cultural backgrounds, are huge, and this raises another, deeper dimension of the term, 'other'. The 'other' can also be understood as that which lies on the margins of or beyond the conventions or traditions of specific formations of the symbolic order that constitutes our understanding. The other is therefore, 'that which is different'. This is not to say that it lies totally outside of any symbolic order, but simply the one in which our understanding is formed. For example, the art practices of other cultures may be so different from our own that we fail to understand them, or, closer to home it is frequently the case that contemporary art is so baffling that we cannot construe meaning, it appears so 'other' to what we have previously understood as art. In my experience of teaching art it is not uncommon to witness students and children producing art work which is also very difficult to understand. However it is through this process of marginalizing, of excluding that which we do not understand, that we often confirm that which we do understand. This seems to be a necessary hermeneutic process, which provides stability, but one that requires disturbing if we are to expand our awareness. We acquire stability through the forms we create to understand the world but we also need to recognise the limitations of these forms if we are to extend our understanding.

The crucial idea that processes of recognition and identification are constructed through relations with the other and thus through difference is noted by Hall (1996):

Above all, and directly contrary to the form in which they are constantly invoked, identities are constructed through, not outside, difference. This entails the radically disturbing recognition that it is only through the relation to the Other, the relation to what it is not, to precisely what it lacks, to what has been called its *constitutive outside* that the 'positive' meaning of any term – and thus its identity – can be constructed (pp. 4–5).

The implications of this statement for understanding the recognition and conferring of pedagogised identities are profound but quite tricky. Seen in these terms identification involves a process of naming and foreclosure, naming is thus an act of power that invokes inclusion and exclusion. We can see this process at work in the assessment of student's art work. The work is recognised and valued according to a set of criteria (the Other) which by implication include and exclude in the sense that certain work is deemed worthy and therefore valued according to the criteria whilst other work is not. The suggestion is therefore that certain subjectivities and experiences are valued over others. The criteria themselves are not 'in the work' but consist of particular signifiers (forms of visual representation and techniques etc.) that are desired. Thus work which reflects this particular Other is included and valued, work which does not is marginalized or adjudged to be weak or even defective. It is this particular Other (the determining criteria) according to which the student's art practice is read which constitutes the student's pedagogised identity. The signifier (a particular assessment criterion) represents the subject (student) for another signifier (the teacher's assessment discourse). Through this identification process the student is given (and usually accepts) a place within the symbolic and normalised order of assessment and is thereby understood as a student by him or herself and by the teacher. Shortly I will discuss the idea of *pedagogised others* in reference to those students whose art practices lie beyond the boundaries of conventional interpretation. But first I want to turn to Judith Butler's point, discussed in the previous chapter, that what we need to consider carefully in relation to the formation of identity are the kinds of *restrictions in production* of identity that such practices invoke.

The subject of discourse and the subject of desire: a rapprochement

In *The Psychic Life of Power*, Judith Butler (1997) describes how the formation of subjectivity always involves an unconscious, that which is repressed or which lies beyond the subject of consciousness as constituted in imaginary and symbolic orders. We might say that the psyche is that which exceeds the imprisoning effects of the discursive demand to occupy a normalised and therefore coherent identity as a person. In an interesting twist she claims that identity and subjectivity are not processes of production but invoke, "a destruction (brought about by entry into the symbolic) on the occasion of which a subject is formed (p. 92)." For Butler therefore subjectivity and the process of identification are not simply a matter of domination by discourse and normalisation but they "designate a certain kind of restriction in production (p. 84)."

If I might be permitted a degree of flexibility of interpretation here I think Butler's point can be applied to our recognition of art work through identification processes such as assessment. The practice of assessment often involves, as I have already discussed, 'a restriction in production' in that a particular set of expectations or criteria are used as the hermeneutic framework in which students' art practice is identified. If we take the assessment criteria as consisting of the conscious norms according to which assessment is understood as practice, those pieces of work that seem unintelligible and therefore outside such norms, could be said to constitute the equivalent of Butler's 'unconscious'. The unconscious here can be understood as the other of consciousness. In some ways this unconscious is close to Lacan's order of the Real, that which lies beyond symbolisation. I will discuss this shortly.

The *rapprochement* between the subject of discourse as articulated by Foucault and the subject of desire postulated by Lacanian psychoanalysis provides a framework in which we can consider the formation of subjectivity and identification in art education. The *rapprochement* brings together the notions of normalisation, power, desire and the other in the formation of pedagogised identities. It suggests that all such identities are formed through identification with a desired other, (the ideal other as constructed by assessment criteria, particular forms of practice), which serves a normalising and regulating function. Identification is thus an act constituted through desire and relations of power. It is a process in which the subject becomes a particular kind of subject through the agency and power of the signifier.

In much of my recent work I have been interested in how we respond to the relationship between this desired other, established by the Other, and those art practices which appear mysterious and which can easily be dismissed (through the Other) as weak or the products of students or children regarded as having little ability in art practice. If we desist from dismissing such work according to conventional ideas of skill and representation it is possible to consider how such 'others' to convention return to trouble the categorisations of the norm (the Other) and so allow us a possibility to counter the relations of power through which particular subjectivities (pedagogised identities) are formed. This suggests an opportunity for promoting new forms of subjectivity and identity by moving beyond the particular restriction in production of older established norms into a new hermeneutic state. In other words, this 'unconscious' other (the Lacanian Real) may disturb and thus create the possibility of new identifications, new subjectivities and the move towards a more inclusive approach to teaching and learning in art education. I would like to provide a practical illustration shortly of what I mean here by looking at another set of drawings.

The Ambassadors

There is a painting by Holbein housed in the National Gallery in London entitled *The Ambassadors*, which has been employed by Lacan (1991, pp. 85–90) and others to illustrate their explorations of identity, representation and meaning. I want to use this picture to illustrate my discussion of the formation of pedagogised identities, that is to say identities of learners and teachers in art education. I will provide my own interpretation of Holbein's painting to suit my purpose. The painting is well known. Two richly clothed dignitaries are standing either side of a set of shelves on which are displayed collections of objects and measuring instruments. They look out towards the viewer. In the central foreground, rising from the base, there is a mysterious form which appears as a smudge, a fuzzy image. If the viewer takes up a position to the extreme right of the painting the smudge is transformed into the representation of a skull. The technical term for this visual manipulation or distortion of form is anamorphosis. It is a technique that interested painters of the period. The interesting point about the painting is that from a frontal viewing position this meaningless shape is surrounded by meaning, that is to say, all around the mysterious shape meaning is abundant in the form of recognisable depictions. This idea of lack at the centre of a field of meaning (the Other), this apparent void in the midst of recognisable form, is something I want explore in relation to the ways in which we recognise and identify art practice through the symbolic order and so constitute subjectivity and ability in art practice.

Assessment and the pedagogised other

In school art lessons some students produce mysterious images that are difficult to interpret, they are rather like the meaningless smudge in Holbein's painting. That is to say, within the discourses and practices through which we form our understanding of art practice and which constitute evaluation and assessment criteria, such productions are a mystery. But if we are somehow able to change our perspective so that we can reflect upon the foreclosing limitations of the hermeneutic structure of our interpretational discourse there may be the possibility of forming a new hermeneutic state, rather similar to taking up a different viewing position before Holbein's painting, so that what was initially meaningless now emerges with meaning. I shall discuss the possibility of a change in perspective in order to effect a more inclusive approach to assessment and, consequently, a radicalisation of perceptions of students as learners.

In my experience assessing children's or students' art work has always been a problematic aspect of teaching art in schools. Discourses of assessment are always predicated upon particular understandings of what art is. There are those who feel that to even consider assessing art work is rather pointless because art is concerned with self-expression and we should value equally each individual's form of expression and representation. Others feel that it is possible to assess student's art work if we select the appropriate criteria and forms of judgement. My purpose is to consider how assessment as a discursive practice can be considered as an apparatus of visibility and surveillance and, to refer back to Butler, a process of restricted production. I want to discuss how assessment in art practice actually constructs or makes visible both students' and teachers' pedagogised identities. Consider the five drawings in Figure 39 (a–d), below. They were produced in a lesson where the students (age 11–12 years) worked in pairs and took turns to make a line drawing of their partner. This is a common drawing exercise in secondary schools in the UK.

Many observational drawings which students produce are assimilated or recognized within codes of visual representation through which they achieve meaning. This is not because the drawing reflects a visual correspondence with reality, a signifier-signified relation (although we might believe this to be the case) but because the drawing is recognized within accepted representational codes, that is to say a signifier-signifier relation. However there are some drawings which jar, their form is mysterious and they are frequently regarded as poor representations that reflect a lack of drawing ability. The effect of the oddness or the singularity of such drawings upon a student's pedagogised identity is that the student frequently occupies a place of *otherness* in relation to the normative forms of accepted drawing practice. The student becomes what I call a *pedagogised other* of the accepted symbolic order of drawing

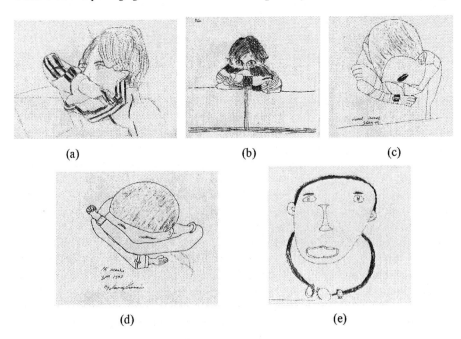

(a)   (b)   (c)

(d)   (e)

Figure 39.

practice. Referring to Butler (1993, p. 22) as quoted by Hall (1996), the student becomes a marginalized subject within the specific discourse in which drawing ability is assessed.

All identities operate through exclusion, through the discursive construction of a constitutive outside and the production of abjected and marginalised subjects, apparently outside the field of the symbolic, the representable, which then return to trouble and unsettle the foreclosures we call identities — (Hall 1996, p. 15 my emphasis)

For me it is drawing (e), the one that troubles and unsettles my foreclosure, which I find interesting in relation to the task of assessment and the subsequent identification of the student as learner.

One possible scenario of assessment might be to regard drawings (a) and (b) as more effective representations than drawings (d) and (e) with drawing (c) lying somewhere between these pairings. Drawing (e) is strikingly different and could be regarded as weak or defective as a representational drawing; a limited representation which indicates that the student responsible for its production could be regarded as less able in drawing practice than the other students. In assessment discourse the student's art work represents the student not simply for others, teachers responsible for assessment for example, but primarily for other signifiers, (the Other) that is to say, for the symbolic network of representational codes or discourses of visuality in which the art work as signifier has to be inserted to achieve meaning. For Lacan the signifier represents the subject not for another subject but for another signifier. We may acknowledge the representational forms of drawings (a) and (b) because they can be easily understood within accepted codes of representation. Equally we can marvel at the linear economy and sophistication of drawing (c), it is indeed a beautiful drawing in which the use of a mainly orthographic drawing system produces a powerful representation of the solidity and positioning of the body. Drawing (d) appears on the margins of the representational codes we tend to employ when assessing such drawings. However, drawing (e) is so different, so singular, that it is not easily understood and it is likely to be assessed as weak or even child-like in relation to the other drawings. But if we regard this drawing as defective we also, by implication, construct its author's pedagogised identity accordingly.

There is a central difficulty embedded in the field of art in education. This relates to the difference between discursive frameworks (the Other) within which we conceive and perceive art practice and the actual event or the act (the Real) of practice. This difference mutates into that between a teacher's understanding of art practice gained from his or her training and work as an artist and the pedagogic requirement to initiate, understand and assess the art practices of students within the institution of art education. Frequently this difference is illustrated by many teachers' open acknowledgement *in theory* of the legitimacy of different forms of expression and representation of children and students engaged in art practice, contrasted with the teacher's imposition, *in practice*, of specific assessment or evaluation criteria of representation and expression. Thus the outcomes of some practices and experiences are valued more than others. The imposition of value on students' art practices impacts upon the construction of both students' and teachers' pedagogised identities.

To return to drawing (e), this can be viewed rather like the smudge in Holbein's *Ambassadors*, in that it appears as a meaningless or marginalised image in the midst of the discourses (the Other) in which we understand representational form. Such drawings are, to quote Bryson (1983, p.147), "so generically unplaceable," however, rather than pathologise the image, we may gain more insight by assessing the lack in our understanding and moving towards a new discursive position, one in which we might effect a realignment of discourse and image. This would entail a radical overhaul of the purpose of assessment in art in education and subsequently the way in which we understand student's art practices. The consequence of this may lead to what Grossberg (in Hall and Du Gay 1996, p. 103) identifies as a "project of constructing a form of knowledge which respects the other without absorbing it into the same, . . ." The difficulty, as Lacan (1991) reminds us though is that:

The signifier producing itself in the field of the Other, makes manifest the subject of its signification. But it functions as a signifier only to reduce the subject in question to being no more than a signifier, to petrify the subject in the same movement in which it calls the subject to function, to speak, as subject (p. 207 my emphasis).

This process of symbolic reduction is inevitable and lies at the heart of assessment discourse and it is according to such reduction that students and teachers understand their practice.

Pedagogised identities: inclusion and exclusion

I have mentioned previously that pedagogised identities arise through processes of normalisation, regulation and desire for the Other. When we evaluate or assess students' art practices, particularly representational painting or drawing, there is nothing behind or prior to the art work which is directly accessible to us, (such as a correct view of a real object, or the student's innate ability), all we have is signification; that is to say, a consensual system of signifiers (the Other) through which we understand art practice and which already precede and extend beyond the art work. In order to establish a more inclusive approach to the different semiotics of children's and student's art practices it is sometimes necessary, though never easy, to pass through the common currency of interpretation into a new hermeneutic state, which of course eventually will be subject to deconstruction. Before I tackle Lacan's order of the Real I will extend my discussion of the imaginary and symbolic orders by considering other Lacanian terms that offer conceptual tools which I have found helpful in my explorations of the formation of teacher and learner identities, and which help to establish a critical stance towards the discourses in which practice is understood.

Identity and objet petit a

Objet petit a the 'little other,' in contrast to the big Other (the symbolic order), can be understood as an object that causes desire, an object which we seek but which we never attain. It is a fantasy or imaginary object, something which has no existence 'in reality' but which nevertheless structures desire. The young child's 'mirror image', as a fantasised ideal object, occurring in relations with others is an early formulation of the objet petit a. It can be conceived as a fantasy object that lies beyond symbolisation but around which symbolisation circles. For example, attempts to reveal the essence of *society, tradition, democracy, intelligence, ability*, in order to expose their hidden kernel of meaning, always in the end fail because such terms are constituted upon an essential lack which is covered over by the term itself. We can never attain the essence of ability, for example, because it is always contingent upon value and context. Each of these terms can be viewed as constituting a fantasy object, *objet petit a*. The current concern for *standards* in education in England is an interesting illustration of *objet petit a* functioning within the politics of educational policy. This term, as Williams (1980, p. 249) shows, when acting as a plural singular is frequently employed for suasive or consensual purposes. When considered closely, unless specific standards in the sense of an ordinary plural are identified for specific areas of practice, the use of *standards* as a plural singular seems to refer to something universal and unquestionable. Indeed, as Williams tells us, it is difficult "to disagree with some assertion of standards without appearing to disagree with the very idea of quality." Sometimes I feel a similar sense of unease when deconstructing assessment discourses thereby provoking the question, 'so do we accept anything and everything as equal?' The concern for standards in education does not signify an unchanging, universal and permanent referent, for as societies change so do values, and even within specific socio-historical periods there are radical disagreements about standards. Thus this popular term has no essential meaning but develops meaning within specific ideological discourses.

In relation to other conceptual objects such as *democracy*, Zizek (1989) writes:

. . . the essentialist illusion consists in the belief that it is possible to determine a definite cluster of features, of positive properties, however minimal, which defines the permanent essence of democracy and similar terms. In contrast to this essentialist illusion, Laclau's anti-essentialism compels us to conclude that it is impossible to define any such essence, any cluster of positive properties which would remain the same in all possible worlds – in all counterfactual situations. In the last resort, the only way to define democracy is to say that it contains all political movements and organisations which legitimise, designate themselves as democratic. . . . In other words, the only possible definition of an object in its identity is that this is the object which is always designated by the same signifier – tied to the same signifier. It is the signifier which constitutes the kernel of the object's identity (p. 98).

Signifiers such as *standards* and *ability* are not points of density of meaning which refer to fixed signifieds, although this appears frequently to be the case. They are conceived and experienced as points of plenitude of meaning whilst in fact their constitution involves the covering over of a certain lack. Such signifiers constitute the Lacanian *objet petit a* in the sense that their apparent reference to specific signifieds is created through a fantasy object of desire (the need, for example, to 'raise standards'). Another way of talking about this is to recognize the relative nature of such discourses within their specific social and historical contexts. In teaching and learning contexts the term *ability* is often used by teachers to identify students' levels of under-standing and practice, as though the word signified some inherent property a student possessed. But considered another way it refers to a particular kind of behaviour which is deemed acceptable or desirable within particular prac-tices and ideologies of teaching and learning. In the field of art in education students who are considered to be able are often those who are able to draw in a particular way, or put differently, are able to employ a particular repre-sentational system. Thus the term *ability* does not identify an essential property but a form of behaviour or practice that is valued within specific paradigms of teaching and learning.

The well-known anecdote recounting the meeting of Zeuxis and Parrahasios provides an illustration of *objet petit a* functioning in the act of interpreting a visual representation. Whilst Zeuxis produced an image of grapes which appeared to fool birds, he is similarly deceived by Parrahasios who had painted a veil on the wall. Zeuxis asks Parrahasios to show what he has painted behind the veil. The key point is that the very 'act of concealing deceives us precisely by pretending to conceal something,' (Zizek 1989, p. 196) and it is this something behind which we seek which constitutes *objet petit a* . . . because of course there is nothing behind the image, only ourselves, our projections. In the practice of assessing students' observational drawings is it the case that we look beyond the drawing to a supposed reality in order to consider the drawing's representational efficacy?

Point de capiton

This term translated into English as 'quilting point' or 'anchoring point' refers literally to an upholstery button, a device which pins down the fabric in upholstery work. Analogously Lacan uses the term to discuss how partic-ular signifiers retroactively stitch the subject into the signifying chain of language. Lacan (1993) writes:

Everything radiates out from and is organised around this signifier, similar to these little lines of force that an upholstery button forms on the surface of material. It's the point of conver-gence that enables everything that happens in this discourse to be situated retroactively and retrospectively (p. 268)

Zizek develops the notion of quilting with reference to the Althusserian idea of interpellation and shows how key signifiers interpellate or hail individ-uals into subject positions, a process of naming. He describes how meaning is structured through key nodal points (1989, pp. 87–100), key terms which articulate the truth of a particular ideological discourse. For example, if discourse concerned with freedom is quilted through communism a particular structure of meaning will develop, relating to class struggle and so on. On the other hand, if this discourse is quilted through an idea of liberal democracy a different structure of meaning develops. The *point de capiton* prevents the endless circulation of signifiers and show that Lacan does not subscribe to the postmodern idea of an unending fluidity of meaning (see Stavrakakis 1999, pp. 59–60). Meaning is produced retroactively by signifiers being attracted to particular *points de capiton* which fixing meaning around a signifying knot and not to a pre-existing signified. In contrast to postmodern ideas on the eternal flux of meaning Lacan uses the theory of *points de capiton* to show how they create the illusion of a pre-symbolic reality, that is to say how they create the illusion of a pre-existing signified. The structural effect of the *point de capiton* is therefore to suggest that meaning is inherent to a particular signified, to a fixed presence.

It is possible to consider the interpretation of the term *art education* within different frameworks of practice in order to see how it is quilted into particular embedding discourses and thus given meaning through particular *points de capiton*. An illustration of this quilting process will be provided in Chapter 8 where I present a series of interviews with teachers in which they describe their rationales for teaching and learning in art education. It can be deduced from these statements that what counts as *art education* varies according to the different perceptions of art practice and understanding that are formed in different rationales for practice. It becomes evident that ability in art practice is conceived differently within different ideologies of art educational practice and that the process of interpellation functions quite differently in such contrasting teaching and learning contexts. This illustrates the point that *points de capiton* do not refer to absolute values or essential meaning but they invoke a political aspect to meaning, which implies hegemonic struggle between competing ideological discourses that are structured by contrasting *points de capiton*.

Zizek argues that, what is at stake in ideological struggle is which of the nodal points, *points de capiton*, will totalize, the structure of meaning. The *point de capiton* is thus a signifier which, as a signifier, unifies a given field, constitutes its identity: it is, so to speak, the word which things themselves refer to recognise themselves in their unity. The importance of this term for the constitution of subjectivity and identity is crucial because individuals are interpellated into subject positions (acceptable or marginalized) through discourses whose structure of meaning is unified by *points de capiton*.

The *point de capiton* is the point through which the subject is sewn to the signifier, and at the same time the point which interpellates individual into subject by addressing it with the call of a master signifier (. . .) – in a word, it is the point of the subjectivation of the signifier's chain (1989, p. 101).

I have shown earlier how the signifier *accuracy* functions in assessment discourse as a *point de caption* in that it presupposes an entire ideological edifice of representational practice concerned with the reproduction of optical truth. According to this ideology of representation student's abilities are interpellated as particular pedagogised subjects and therefore provided with specific pedagogised identities. In Chapter 7 I also describe different paradigms of art education in England showing that each paradigm is underpinned by specific discursive terms that form their respective ideological quilting points.

This has crucial bearing upon how we recognise and identify others. By implication it bears on how we form our understanding of students' art practices within the parameters of the art curriculum and associated teaching and assessment practices. We can only identify students' art practices through our discourses and understanding of visual practice which we have acquired and through which we understand the field of art practice in education. The implications of this last sentence for teaching and learning in a plural social context are profound. We understand students' art practices not by gaining direct access to students *in-themselves*, or through direct access to their *intentions* but through conversations and readings of students' work which are constructed within specific ways of understanding art practice (the Other) which we have inherited and absorbed. Under the gaze of such institutional discourses both students and teachers become subjects of specific practices and forms of knowledge that make up the field of art in education. In such practices and forms of knowledge students and teachers are positioned and regulated as subjects of the gaze of this pedagogic field.

In my discussion of the video sequence in the previous chapter I highlighted the discourse that teachers used to identify the more successful of two drawings and, by implication, the more able student. Key terms of their discourse such as *proportion*, *composition*, *balance* and *perspective* stitch the drawings and the students into a particular discourse of visual representation which constitutes a specific structure and metonymic chain of meaning within which both drawings and students are made visible. The important point is that the identification of the student's drawing ability or the drawing's representational form does not refer to something *in the student* or *in the drawing* but is recognised and produced through a specific discourse of visual representation and practice. It is through the gaze of this specific discourse, employed by the group of teachers, that both the drawings as visual representations and the students as art practitioners are constituted.

The notion of power-knowledge from Foucault and the Lacan's theory of *points de capiton* can be combined in order to consider the productive effects of practice and discourse in educational sites such as art education. In quilting understanding of teaching and learning through specific terms and concepts of practice a particular discourse operates a form of power-knowledge. Walkerdine (1990) describes the positioning and regulating process through which individuals come to recognise who they are:

Modern apparatuses of social regulation, along with other social and cultural practices, produce knowledges which claim to 'identify' individuals. These knowledges create the possibility of multiple practices, multiple positions. To be a 'clever child' or a 'good mother', for example, makes sense only in the terms given by pedagogic, welfare, medical, legal and other discourse and practices. *These observe, sanction and correct how we act; they attempt to define who and what we are* (p. 199, my emphasis).

Fetishism, assessment and identity

A traditional understanding of the term fetishism denotes the ascription of certain qualities or powers to inanimate objects. In many religions, for example, particular objects or creatures are believed to possess specific powers. In the world of advertising the production of similar beliefs can also be perceived whereby particular products are marketed as possessing, or will provide the purchaser with certain qualities. Such religious objects and consumer goods are therefore fetish objects. Fetishism also extends to inter-personal relations between people, between, for example, a monarch and her or his subjects. They confer upon the monarch the aura of 'kingliness' or 'queenliness' though they act as though this aura is a natural property. Similarly relations between teachers and students are fetishised in that the teacher is projected as 'the subject supposed to know,' the person with authority who possess the knowledge or skills which the student desires. The student on the other hand is often considered as the one who lacks knowledge. Marx's celebrated account of commodity fetishism refers to relations between things replacing relations between people, as is evident in the attribution of fiscal value to consumer commodities. In all these instances of fetishism the fetishist illusion consists of misperceiving as natural or inherent properties of the fetish-object which we confer within our socio-cultural and symbolic structures. The process of fetishism is, essentially, a process of identification, or put another way, identification can be considered as a fetishising process.

The formation of individual identity can be understood as a fetishising process. This is perceivable in Lacan's theorisation of the mirror phase where the young child invests his or her mirrored image, established in relations with others, with a sense of identity and unity. It can also be perceived in his theory of the Other, the symbolic order, where the signifier creates the transferential illusion of a definite signified. Althusser's idea of interpellation, discussed in the previous chapter, also involves fetishism, whereby the process of naming, particularly within racist, sexist or gender discourses posits certain qualities upon or within the one who is named. Fetishism also pervades identifications that are formed within school practices such as those formed within the evaluation or assessment of art work. When we believe that we recognise ability *in* students or *in* their art work this is a fetishising process. Our pedagogic practices are regulated by specific discourses and systems of art practice that allow the process of assessment to proceed in the belief that we are involved in direct relations with students. In other words we forget or are unaware of the regulatory effects of assessment discourse and the perceptions of practice it invokes. In such pedagogic relations 'ability' seems naturally evident and we fail to notice the fetishist screen of discourse (the Other) through which ability is conferred. Earlier I referred to the use of the word *accuracy* in discourses concerned with the assessment of observational drawing and painting. It could be argued that the desire for accuracy in this discourse is driven by two fetishised illusions, one consisting of a belief in an objective world which we can perceive 'as it is' and the other in a belief in the efficacy of a representational form to reproduce this perceptual experience.

In the exemplars of fetishism above there is an implicit distinction between the 'fetishist aura' and the object 'in-itself'. However, Zizek (1997, pp. 86–126) shows how the conception of the object or person 'in-itself', that is to say the very idea of objectivity, should also be conceived as a fetish, because it is a notion whose appearance of a detached, prior reality conceals subjective mediation. Zizek argues that the very idea of an object's external and material being (the way things *really* are) is the ultimate fetish, hiding its subjective production in the symbolic order. This refers to my earlier point of the signifier producing the illusion of a pre-existing signified. The idea of fetishing as being a process of identification is important in that it pervades our conceptions and comprehension of art practice and the art object. We attribute value to particular forms of art work, particular artists and partic- ular skills and techniques, we also downgrade or ignore others. A recent article in the newsletter for the National Society for Art and Design in the UK (A'N'D Summer 2001) illustrates my point. The author (Colluney 2001) writes with some passion about what he perceives as the demise of fine art traditions with the emergence and growth of digital art. Essentially the argument runs along the lines that in the latter the computer replaces human skills; human productions and conventions of painting and drawing are replaced by pro- ductions of computers and printers. The interesting point about the letter is the implicit fetishising of conventional skills such as representational drawing and painting as being natural and modern digital technologies as alienating. The involvement of the body, of hand-eye coordination and tactile elements constitute a natural human process whilst in digital art computer and printer replace 'human' and conventional practices. It is easy to forget that we often reserve the word technology to refer to new inventions and media whilst regarding older technologies such as those associated with drawing and painting (pencil, paintbrush, etc.) as natural.

If we return to the practice of observational drawing and pull together the ideas on fetishism I have described, there is a tendency to misread such drawings in terms of their fit with the perceptual experience of a viewed reality. We fetishise the experiential presence of a particular perceptual experience behind, prior to or complementary with the drawing. Because the observational drawing cannot directly represent perceptual experience then equally we can argue that assessment cannot be based upon a direct correlation between perceptual experience and representation. Assessment therefore can only comprehend a student's ability in art practice by *constructing* it, not revealing it, within specific discourses predicated by particular codes of representation, (such as those already described in my discussion of the video sequence in the previous chapter), in which the work becomes knowable.

It could be argued therefore that assessment criteria such as the term 'accuracy' in drawing presuppose particular ontological orientations to perception and practice that are based upon a normalised and universal perceptual process. Such presuppositions can fail to acknowledge local semiotic/representational practices that arise within different ontological orientations to practice and representation. If we return to the five drawings in Figure 39 above it is possible, as already stated, to evaluate and assess them according to codes of representation with which we are familiar but is the ontological status of such codes commensurate with the ontological orientations of each student's art practice? This introduces a question of ethics in the sense that it asks: in employing particular modes of assessment are we reducing the student's ontological orientation to practice to a specific ontological identity presupposed by the assessment criteria? The short answer may be yes.

Identity and the Real

The Real, in relation to the imaginary and the symbolic, is perhaps the most difficult Lacanian order to describe, one reason being that Lacan employs the term in different ways in his writing. Lacan distinguishes between reality as we know and understand it through the symbolic order and the Real which lies beyond symbolisation but which is always present. I will describe two interpretations that I believe are helpful for gaining some insight on the issues of assessment and the formation of pedagogised identities in art education. Although different both interpretations are connected as I hope to demonstrate. Firstly the Real refers to, 'that which resists symbolisation absolutely' (Lacan 1988, p. 66). The most uncomplicated sense refers to brute existence, to a 'hard impenetrable kernel that resists symbolisation.' Experience is generally comprehended through representational processes formed within socio-cultural contexts. However there are occasions when what we experience is difficult to comprehend, when our symbolic order fails. This is noted by Miller (in Zizek 1989, p. 171):

The Real is a shock of a contingent encounter which disrupts the automatic circulation of the symbolic mechanism; a grain of sand preventing its smooth functioning; a traumatic encounter which ruins the balance of the symbolic universe of the subject.

Bowie (1991) also describes the distinction between the Real and the symbolic:

The network of signifiers in which we have our being is not all that there is, and the rest of what is may chance to break in upon us at any moment (p. 103).

It is 'the rest of what is' which constitutes the Lacanian Real and which we experience purely as contingent encounters that disrupt our symbolic frameworks. On encountering the Real Bowie argues that, "The mind makes contact

with the limits of its power, with that which its structure cannot structure"
(p. 105). This has important implications for assessment and identity, for
example, when we are confronted with art work which we find difficult to
comprehend. I have already discussed drawings that present such difficulty
in that they appear to lie beyond the symbolic frameworks that form our
comprehension of representational practice. 'We can only speak about what
we notice but what we don't notice happens to us most of the time (Brookes
personal communication),' what we don't notice could be considered as the
Real of existence.

The Real can therefore be understood as a contingent encounter in which
our frameworks of understanding are punctured. Peter Weir's film, *The Truman
Show*, discussed in the last chapter, provides a graphic illustration of this
process when several inexplicable events occur in Truman's life for which
he can find no explanation. These events disrupt Truman's comprehension
and create instability within the symbolic order which gives sense to his
existence. Although I have described the Real as a disruption of the symbolic
order it is important to understand that the symbolic order introduces a cut
in the Real (see Evans 1996, p. 159). The Real is always primary, always there,
but largely overwhelmed by our ideas of reality which are the products of
the symbolic order. So as well as denoting that which lies beyond symbolisation, the Real, by implication, refers to that which is lacking in the symbolic
order, a foreclosed element which can never be grasped.

Rather than interpreting the drawings in Figure 39 (e), and Figure. 5, as
weak, defective or mysterious representations we might think of them as
Real objects that disturb the discourses in which we understand the experience of drawing practice. Extending this line of thought, we might then be able
to consider the point that assessment is not identifying natural qualities in
students or their art work, but is concerned rather with a particular restricted
kind of identification process. This reading opens up the possibility of evaluating the discourses and classification systems that constitute our
understanding of art practice and how the pedagogised identities of teachers
and learners are formed. Consequently we may then be able to move towards
a more inclusive comprehension of the difference of students' art practices.
The contingency of such encounters with art work that is difficult to comprehend, which is not uncommon in teaching art in schools, suggests to me
that we need to develop systems of comprehension and assessment which
respond sympathetically to the heterogeneity of practice and the different
ontological orientations to practice; where the singular is not reduced to the
norm. However, assessment is always a reductive process in which a high
variety complex is reduced to the control form of assessment criteria, perhaps
what we require are systems which can cope with variety more sympathetically. We can view assessment as a kind of stochastic process (see Bateson
1980) that is to say as a process in which a high variety is combined with a
selective process so that only certain aspects of the variety are deemed valid.
What is required is a more flexible control operator.

Stavrakakis (1999, p. 86) asks if it is possible to approach the Real before symbolisation creates reality? Quoting Evernden (1992, p. 110) he writes, "How can we return to things before they were captured and explained, in which transaction they ceased to be themselves and became instead functionaries in the world of social discourse?" Similarly in relation to drawing (e) in Figure 39 and other mysterious art work produced by children and students, is it possible to approach art practice before thinking of it as Art, that is to say before it is captured by those discourses in which we understand art practice. The short answer is no, but it is in those instances when art objects dislocate our discourses of understanding art practice, when the Real pushes against the boundaries of the symbolic, that we may begin to see the limitations of the symbolic and redraw its boundaries.

The second interpretation of the Lacanian Real concerns the idea of a real, but impossible object (Real-impossible). Reference to cinema may help to provide an illustration. Zizek (1989, p. 112) illustrates the idea of a Real-impossible through Alfred Hitchcock's thriller, *North by Northwest*. The film begins in the reception lounge of a large hotel. Richard Thornhill (played by Cary Grant) is reading a newspaper when a bell boy announces, "Message for Mr Kaplan." At the same time as this announcement Thornhill rises and advances towards the reception desk. Two foreign agents spot his movement and take him to be George Kaplan, the man they are chasing. However it turns out that George Kaplan is a fictitious character invented by the American security services but the point is that all the action of the film rests on the fiction that George Kaplan exists. The name George Kaplan is thus a signifier without a signified and constitutes a Lacanian Real-impossible object. Put another way the name George Kaplan identifies the presence of a lack in the symbolic order which at the same time appears real due to the body of Thornhill. Thus we can say that the entire logic and sense of the film is grounded upon this essential point of lack, this desired Real-impossible object which appears real through the accidental presence of Thornhill.

Is the act of interpellation described here, where a presence (a name) signifies a lack that is embodied by the body of another, of relevance to the formation of identity in art assessment? The idea of embodiment is worth considering in relation to the forms of knowledge and practice that are established and perpetuated by curriculum discourses. If I be allowed a degree of interpretational license, it could be argued that the description of practice provided by the discourse of the National Currriculum for Art in England or, equally, the assessment discourse of the GCSE examination, provides a specific disembodied discourse of practice which assumes an idealised body, an idealised pedagogic identity which has no ontological consistency but which has real effects upon the designation and determination of ability in art practice. That is to say, when students come under the purview of the GCSE examination assessment matrix their identity as subjects of practice is constructed. The ideal identification of practice with no ontological consistency subjects the real practices of students and their different ontologies to its power.

Zizek extends this idea of a Real-impossible by considering,

. . . The Real as an act which never took place in reality but which must nevertheless be presupposed, 'constructed', afterwards to account for the present state of things (pp. 168–169).

Perhaps we can get something of the sense of this statement by thinking again of the way in which we respond to strange or mysterious outcomes of observational drawing practices and how we categorise them. We can only interpret such mysterious art work retrospectively, according to the symbolic frameworks in which we understand drawing practice; when faced with such art practice we struggle for meaning as a consequence of the effects of disturbance to our assimilated forms of comprehension. A quick response to account for the mysterious form of such drawings is to construe them as weak representations, the product of students with 'little drawing ability'. A more considered response might switch the focus from the mysterious representational drawing onto the discourses in which we comprehend representation. How the dynamics of such a switch arise is not easily described particularly when this involves breaking away from the pattern of values that hold and inform our interpretations. Both responses involve a retrospective filling in of the void in our comprehension created by bumping up against the Real. The latter response has the possibility of leading to a more inclusive and enlightened hermeneutic state even though it is still at some distance from the Real which is impossible to attain. A new hermeneutic state would not only involve a change in practice (of assessment) but also a change to the background against which we understand practice. These changes invoke a questioning of practice, a questioning of values and a questioning of representation. By providing this particular reading of the Real-impossible Zizek seems to be pointing to the unbridgeable distance between the experiencing of mystery and the way in which it is symbolised, this is close to Brookes's ideas on mystery and resolution described in Chapter 3.

Summary

There may be those who would argue that my application of Lacanian terminology is simply a case of wallowing in theory for its own sake, that such writing is of little relevance or value for reflecting upon issues of practice in the field of art in education. If that is the impression I create then I have been unsuccessful in my venture. Lacan's work when applied to processes of identification and subjectivity in education is valuable, I believe, because it illustrates the importance of the signifier (the Other). In breaking the link between a signifier and a pre-existing signified we can begin to see how terms such as *ability*, *teaching*, *learning*, and *assessment*, are signifiers which do not refer to pre-exiting states (though this appears to be the case) but construct the subject within specific discourses. In other words these signifiers represent the subject for other signifiers. Within such discourses the subject becomes an ideological subject in which inclusions and exclusions, or legitimate and illegitimate practices are established.

However, unlike social constructivism or post-structural theory Lacan works with the idea of the Real and thus avoids any essentialism or determinism implied by a reduction of experience to the symbolic. If everything is determined by discourse then how do we account for new constructions of reality? The Real is that domain which exceeds the symbolic order and by bumping up against it can effect changes in the symbolic construction of reality. The Real cannot be revealed but its effects can illustrate the lack in the symbolic order, that is to say the ways in which we understand reality. I have discussed how the symbolic order in which we understand observational drawing practices can be disrupted by those drawings that are inexplicable but it depends upon the degree of disturbance we experience as to whether we dismiss such drawings as inadequate, or start to think about the ways (discourses) in which we understand such drawings. Thus Lacan's notion of the Real alerts us to the fact that the symbolic is not all there is and it tells us to be vigilant of assessment discourses, recognising that what is lies mainly beyond their purview. According to Stavrakakis (p. 69) we could consider Lacan not as a social constructivist, nor as a post-structuralist, but as a Realist. But this is not the conventional idea of realism whereby there is a definite link between signifier and a signified referent, it is the opposite, in that the Real is unknowable but has the power to disrupt reality.

With Lacan we become aware of the fact that the hermeneutic process is far from straightforward. Gadamer seeks to achieve understanding and agreement through a fusion of horizons within dialogic relations. Lacan shows how this is impossible by showing how the symbolic order in which dialogue functions is always lacking and consequently how the subject is lacking. He also shows how the other person is always fundamentally 'my other', an imaginary identification surrounded by fantasy and misrecognition. Habermas's project of communicative action, the attempt to achieve a post-ideological state of emancipation is also denied by Lacan because the subject can never escape the defiles of the signifier, that is to say the subject, being constructed within imaginary and symbolic orders (a subject of language) will always and inevitably be an ideological subject, it is through such ideological forms that the subject acquires stability as a particular kind of subject. Thus in relation to identity and subjectivity, for Habermas it seems to be a case of eliminating ideology by using rational discourse to undo its distorting effects in order to achieve a state of emancipation. For Lacan however, it is impossible to achieve Habermas's meta-state of emancipation because the Other is always lacking, there is no purified discourse, no signifier in which the subject can achieve a full identification. For Lacan the search for identity and subjectivity is a case of hegemonic struggle to achieve stability through a particular ideological signifier.

The conceptual tools offered by Lacan help us to explore those discourses and practices in which teachers and learners acquire their identities and subjectivities in order to expose the ideological construction of such identities. In so doing my purpose is to try to work towards developing an ideological framework that is more commensurate with difference and diversity in art practices. Such conceptual tools help to prize open the naturalising power of established discourses and practices and thus allow the possibility of viewing them as ideological and not natural productions.

CHAPTER SEVEN

THE FIELD OF ART IN EDUCATION

The explorations of the formation of identity and subjectivity developed in the previous two chapters raise a variety of issues relating to how we initiate and assess students' art practices that in turn relate to how we conceive art practice itself and how we conceive our own practices as teachers of art and design. In England we have a National Curriculum for Art and Design (DfEE 2000) according to which all primary and secondary schools must structure programmes of study and assessment of children's and student's art practices. Ostensibly the conception of a National Art Curriculum suggests a uniform structure and provision for teaching, learning and assessment. This is of course an illusion that is not difficult to dissolve when we take a close look at what is actually happening in different art departments in secondary schools and in the provision of art education in different primary schools. It will not surprise anyone, or almost anyone, that in different schools teaching, learning and assessment in art education can be quite varied. The implications of this variety for the constitution of pedagogised identities in art and design are significant.

An art curriculum that concentrates mainly upon traditional skills and techniques of observational drawing and painting and other art activities developing from these 'foundational practices', will produce quite different pedagogised identities to a curriculum which concerns itself with encouraging students to develop art practice to explore contemporary social and cultural issues. Equally a school art curriculum in which emphasis is placed upon teaching specific skills and forms of knowledge, what one might term a transmission view of teaching and learning that in England is summed up by the rather facile and mechanistic phrase, 'the delivery of the National Curriculum,' will produce quite different pedagogised identities than those generated by an art curriculum which places emphasis upon acknowledging students' experiences, interests and local skills as the fulcrum for developing enquiry and learning. Many would argue that in teaching art there is a need to be able to respond to the personal power and potential of children's and students' art activities whilst also initiating them into socio-cultural traditions of practice and forms of knowledge. Concentrating on the latter can invoke a closure whereby the former is undervalued.

In this chapter I will consider some of the different constituents of the field of art education in England in order to develop my ideas on the production of pedagogised identities and subjectivities I have discussed in Chapters 5 and 6. However in this Chapter I will be concerned with the formation of pedagogised identities as anticipated in the text of the National Curriculum for Art in England, which will be contrasted with how such identities are formed in different secondary school art departments. I will begin with a critical reading of recent pedagogies in art education and then focus on the discourse of the National Curriculum for Art. Then I will consider this discourse through a description of Bourdieu's sociological analysis of field and habitus, which provides a theoretical format for considering art in education as a specific field of production of both practice and subjectivity. I will then offer a transcription of a series of semi-structured conversations with art teachers. I will analyse these teacher's responses as narratives within which they are describing their identities as teachers and by implication the formation of their student's pedagogised identities. My purpose here is to contrast the almost seamless and disembodied discourse of practice constructed by the text of the National Curriculum for Art with the different hybrid practices and experiences of teachers. This contrast brings out the difference between the decontextualised epistemology of the National Curriculum text which prescribes specific learner identities, and the local ontological structures of teaching and learning as manifested in different teaching-learning realities. The task for any teacher is thus one of mapping his or her students' or children's art practices onto the National Curriculum levels of achievement which for some teachers may be disturbing whilst others perceive little difficulty.

RECENT PEDAGOGIES FOR ART EDUCATION IN ENGLAND

Before I tackle the National Curriculum for Art directly I want to refer briefly to recent previous approaches to pedagogy in art education in England and how these were instrumental in forming teacher and learner identities in the field. During the 1970s and 1980s children's and students' art activities were described and conceived as acts of self-expression. Self-expression, or 'self-realisation', were common terms that underpinned rationales and justified the purpose of art education. Many art educators still regard the idea of developing children's and students' self-expression as the most important justification for their work. In numerous interviews with PGCE students they site self-expression as a fundamental purpose of art practice. This concern with the expression of self and with associated conceptions of 'uniqueness' and 'individuality' are central to modernist conceptions of artistic practice and of the artist as a creative and imaginative individual. Such concerns can be found in the writings of Ruskin, but, as Burgin (1987) indicates:

The concept of art as expression is given its twentieth century form most notably in the writings of Benedetto Croce, whose most influential teaching – derived from Kant, and now an unquestionable received wisdom of common sense – is that 'science' is the expression of concepts, while 'art' is the expression of feelings (p. 148).

During the mid to late 1970s in England, Robert Witkin's book, *The Intelligence of Feeling* (1974) provided an application of Croce's dichotomy to the field of arts education arguing similarly that education in the arts is concerned with the education of feelings whereas education in the sciences is concerned with understanding objective facts and conceptual knowledge. In a Schools Council publication entitled the Arts and the Adolescent Working Paper 54 (1975) Witkin writes:

Expressive action is the means by which an individual comes to know the world of his own feelings, of his own being – a world that exists only because he (she) exists (p. 57 my bracket).

Building upon the theoretical framework of *The Intelligence of Feeling*, Malcom Ross (1978, 1980, 1983, 1984), produced a substantial body of work that advocated the expressive and creative value of arts education, more recently advocated by, *All Our Futures* (2000), a report by the National Advisory Committee on Creative and Cultural Education (NACCCE) into creativity, culture and education. The child or student is placed at the heart of educational thinking and practice and the intention is to promote individual creativity and sensitivity through expression in art media. The influence or spectre of Herbert Read, who argued that education through art is concerned with the "expression of feelings in communicable form", can be detected in both Witkin and Ross. Peter Abbs (1987, 1989) also provided a philosophical argument for the centrality of developing the senses and feelings through arts education and the central position the arts should occupy in the curriculum. In support of this approach to individuality and self-expression Maurice Barrett (1979) in the late seventies and early eighties argued that:

Art education is concerned with the development of the senses as our ways of 'receiving' our world, and the process that we use to symbolize, externalise, understand, order, express, communicate and solve its problems (p. 45).

The approach to pedagogy and practice which Witkin, Ross, Barrett and others promoted therefore was grounded in the idea of the sensing and expressive individual who, through art practice, is encouraged to externalise ideas, feelings and responses in expressive media. The process of expression is modified and refined through a process of 'reflexion' in which the initial impulse, idea or feeling (Witkins's sensate experience), is expressed through art media, a process which in turn generates further sensate experience as the individual responds to impulses that are generated through manipulating the art medium. This approach assumes an external world that the senses 'receive', or an internal world of imagination, which the individual experiences in his or her unique way and then transmits this uniqueness through expressive media. There is little emphasis in this body of work on the socio-cultural construction of ideas, feelings or responses or of the socio-cultural construction of the 'receiving' of our world. Key terms such as expression, feeling, sensation and impulse constitute a specific discourse in which human experience and art practice are comprehended and they form the conceptual fulcrum of a pedagogic rationale for teaching and learning in art education. In relation to the work of Lacan described in the previous chapter, these key terms constitute Lacanian points de caption, they are the metaphysical quilting points that structure the pedagogic discourse in whose terms both teachers and their students are made visible as pedagogic subjects.

In Rod Taylor's influential book, *Educating for Art* (1986), based upon the *Critical Studies in Art Education Project* (1981–84), sponsored by a variety of Art, Craft and Curriculum bodies, a different pedagogic emphasis is developed in which the aim is to encourage students to acquire and develop a critical language and response to art work. There was a growing perception amongst some concerned with art in education that too much emphasis was placed upon practical activity to the detriment of developing children's and students' ability to comprehend art and to discuss and communicate their ideas about art. The aim therefore was not to diminish the value of making in art practice but to encourage a critical and reflective awareness of art so that children and students could acquire a broader understanding of their own art practice in relation to the diverse practices of others and to different cultural traditions of art. This work spawned a rich development in what might be loosely termed museum and gallery education in the field of art in education. It is reasonable to suggest that Taylor's work led to a significant expansion of education departments within art galleries and museums, to the quality of services they provided and to a burgeoning increase in the number of school visits in order to introduce children and students to artefacts and develop their ability to question and comprehend them. Many of the major galleries and museums in UK cities, for example, now have strong professional development programmes for the professional development of teachers and they provide valuable resource materials to support teaching projects.

There was a significant shift of emphasis from the child or student-centred pedagogy of Witkin et al., concerned with the development of expression and feeling in art practice, to Taylor's child or student centred approach that placed emphasis upon developing a critical and reflective awareness of art objects and processes. Equally there is a significant difference in the key terms that constitute the two pedagogies for art education. In contrast to terms such as, expression, feeling, sensation and impulse, that underpin the pedagogy of Witkin et al., we find Taylor employing different terms: critical awareness, understanding, appreciation, illuminating experience, judgement. The expressive individual of practice is counter-balanced in the pedagogy of Taylor by a critically aware individual. Taylor's work was instrumental in promoting the conception of visual literacy (see Allen 1994) which became a central concept in the 1995 National Curriculum for Art in England, although the term was rarely employed by him preferring instead the idea of critical response.

THE NATIONAL CURRICULUM FOR ART IN ENGLAND

The National Curriculum for Art that developed throughout the nineteen-nineties incorporated the idea of a critical individual advocated in Taylor's work but it did not foreground the ideas of self-expression and individuality central to the pedagogy of Witkin, Ross, Barrett and others. Since its

inception this curriculum has promoted a pedagogy grounded more in technical achievement and the acquisition of bodies of knowledge. It is a curriculum
led by assessment of children's and students' progress through specific age
related Programmes of Study. Progress is assessed according to Attainment
Targets that delineate expected levels of attainment. The latter identify the
techniques, practices and knowledge children and students are expected to
acquire and demonstrate by the end of specific periods of teaching and learning,
these periods ending at years 7, 1, 14 and 16 are called Key Stages. There have
been three art curriculum orders since 1992, the second version from 1995
to 2000 placed particular emphasis upon developing visual perception and
visual literacy (DfEE 1995). Emphasis was placed upon teaching children
and students a range of art practices and forms of knowledge. There was no
description of a pedagogical rationale although it could be argued that this was
implicit to the Programmes of Study and Attainment Target descriptions.
Thus this curriculum provided a discursive framework that stipulated a regulated agenda for the content of art education and a list of expectations of
achievement. The phrase "pupils should be taught to . . ." highlighted
throughout this curriculum document, and which figures prominently in its
successor, curriculum 2000, indicates a rather prescriptive educational agenda
in which conceptions of inner creativity and expression, the cornerstone of a
curriculum based on self-expression, are relegated to a less significant position.

It is instructive to consider the language of the 1995 art curriculum in
contrast to the key terms of the pedagogies of Witkin et al. and Taylor. Ross
(1995) invoked a scathing attack upon the document by concentrating upon
the concepts being promoted. He draws our attention to recurrent terms:
identify, recognise, record and select, that for him, 'signal the world of technical rationality.' He claimed that this curriculum promoted a view of art as,
'craft, technique, product, knowledge and know-how.' In contrast Ross argued
that other terms once highlighted and central to previous art education discourses: creativity, feeling, expression, aesthetic, emotion and symbol, are
dramatically underplayed. Of course there are those who would disagree with
Ross's analysis arguing that the National Curriculum for Art is an effective
device for ensuring that all children and students in England up to the age
of fourteen are provided with the opportunity to engage in learning through
art practice which is organised according to specific learning targets that are
assessed on a regular basis. But it is fair to say, I believe, that when we consider
the SCAA Exemplifications of Standards for Key Stage 3 document which I
have already discussed in Chapter 5, that was produced for teachers to promote
consistency in assessment, a particular technical construction of ability in
specific art practices is promoted by the National Curriculum for Art literature. In my earlier discussion on this point I argued that teachers were being
encouraged to assess their student's technical and expressive skills in observational drawing and painting according to a simple mimetic understanding
of representation presupposed by the term 'accuracy'. This term presupposes
in turn an idea of vision that is a universal and unmediated experience and

that representation of this experience is a matter of technical proficiency. Variation in this proficiency is put down to personal 'noise' or 'lack' in the transition from perception to representation. Given that visual experience is universal it is therefore down to the teacher to judge along a sliding scale how closely a student's drawing or painting approximates the truth of perception (see Bryson 1983, p. 10). It is within this demonstration of particular techniques of representation that the student becomes visible as a pedagogic subject.

The new National Curriculum for Art and Design in England (DfEE 2000) retains the emphasis upon skills, techniques and knowledge which children and students should be taught through specific Programmes of Study. The assessment framework consists of an Attainment Target of eight levels (DfEE pp.38-39) each consisting of a series of expectations of learning and understanding which, according to the document, identify 'increasing levels of difficulty' (DfEE, p. 38). Progression in learning in art is thus conceived as a process of overcoming predefined levels of difficulty. Children and students at the end of each Key Stage are expected to attain particular levels of attainment so, for example most students at the end of Key Stage 3 (age 14 years) should attain levels 5 or 6. The text of the curriculum states that, "Each level describes types and range of performance that pupils working at that level should characteristically demonstrate (DfEE, p. 7)." The description of Attainment Level 5, for example, states:

Pupils explore ideas and select visual and other information. They use this in developing their work, taking account of the purpose. They manipulate materials and processes to communicate ideas and meanings and make images and artefacts, matching visual and tactile qualities to their intentions. They analyse and comment on ideas, methods and approaches used in their own and other's work, relating these to its context. They adapt and refine their work to reflect their own view of its purpose and meaning (DfEE, QCA, p. 39)

The first sentence of each Attainment Level description relates to 'exploring and developing ideas'. Level 1 states: Pupils respond to ideas; Level 2 states: Pupils explore ideas; Level 3 states: Pupils explore ideas and collect visual and other information for their work; Level 4 states: Pupils explore ideas and collect visual and other information to help them develop their work; Level 5 states: Pupils explore ideas and select visual and other information; Level 6 states: Pupils explore ideas and assess visual and other information including images and artefacts from different historical, social and cultural contexts. And so on. A similar list of the next sentence in each Level description concerned with 'materials and processes' could be cited. My point is that it is difficult to conceive in these hierarchical level statements a consistency in terms of increasing levels of difficulty or in terms of progression and I suspect that many teachers and trainee-teachers experience difficulty in using the statements to assess their children's or student's progress.

It could be argued that the eight levels of attainment position and regulate the heterogeneity of children's experience and practice within a normative series of statements so that variety and difference are homogenised according to the level descriptions. These "level descriptions provide the basis on which to make judgements about pupils' performance . . . (p. 7)." Thus the norms of practice encapsulated within the Attainment Target level descriptions form a logic through which children's and student's art practice is both conceivable and understood as art practice. They therefore construct art practice as a specific kind of practice and, consequently, they construct specific, if somewhat muddled, identifications of students as learners and teachers as teachers. In other words the level descriptions construct both student's and teacher's pedagogised identities. These curriculum discourses constitute part of the inter-textuality of art in education within which teachers and students become visible and are understood.

In contrast to the text of the Programmes of Study and Attainment Target levels, the new curriculum for art and design in England contains some laudable statements (DfEE, pp. 24–32) about the need to respond to students' different and diverse learning needs in order to develop a more inclusive curriculum. The focus upon inclusion is a new generic constituent of all National Curriculum subject documentation in England. Three principles for creating a move towards inclusion are established (p. 24). Two of these refer to: "responding to pupil's diverse learning needs," and, "overcoming potential barriers to learning and assessment for individuals and groups of pupils."

Teachers should be aware that pupils bring to school different experiences, interests and strengths which will influence the way in which they will learn (p. 25).

They should use appropriate assessment strategies which . . . use materials which are free from discrimination and stereotyping in any form (p. 25 my emphasis).

These two statements are surely to be welcomed in the move to establish a more inclusive art curriculum for the twenty-first century. However the second raises some important issues in relation to the Attainment Target level descriptions on which I have just commented. It could be argued that stereotyping and discrimination actually underpin the eight level descriptions of practice through which progress is assessed. In other words these level descriptions constitute a form of epistemological stereotyping and discrimination which enforces a particular understanding of art practice according to which students' "different experiences, interests and strengths" are measured and valued. Students' ontological differences are thus filtered through the values of a particular epistemology of practice that underpins the expectations of the standards according to which outcomes of process and practice are assessed. Thus it could be argued that the exemplary desire for an inclusive curriculum is actually negated by an assessment process that values and expects particular forms of practice whereby some students' practices are valued more than others. There appears then to be a conflict between the principles of inclusion and the politics of assessment.

Perhaps it is worth considering the implicit temporality of the level descriptions of the new art and design curriculum in contrast to the local temporality and outcomes of student's art practice. The former consists of a series of normative categories and expectations grounded within a decontextualised and homogenous temporality in order to be able to classify practice along a projected continuum of difficulty. The latter involves a temporal heterogeneity, it invokes the existential and experiential temporalities of different art practices within their socio-cultural differences. In the practice of assessment the former is placed over the latter like a template so that local experiences of practice, which include local semiotic structures of expression and signification, are reduced to the normative discourse of the level descriptions. Another way of describing this contrast is to think of it as a contrast between the disembodied and idealised description of practice of the attainment levels and the different embodied art practices of children or students.

It could be argued that this conception of pedagogy in art education is far removed from that espoused by Witkin et al. in their humanist advocacy of art practice grounded in ideas of self expression individuality and uniqueness. Understandably there are critics of the very conception of a national curriculum structure (see Swift and Steers 1999) who would want to see a variety of curriculum models in operation and who advocate a more experimental, diverse, plural and risk-taking approach to art in education. There are others who are happy to work with the project of the National Curriculum but recognise the difficulty of assessment posed by the Attainment Target level descriptions. However if we are serious about creating a pedagogy and practice of inclusion in art and design education then we require discourses that are commensurate with and respond to a high variety of functioning in this field and which do not reduce this variety to a specific view of practice. I shall explore ideas and suggestions for curriculum change in art and design when I describe more innovative approaches to teaching and learning in Chapter 8.

I have described how the formation of teacher and student identities in art education is dependent upon the discursive frameworks within which practice is understood. In my brief review of pedagogy in art and design in England since the nineteen-seventies I have demonstrated how different discourses of practice and assessment and their key discursive terms (points de caption) have produced contrasting pedagogised identities. My analysis reinforces the theorisation of the formation and regulation of subjectivities and identities in Chapters 5 and 6. It shows that pedagogised identities are historically located, discursively constructed and regulated. The child, student and teacher are not therefore to be viewed as independent autonomous selves who are affected or informed by an external social and cultural context. Rather they can only be understood within the changing discourses and practices that make them visible and knowable as children, students or teachers. This conception of subjectivity rejects the dualism of individual and society, and invokes a fusion or a folding whereby the 'outside is already inside', whereby the child, student or teacher can only exist or be known as such through the social discourses and practices in which they are constituted.

BOURDIEU'S NOTIONS OF FIELD AND HABITUS

The different discourses of teaching and learning in art education to which I have referred briefly can be said to make up part of the field of art education. Within this field these different forms of teaching and learning produce different kinds of subjectivity and pedagogised identities. Pierre Bourdieu's work on the notions of field, power and habitus is helpful for understanding how processes of subjectivity and identity are formed in particular fields of social production. In *The Field of Cultural Production* (1993) Bourdieu describes the idea of field as consisiting of a "separate social universe having its own laws of functioning" (p. 162). A field is a field of production that is made up of specific forms of practice, methods and principles of evaluation of both practice and work produced in the field. The laws or regulative devices which organise its functioning involve power relations between those who occupy dominant positions in the field and those who are dominated. Such relations are invoked through the acquisition of cultural capital which relates to those forms of knowledge and practice which are valued as well as educational qualifications, and symbolic capital, which relates to the prestige and recognition gained through success. Those who are able to acquire the cultural capital within a particular field possess the means for advancement (symbolic capital) within the field and beyond. Practices and forms of knowledge which are valued and which therefore constitute cultural capital exert hegemonic power over other practices and forms of knowledge that are viewed, within the field, as inferior or are not recognised in the field. In relation to my descriptions of the National Curriculum for Art in England, the Attainment Target Level descriptions constitute the discursive framework through which cultural capital is formulated leading to the acquisition of symbolic capital. Changes to what is perceived as cultural capital become evident when we consider the different dominant discourses that structure art in education at different historical periods. For example, *self-expression individuality* and *uniqueness* are terms that establish a different discourse to the terms knowledge, skills and understanding.

Bourdieu's notion of habitus concerns those particular dispositions and attitudes towards practice which a person acquires unaware of their constitution according to particular rules in the sense that such dispositions seem natural. These dispositions relate to modes of perception, thinking and ways of evaluating actions and those of others. They are inculcated from early on and thus mould practice, behaviour and understanding in particular fields. These dispositions towards practice produce what Bourdieu terms a bodily hexis, which is to say a particular organisation of the body in practice. Thompson, in his introduction to Bourdieu's *Language and Symbolic Power* (1992), writes of the relation between habitus and bodily hexis: the habitus, he remarks:

'orients' [. . .] actions and inclinations without strictly determining them. It gives them a 'feel for the game', a sense of what is appropriate in the circumstances and what is not, a 'practical sense' (le sens pratique). The practical sense is not so much a state of mind as a state of the body, a state of being. It is because the body has become a repository of ingrained dispositions that certain actions, certain ways of behaving and responding, seem altogether natural. The body is the site of incorporated history. The practical schemes through which the body is organised are the product of history and, at the same time, the source of practices and perceptions which reproduce that history (p. 13)

The organisation of the body through specific forms of practice and attitudes towards practice is a product of history which reproduces specific attitudes and perceptions of practice. Bourdieu's analysis of habitus and bodily-hexis is close to Foucault's explorations of biopolitics and biopower which refer to the technologies, knowledges, discourses and practices in which individuals are positioned and regulated within institutional and other social sites so as to produce particular kinds of behaviours, including learning. It is possible to argue that learning to draw or paint, that is to say, to engage in art practice in a certain way can be understood as organising the body through a particular form of practice which will produce a particular form of cultural and symbolic capital. The current Attainment Target level descriptions and the Programme of Study outlines in the English National Curriculum for Art invoke a series of descriptions and expectations of art practice which, when viewed from Bourdieu's notions of habitus and bodily hexis, constitute a specific organisation of the body-in-practice. Thus art in education can be conceived as a specific technology for managing and normalising the body-in-practice through specific forms of art practices and ways of comprehending art practice.

The particular forms of practice and understanding which a person acquires are due to the relation between the habitus (incorporating the bodily hexis) and his or her positioning within a specific field of production. Now my point is that we can use Bourdieu's notions of field, habitus, cultural and symbolic capital to theorise the production of subjectivity and pedagogised identities in different sites of art education. We can apply the notion of cultural capital to those forms of practice and knowledge that are valued within a particular school art department, so that gaining success in such practice, through assessment and examinations, produces symbolic capital. We can view art education in schools as a general field of cultural production that consists of particular sub-fields (different art departments and their practices, curriculum policies, examination systems and so on), which articulate different dispositions, attitudes towards, perceptions and understanding of art practice.

According to Bourdieu (1993, p. 183) within a field there will be orthodox as well as more heterodox forms of practice and perceptions of practice that vie for positions of power and dominance and the struggle for cultural and symbolic capital. Perhaps we can see this struggle as manifested in historical changes in the field of art education, from discourses and practices of 'basic-design' to 'self-expression' and to 'skills and understanding'. Once dominant discourses of practice are overtaken by others but the former do not disappear entirely. This process can be observed when we consider current forms of practice in art education in which traces and manifestations of once dominant forms of practice still exist in school curricula. For example, art work in many schools consists of a mixture of practices from different historical and cultural settings, such as observational drawing and painting or design and exploration of visual forms.

CHANGE IN THE FIELD

Within a field there exist different positions and relations but the historical constitution and sedimentation of a field will provide the possibilities for practice and perception of practice. These positions include dominant-dominated relations indicating those who acquire cultural and symbolic capital and those who do not. They also include by implication practices and forms of perceiving them that are well established and practices which are new or avante-garde that seek recognition and acceptance. Change in the field depends upon its current state of possibilities which is a production and accumulation of past and current practice,

The impetus for change in cultural works – language, art, literature, science, etc., – resides in the struggles that take place in the corresponding fields of production. These struggles, whose goal is the preservation or transformation of the established power relationships in the field of production, obviously have as their effect the preservation or transformation of the structure of the field of works, which are the tools and stakes in these struggles (p. 183).

Change is therefore dependent upon the specific interests of people and the positions they occupy in the field in relation to the 'dominant pole or the dominated pole of the field':

-towards more open and more innovative possibilities, or towards the most secure and established possibilities, towards the newest possibilities among those which are already socially constituted, or even towards possibilities that must be created for the first time (p. 183).

This quote refers to what might be called in systems theory the state of a system, that is to say how it is likely to develop in time. Bourdieu refers to two positionings within the field that exist on a continuum that runs from conservation and tradition towards revolution or radicalism. The power relations between the more conservative and the more radical positions in their attitude to change are dependent not simply on the field but on the effect of external struggles and the 'reinforcement that one may find from without' (p. 185). The contrasting positions in the field which are determined by people's interests *vis a vis* the acquisition of cultural and symbolic capital can be considered and understood through the use of a different metaphorical language employed by C.H. Waddington in his analysis of the development of complex systems. I believe there are close correspondences between Bourdieu's sociological theorisation of field, habitus, power and capital and Waddington's (1977) cybernetic analysis of what he termed *chreods* (or pathways of change), and *epigenetic landscapes*, which describe the growth and development of a system.

CHREODS AND EPIGENETIC LANDSCAPES

We can think of the field of art in education as a complex, consisting of many spaces of action, for example, teachers in their different teaching contexts, which consists of their different dispositions to and organisation of practice. This is a complex dynamical system in which different attitudes to teaching and learning in art from conservative to more innovative or radical approaches coexist. The stability of many approaches to teaching art however is often concerned with maintaining forms of practice, traditions that have been established and which are valued. The preservation and valuing of particular practices through time provides stability along a certain pathway of practice. Waddington (p. 105) suggests that we can picture such pathways as attractor surfaces that control the flow of practice. The attractor surface is made up, for example, of a series of values relating to forms of practice, discourses of and those relating to practice as well as ways of perceiving and perpetuating practice. The historical constitution of the attractor surface provides therefore both the momentum and justification for practice and perception.

The pathway can be termed a chreod, a Greek word meaning 'necessary path' (p. 106), a pathway in place and time. We can think of the attractor surface of a chreod in the form of a valley, so that a deep valley with high walls produces a highly stable chreod whilst a shallow valley is a less stable chreod and more susceptible to change. Waddington states that, "Different canalised pathways or chreods may have rather different types of stability built into them (p. 106)." For example a deep chreod would consist of an attractor surface which is highly conservative and resistant to new forms of practice and understanding, a shallow chreod on the other hand would be more flexible and less resistant to new practice. The attractor surface that makes up the chreod is similar to Bourdieu's notions of habitus, cultural and symbolic capital, which refer to the inculcation of dispositions towards practice and the valuing of specific forms of practice. The terms of language that are used to describe, evaluate and assess art practices in schools, such as those described in my analysis of the video sequence above, form a particularly deep chreod in the sense that they constitute a particular and highly stable way of conceiving practice which is so well established it almost seems natural. There are links also between Lacan's points de capiton, which create stable knots of meaning, and Waddington's notion of attractors.

Bourdieu's description of the continuum of positionings which make up the field of cultural production, consisting of conservative to radical poles can be translated into Waddington's notion of an epigenetic landscape. Epigenesis in general terms refers to the development or growth of a system. Different positions in the field (conservative to radical) and their respective dispositions and attitudes (habitus) equate to different kinds of chreods and their respective attractor surfaces which together make up an epigenetic landscape. A social system such as the field of art in education can be viewed therefore as an epigenetic landscape in the sense that it is composed of different components: teachers, curriculum policies, examination systems, inspection regimes, teacher-education, etc., each incorporating sets of values some of which are deeply entrenched while others are more susceptible to change. We could say that the chreodic development of a particular method of teaching art in a school consists of an attractor surface which includes the teachers' dispositions towards art education, their particular understanding of art practice and the art practices that are encouraged, demanded and valued. Such attractor surfaces mould the development of students as learners within the department. The chreodic development of different art departments and their differing value systems relating to pedagogy in art education can thus be viewed as composing part of the epigenetic landscape of art education in schools. Other factors already mentioned which constitute this landscape include government curriculum policies and strategies, initial teacher education, continuing professional development courses, texts on art education, gallery and museum art education links and so on.

The impetus for change in the way art is taught in school and, consequently the way art practice is perceived and understood, arises within a contest in the field to preserve or to transform established practices and their hegemony. The struggle to introduce new forms of art education can be considered as a struggle for cultural capital and the subsequent symbolic capital which accrues. In the terms of Waddington's cybernetic discourse, this struggle can be viewed as a disturbance to the attractor surface of an established stable chreod, that is to say a disturbance to an established form of teaching and learning in art education. If the disturbance is large enough change may eventually occur, if it is not then the disturbance is likely to be absorbed and assimilated by the current values of the system. There are analogies here with the dynamic Piagetian notions of assimilation, accommodation and equilibration. In the field of art education it might be argued, for example, that the external impact of issues of culture, race, gender and sexuality, has produced a disturbance to the field that has effected significant changes in practice and perceptions of practice, though by no means universally. Waddington's terminology may appear slightly obscure but it does seem important to me to explore ways of thinking about change which try to embrace ideas of coexistence, stability and transformation. The field of art in education does require the recognition that teachers coexist but function in quite different ways that provide local stability to their teaching. Teachers also transform their teaching at different rates and at different times and in different degrees. Changes in curriculum policy impact upon these local practices of teaching in different ways and degrees. The field or epigenetic landscape of art education is highly complex and my reference to Bourdieu and Waddington concerns the need to struggle for an appropriate language in order to get to grips with its dynamic complexity. The energy that sustains the field is therefore multi-dimensional and multi-modal and is manifest in teacher attitudes and practices as well as curriculum policies and educational theories, which are the equivalent of game rules that provide potential energy to the field. It seems important then to

risk the tentative possibility of a dynamic geometry that allows for difference and co-existence, stability and transformation in the practices of teaching
and learning in the field of art and design education.

In our quest perhaps we can learn from the field of mathematical discourse. Over many years I have discussed these ideas in conversation with
W.M. Brookes, of the University of Southampton, who introduced me to
thinking about complex systems and change. In Mathematics one of the
powerful concomitant notions to field is that of 'potential'. 'Field' in applied
mathematics usually means 'potential field' and hence the deepest valleys
require more energy to be expended if they are to be vacated or destroyed.
This is not easy because the very configuration of the field is the pattern of
forces operating! If we think of 'field' as in 'field of battle' or 'playing field'
it is simply a description without dynamics. Potential energy is provided by
game rules or by the form of battle. In relation to art education practices of
teaching and learning the point here is that the dynamic of practice and
comprehension is generated by the dispositions of the teacher and student,
which energise the teaching-learning relation and the production of work.

These attempts to theorise the complex systemic developments within and
between fields of production are quite involved but equally I believe they
are important. For instance, when we consider avant-garde developments in
the field of art production we are often faced with an almost irreconcilable
situation. When the semiotics of new art work lies beyond the assimilated codes
of decipherment, as happens frequently today, illustrating the point that we live
in a period of frequent rupture, problems of meaning and interpretation are
not uncommon. The transformation in modes of art production thus precede
modes of interpretation, which are much slower to develop. A transforming
of interpretations is not developed by everyone at the same time as can be
acknowledged in frequent dismissive attitudes to contemporary art. New work
is often perceived through established codes and dispositions (habitus) these
modes of perception are "precisely those against which the new work has been
created (Bourdieu 1993, p. 226)." The introduction of contemporary art
practices to art in education can be equally problematic, as I have already
discussed in relation to GCSE moderation, when one external examiner found
some work in one school 'very conceptual'.

In the following section I will present some conversations with art teachers
in secondary schools in England. My purpose is to contrast the expectations
and description of practice in the English National Curriculum for Art and
its implicit construction of teacher and learner identities with these local narratives of teaching and learning and their respective constructions of teacher
and learner identities. These narratives of teaching and learning reveal, in
Bourdieu's terminology, quite different productions of cultural and symbolic
capital.

TEACHER AND LEARNER IDENTITIES IN THE FIELD OF ART EDUCATION

I recorded a series of conversations with teachers of art and design in English secondary schools, my intention was to explore their attitudes, rationales and beliefs about teaching and learning in this curriculum area. For me the interesting point about these conversations is that in describing different approaches towards practices of teaching and learning they are hinting at the construction of different pedagogised identities. I have chosen those extracts from each conversation that I believe best illustrate each teacher's pedagogical approach and I have annotated the recordings slightly to help my presentation. As recordings the responses made by each teacher can be considered as forming narrative identities of themselves as teachers of art. In the language of Waddington each narrative hints at a different chreodic structure and organisation of teaching and learning in art education. Each narrative describes a different pathway of teaching and learning structured by its respective values. In the language of Bourdieu these narratives hint at the different habitus and bodily hexis of each teacher, that is to say, their different dispositions and attitudes to teaching art and the way through teaching and learning practices the body is organised as a body-in-practice. There are many possibilities for a study of the kind of bodies-in-practice teacher narratives of practice invoke in relation to issues of race, gender, class, sexuality and disability, but a detailed account will not be possible here. However, this does indicate the need for further study into what kind of bodies are presupposed by different practices of teaching and learning in art in education.

NARRATIVE 1

In the first narrative the teacher describes the situation he found when arriving at his present school.

"When I came to this school the work was just like I was doing at my previous school, there was lots of work on the wall that displayed beautiful renditions of observational drawing and painting. A classic case which illustrates how students operated at GCSE level was if someone was doing something on sport, say basketball, they would collect lots of photos of sports pictures and produce beautifully rendered drawings from the photos. The final piece would then consist of a compilation of these different drawings on one sheet of paper. It was difficult to break this approach to work because that's the way in which they were used to working. We did tricks like you would get someone's work, say some coloured pen work and cut it up in front of the class in order to show that small sections could be developed into exciting work. This was difficult to do but as long as they have confidence in you and what you are trying to do then you can get away with these kinds of tactics. . . . So now instead of copying photographs we would give them a camera and tell them to go and watch a

game of basketball and take their own photographs which they can then work on . . ."

This teacher is obviously concerned with locating art practice and learning through art within the personal experience of the children and students. He is obviously keen to avoid the use of secondary material such as magazine images but quite happy for students to take their own photographs on which to base their work. His pedagogy in relation to developing skills and techniques is revealed in the following remark:

"As a department we place emphasis on using art as a tool to explore the world around them and self-exploration and less of an emphasis upon just developing skills and techniques. . . . At GCSE level the emphasis upon group taught skills becomes increasingly less a part of our teaching. . . . We need to break down preconceptions about ways of working . . . when you are dealing with 20 students each needing to justify to themselves what their ideas are there's a constant sense of edge . . . so its not just 'how do I mix plaster?' they are all asking 'is this a good idea?' or, 'if I do it this way what do you think?' . . . its difficult to cope with everyone but we do it here because of the ethos we have built up . . ."

A remark about the National Curriculum for Art also illustrates this teacher's approach to skills teaching:

"I've never allowed the National Curriculum for Art to get in the way of what my Department wants to do. . . . We don't provide a good art education by constant reference to the National Curriculum. . . . In the National Curriculum there is an emphasis upon observational drawing which we don't have, we do it but its not a big part of our teaching. . . . I wouldn't want to shift our approach to feel that we were mapping out all these skills as outlined by the National Curriculum because I think teachers would become too concerned about whether they are covering all these skills, and that is a problem. . . . I'm conscious about the curriculum we use and have established here which is about an ethos we have developed rather than something we have written down on paper. . . . It's there because we believe in it, the student's believe in it but its not a great heavy structure. . . . I'm conscious of the fact that it's difficult to put on paper what our ethos is . . ."

He continues to describe the ethos of his art department in relation to A Level work and critical studies:

"The ethos of our department is strongly reflected in our A Level personal study component, we don't tend to follow the lush sketchbook practice of many A Level courses in which students produce an illustrated sketch book study of an artist . . . instead we do dissertation studies of 5000 words which

is an illustrated piece of writing . . . this writing is writing which is personal and important to them about art and design. . . . We don't encourage the 'life of Van Gogh' or 'Picasso' approach but instead they will write about personal life journeys. . . . One student wrote about his journey through art education from junior to secondary school and described how on coming to secondary school his ideas were turned upside down. . . . The important thing was that his writing was about his personal experience of art education and what he thinks art and design is, which is quite a profound thing for a 17–18 year old. . . . We were talking about multiculturalism a while ago well we had a refugee, not poor but quite well off, whose family fled their home country and her dissertation was about how she perceived her home culture (indigenous) after two years in this country. . . . It would have been an easy option for her to write about Islamic art and produce a straight-forward study but she chose to write about how she saw herself as a woman in Iran and as a woman in North London in a project on identity . . ."

NARRATIVE 2

The second narrative illustrates a different approach to teaching and to learning, like the last teacher there is a deep concern for individual expression and enquiry but with this teacher art practice takes on a different inflexion.

"When I begin work with kids I start by questioning and talking and we end up with a question, "Why are we doing this work?" The answer emerges in the next few lessons and in many ways as a teacher I will answer this question . . . I have no distinct idea about what they will produce at the end of the project. I want to encourage kids to make work that is reflective and which has meaning and the vast majority respond, a minority fit into what I call those who want to work in a linear beginning-to-end sequence, but often when they see how others are working they begin to see a different way of making art and what is acceptable as art. Once they see that art can be other to what they expect its as though they see their world in different ways. Often when they arrive here the art kids most generally do is all about looking and rendering. I try to get them to look differently, to put themselves in different positions physically to begin with for example by standing on tables or lying underneath or looking from a corner of the room . . . in other words to change their perspective. This leads into looking at their own world, we start to talk about who they are, where they are from and so on. Since coming here I developed a way of working which is concerned with different levels of awareness, I'll try to explain:The school has a strong Irish community and whenever you probe ideas about who they are students stop at their mums or dads and the high street. They don't think of London or England, they think of the school and others in the neighbourhood. What I try to do is develop three

levels of thinking; level 1 is the high street, mum and dad, holidays in Spain,
supporting Manchester United. The images for this level are easy to find.
Level 2 is to look beyond mum or dad, to get out a map and look where
Eltham is in London and England and so on. In level 3 they find out about
grandparents, who they are/ were, where they come from, and so on."

When asked about teaching specific skills and techniques this teacher
responded:

"It is a symbolic way of working, it isn't based around drawing and
observation. We often begin with words. It's about the invention of symbols
and the reinterpretation of symbols. The backbone of skills come in here
so that images at level 1 are developed by working deeper into a painting
and inventing or re-using symbols, we will talk about composition and
lay-out for example and the skills will develop around the reason for
making."

When asked how to describe the purpose of art in education this teacher replied:

"The key can be seen in a number of things. It can be seen in grades. But
let's look at this student. She came in to ask if she could talk to me. She
said she had an idea, just an idea, but she felt there's not much to the
work. She said, "Its about foot and mouth Sir, about the way animals are
being slaughtered, you see it on TV, It's awful because animals are being
killed for our mishandling of them, for profit." "Well," I said, "That's
your issue so tell me what you want to do". She said, "We move animals
around the country to be slaughtered because its cheaper to kill them in
certain places. I want to go to the butchers on the day of the examination
and I want to get a cow's heart and I want to suspend it in a cage . . .
and I want it to be frozen so that as it dissolves the blood runs out of the
heart . . . and I want a map of England with the blood splashing onto it
and running over the map. Do you think I will get a bad grade for this?"
For me that is what the aim of art education is . . . it's not about the
grade its about the idea, about the reason for making the work. If you
feel passionately enough about something to be able to go beyond thinking
about it and actually make and see something physical in front of you,
then we have delivered I feel...that sums it up for me. Art can bring you
to a place which you wouldn't get to otherwise within the confines and
structures of educational institutions."

The teacher continued:

"I think that art would be much better not being called art . . . the problem
is that . . . and I'll say something contentious here . . . I think the national
curriculum was written for poor teachers of art because you loose the
idea of what art is or can be . . . and that is the problem with the language

of the document it creates a particular idea of art and what it is . . . but what is art? There's no answer. When we construct a curriculum and so on we like to have answers, a packaged item so that people like inspectors can know what it is to look for. There seems to be a particular emphasis upon observation, of beginning art in this way. Why is this? I worked in an art department in one school where every scheme of work was planned in great detail according to what they felt the national curriculum was expecting . . . it's as though we bring the curriculum already sorted out to the students . . . I'm not sure if this is right because I think it negates the individuality of the child."

NARRATIVE 3

The third teacher was more concerned with a traditional way of teaching art practices and their respective skills and techniques:

"My purpose in this school, which is quite traditional, is to give them some traditional art training at the beginning and then through that let their expression take over. Hopefully by A level and GCSE it's evident that they have the skills that backs all the work up."

When asked what he meant by traditional he replied:

"Well traditional drawing and painting as a starting point. Drawing from observation but not necessarily still-life, drawing from observation of their sources, we allow them to use photographs for example . . ."

A major issue for this teacher is therefore in the early years of secondary education to develop childrens' learning in specific art practices and techniques.

"Techniques yes, we're a boys school . . . boys like to draw things that look like they're meant to in their minds . . . later on you can expose them to other things but at the beginning they do like to have a grip on what they are doing."

When I asked if the National Curriculum for Art was something he welcomed he replied:

"I think its been good, it's a great leveller. My own art education was four years of drawing crushed coke cans, . . . if you couldn't do it you couldn't do art . . . There was one person perhaps who could probably do it but the rest of us were lost . . . so I think it (NC) is quite good, its given a kind of structure to education to the arts. . . . I don't think its limiting I think you can use it as a starting point . . . I'm using the QCA schemes of work at the moment because they relate to themes we use a lot. . . . If we are trying to get some kind of standardisation across the country you've got to have some kind of basis I think for starting out. Hopefully when it

comes down to attainment levels we are all assessing at the same kind of level."

However, pursuing the idea of standardisation a little further, I asked this teacher, who visits many schools in his position of GCSE moderator, what he felt about the work he noticed in other schools, he replied:

"Using my assessment experience I'm finding that everything is up and down everywhere. Most work I see leaves me cold. I am amazed at the lack of letting the kids have ago, in some schools, the work is very formalised , scale wise, material wise and actually looking at other artists' work it is pretty weak. . . . I'm going to shoot myself in the foot here aren't I, I'm going to say traditional aren't I? I think a lot of people are reading the National Curriculum wrongly . . . there is far too much orthodoxy, not letting kids take chances."

The contrast between this teacher's approach to teaching and learning in art and the teacher's comments in narrative 2 is quite striking. The phrase 'to give them some art training' perhaps typifies the way teaching and learning are conceived by this teacher. Whereas in narrative 2 remarks such as, 'skills will develop around the reason for making,' or 'I try to get them to look differently', or, 'it's not about the grade it's about the idea,' indicate a different emphasis. Whereas for the more traditional teacher in narrative 3 developing skills and techniques is a primary objective because they facilitate representation and expression, for the teacher in narrative 2 it is ideas that are primary followed by the search for symbolic form. This contrast is manifested in the art work produced by students in each school. Students from the school in narrative 2 are making work which is often termed 'issues-based' in that the work reflects student's reaction and response to personal experiences or social events. Much of the work is mixed-media, three-dimensional or involves installations. Students from the school in narrative 3 produce highly skilled and technically proficient paintings, prints and drawings.

NARRATIVE 4

The fourth teacher expresses her rationale for teaching art:

"My role as an art teacher is presenting, not just art, but presenting the world that the kids are in . . . in a way that they can perceive it in different ways because when you grow up you are nurtured to . . . trained to see things in a certain way . . . my role as an art teacher is to encourage them to question and to explore and to be very inquisitive not only in terms of their own art work but to take this into other areas of their work . . . I try to encourage this the whole time."

I asked her how she felt about teaching specific practices and their related skills, her reply concentrated on drawing and to some extent echoed the last teacher's more traditional approach.

> "*We have increased observational drawing. We have a range of abilities, some children are able to click in to the whole process, they can draw as they see things, others have drawing styles which are quite different. Some would say they are immature or are typical of drawings done by children of a younger age. They draw very one-dimensionally, drawing what they know rather than what they see, I think that's the difference. We try to get them to pick up on the skills they can learn from drawing in a more realistic way . . . and rather than put down what they are doing I try to build this in to enhance their drawing . . . because they see what they are doing as quite different they assume that what is expected is something that is realistic looking . . . , they are reluctant to engage in the whole process of drawing . . ."*

When reflecting upon the different pedagogies for art in education that are implied in each of these narratives, they illustrate quite different dispositions and attitudes towards teaching and learning. The organisation and content of learning experienced by students in each school is therefore different, suggesting a different formation of pedagogised identities in each school. Students' comprehension of art practice will therefore vary according to educational context.

What I am attempting to work with here is the contrast between art practice and attainment anticipated by the text of the National Curriculum for Art in England and each of the above narratives of teaching which articulate different approaches, intentions and pedagogies. My point is that whilst the National Curriculum text anticipates particular kinds of learners and teachers in its descriptions of programmes of study and attainment levels, these narratives signify divergent practices that imply the formation of different pedagogised identities in art education. The contrast between the National Curriculum text and teacher narratives reflects a difference between a disembodied epistemology and different ontological structures of teaching and learning practices. The regime of classification, which is insinuated in the National Curriculum text through the description of levels of attainment, is preoccupied with a particular status of practice and knowledge, that is to say with what constitute different levels of valid attainment of art practice and knowledge. The teacher narratives in contrast reflect different phenomenological ways of making sense tied to contrasting practices of teaching and learning. They seem less concerned, in their different approaches, with classification systems which stand above their practice, and more concerned with responding, in their different pedagogies, to the diversity of children's and student's responses, although the description of teaching in the last two narratives suggests a greater concern for students to acquire traditional skills and techniques. It seems to be for each teacher therefore a case of mapping what has to be disclosed onto the National Curriculum framework in order to appear compliant, and for some teachers, (perhaps represented by the teachers in the first two narratives), the mapping process will prove more problematic than others.

If we think of the different narratives of teaching and learning presented above we can perhaps see that within them the ideas of progression, development, achievement and attainment in relation to learning are quite different and do not sit easily with the more decontextualised discourse of the attainment level descriptions. The second narrative, for example, implies a different conception of development of learning through art to narrative three. The former is concerned with the development of ideas, the ability to interrogate images, the ability to understand and manipulate visual symbols in order to make art work. The latter places emphasis upon the acquisition of traditional techniques and skills in order to provide students with the tools for representation and expression. Both teachers however have to comply with the National Curriculum attainment level descriptions for reporting on children's and students' attainment, in doing so their different pedagogies and practices are compressed onto a universal discourse which hides their difference and suggest the idea of standardisation. These narratives hint at the habitus and bodily hexis of each teacher, their different dispositions and attitudes towards teaching and learning through art, such dispositions assume different modes of perception, understanding and ways of evaluating the art practices of their students. The narratives hint at a different organisation of practices of teaching and learning which seem natural to each teacher. It is within the different realities to which these narratives point that pedagogised identities are formed.

DIFFERENCE AND PRACTICE

In Part Three I return to art practice in schools by considering mixed media work made by students in four London secondary schools. In Chapter 4 I discussed the notion of visuality and how this notion could help us to consider children's drawing practices as visual productions constructed within local signifying practices. In Chapter 8 I take a similar approach to students' mixed media work by considering it as a production of meaning in visual form. I discuss this production process in relation to the idea of intertextuality, previously mentioned in Chapter 1, whereby meaning and practice emerge in dialectical relations with other signifiers, that is to say, other art practices, media images and texts.

In Part One I offered a way of considering children's and students' drawing practices as local signifying processes in which they are able to construct meaning. If we view such drawings as semiotic practices that in some way establish representational significance for the child or student, even though this may not be clear to others, this opens the door for contemplating the possibility of semiotic diversity and a semiotics of visual production grounded within local ontologies of art practice. Such art work is therefore not valued or measured according to its fit with a prior reality (imaginary or real) but it is viewed as a semiotic practice which interacts with a variety of such practices, some of which have become naturalised and conventional, whilst others are regarded as unconventional, unusual, different or mysterious. The importance of hermeneutics relates to the interpretational stance we occupy when needing to respond to children's and student's art practices. In describing a series of hermeneutic strategies I showed how each could be employed to interrogate as well as support the pedagogic relationship. Gadamer's notions of 'dialogic relations' and 'fusion of horizons' were shown to offer a productive pedagogic strategy in which art practice and its development are negotiated reflexively in contrast, for example, to the imposition of specific practices and meaning by the teacher. On the other hand post-structural hermeneutic strategies, in different ways, provide a critical pedagogy through which it is possible to expose forces of regulation and normalisation in which both teacher and student identities are formed in the field of art in education.

In Part Two I considered the discourses, such as assessment discourse, in which both teachers' and students' pedagogised identities are formed. This entailed recognising that such identities cannot be traced to some biological or psychological substratum but that they are constructed within social and cultural practices. By foregrounding the notion of signification in contrast to representation I endeavoured to show that drawings from imagination or observation cannot be traced back to a prior origin or referent which is knowable 'in-itself' in order to assess ability because any attempt to do so always ends up as another representation. For example, judging or assessing an observational drawing of objects according to its fit with a particular experience of viewing objects, is inevitably displaced into assessing the drawing according to another signifier, that is to say a mode of representation, such as perspective, which we believe represents visual experience. This means that we can never get behind representation or signification to a position of apodictic truth.

In such assessment discourses children's and student's art work, and their identities as learners, become textualised according to specific discourses of representational practice through which they are read. I showed, with reference to the work of Lacan how the signifier represents the subject not for another subject but for another signifier. I also provided a critical review of the National Curriculum for Art in England and some of its more recent pedagogical predecessors in art education in England in order to consider changing constructions of pedagogised identities. Within contrasting pedagogies and rationales for art education the subject becomes a different kind of pedagogised subject by being interpellated through different curriculum signifiers. This was followed by presenting a series of extracts from conversations with teachers in which they described their rationales for art and design education. My intention here was to explore and contrast these teacher narratives that articulated different pedagogies in which practice is conceived and how, as a consequence, students' and teachers' identities are formed accordingly. My explorations opened up a temporal as well as a number of philosophical/ideological differences between the text of the National Curriculum for Art and the teachers' local practitioner-based narratives.

Both Foucault and Lacan, in different ways, problematise humanist ideas of subjectivity and identity. They abandon any notion of an essential self, Foucault stressing the production of the subject within discursive practices, Lacan stressing processes of lack and desire in processes of subjectivity. In contrast to Foucault, Lacan's work suggests the impossibility of identification in that there is no signifier for the subject, no signifier can represent the subject in-itself, so that identification is always bedevilled with misrecognition. Both writers present us with a problem regarding the idea of experience. For Foucault experience is historical, which is to say that we should not think of experience as relating to a physical or mental origin which pre-exists representation, but that it is structured and produced within specific discursive practices which change in time. For Lacan it is impossible to attain direct access to experience because it always has to pass through the defiles of the signifier, however for Lacan, the Real hints at a pre-discursive domain of existence, which occasionally disrupts the symbolic order and our ways of understanding reality.

Within contexts of teaching and learning reference is frequently made to experience, for example, to make the curriculum more relevant to pupils' experiences, as if these are expressible or representable directly. But how can we consider this term if it is not possible to gain direct access to biological, psychological, social or cultural origins which the term appears to suggest? In Part Three I will extend the theoretical work of Part Two by considering the idea of experience through the work of Jacques Derrida who in some ways is close to Lacan but who provides a different theorisation of subjectivity and identity based upon the idea of presence.

CHAPTER EIGHT

EXPERIENCE, DIFFERENCE AND PRACTICE

In this chapter I will describe some students' art practices which could be said to challenge more traditional conceptions of art practice and representation in schools and which therefore invoke a need to contemplate the possibility of new directions for creating and understanding art in education. This is not to denigrate more traditional practices in art education but to think about extending practice in the light of contemporary art and new forms of visual signification. Much of this work relates to semiotic practices of contemporary art that explore issues of identity such as gender, race, class and sexuality. In many ways such work is concerned with a semiotics of identity and difference within a social world of increasing complexity and inter-cultural relations. But before I tackle the art work I will provide a brief philosophical grounding in order to preface and situate my descriptions. This grounding will consider ideas of difference, experience and practice, which will then be applied to contexts of teaching and learning in art in education.

FORMS OF LIFE

In his book Philosophical Investigations, Wittgenstein (1953) offers the idea of 'language-games' to describe the use of language and the formation of meaning as a practice that takes place in a multitude of social contexts. For him a language game denotes a form of life. For De Certeau (1984) 'forms of life' are equivalent to 'stories' that denote the practices of everyday life, whilst Ricoeur (1991) investigates identities as 'narrative identities which constitute us' (see also Valdez 1991, pp. 436–437). The importance of the idea of language or narratives that denote forms of life for art practices in education is that we can view such practices as visual narratives or productions which emanate from and which therefore connote particular forms of life. This suggests that we can contemplate the possibility of an infinity of narratives, or semiotic expressions, in relation to diverse forms of life (experiencing). Furthermore the possibility of semiotic diversity provides a powerful antidote against the regulative power of normalisation and orthodoxies of practice, which develop in conservative systems such as curriculum, and examination practices. Wittgenstein always encouraged us to consider the possibility and legitimacy of other or alternative meanings, which describe different forms of life, so that language and meaning are never fixed but always contingent upon context and use. To use an analogy from the work of the Swiss linguist, Saussure, he (Wittgenstein) was concerned with the importance of *parole*, that is to say the living use of language in speech in contrast to the linguistic code (*langue*).

Here the term "language-*game*" is meant to bring into prominence the fact that the *speaking* of language is part of an activity, or a form of life (PI 23).

Personal histories and different cultures indicate that linguistic terms have a multitude of uses and, as I have shown in my discussion of children's drawings, so do visual structures. Wittgenstein's work is full of accounts that describe and challenge fixed meanings. When he writes of forms of life I take this to refer to ontological contexts of practice, which by implication can therefore be applied to ontological contexts of art practice.

We remain unconscious of the prodigious diversity of all the everyday language-games because the clothing of our language makes everything alike (PI p. 224).

The importance of this statement when applied analogously to the context of art education is that it entreats us to develop an awareness of local differences of art expression (the *parole* of art practices) and their visual products as well as encouraging children and students to explore the boundaries of their practice in order to contemplate new forms of practice and semiotic production, which might be termed new forms of life.

TWO NARRATIVES

In his book, *Another Modernity a Different Rationality*, Scott Lash (1999) describes two rationalities, which I prefer to call two narratives, that exemplify firstly the high modernity of the Enlightenment and secondly the modernity of what could be described as post-Enlightenment. Both narratives, Lash observes, pervade our social contexts today, it is not the case that they follow each other chronologically. The first narrative ascribed to Enlightenment thought is dominated by a concern for epistemology. It is concerned with developing logics of classification and reason. Knowledge is classified into specific forms of knowledge about the natural or social world: economics, linguistics, natural science, and so on. Each field of knowledge develops its own system of classification into which its subject matter is classified. Hence in the study of language, plants, medicine or law, systems of classification develop which structure these different kinds of knowledge. Such systems are explored in depth in Foucault's *The Order of Things* (1970) and *The Archaeology of Knowledge* (1972) that describe the growth and development of the classification of different fields of knowledge.

This narrative of rationality spawned the age of reason, the Cartesian *cogito*, the Newtonian universe, it denotes the age of the universal subject, the period we know as the Enlightenment. The science of Newton proposed a universalised and homogenous time and space. Human beings are viewed as transcendent over nature and able therefore to discover universal truths about the world by employing the laws of reason, calculation and measurement. The painting entitled *The Geographer*, by Vermeer, cited by Crary (1996, pp. 43–46), is a vivid depiction of this outstanding age of western intellectual development. In it a male scientist holding a pair of dividers is depicted fully immersed in studying a map that is lit by the flood of light (the light of reason) from the window. It is significant that he does not study the real world of extension but a calculated model constructed by man (a patriarchal reality) in his search for an accurate depiction of the world. It is, as Crary (p. 46) indicates, the calculated model through which the exterior world becomes known, "rendered intelligible to the mind by the clarity of the representation."

The second narrative to which Lash refers concerns a shift from the transcendence of the universal (patriarchal) subject, equipped with the infinite power of reason, to a singular finite and embedded subject, a phenomenological subject grounded in life-world contexts of experience(ing). This narrative does not turn away from epistemology but places more emphasis upon ontology. In this narrative form where *experiencing* dominates, time and space are no longer universal; here temporalities are grounded in local experiential domains, thus temporality is relative to context. Universal meaning and classification are countered by singular experiences and existential meanings. We glimpse this contrast between abstract rational and experiential temporalities in Bergson's (1913) *Essay on Metaphysics*, where he distinguishes between rationalised clock time and the *durée* of experiential time. The seminal work of Husserl in phenomenology affected many others in the study of ontological orientations of meaning including Alfred Schutz's (1962) explorations of meaning in the multiple realities of life-world contexts.

In some ways the shift from the disembodied Cartesian rational subject to a concern with embodied experiencing even invades the territory of the natural sciences. Waddington (1970) asks the question, "Do our scientific theories provide knowledge about exterior nature uninfluenced by individuals, or do they on the other hand, merely show us the way in which the human mind happens to work in its interaction with the rest of the universe (p. 105)?" In the study of space-time in quantum physics the Enlightenment notion of homogenous and universal space and time in which phenomena are objectively perceived, calculated and known by rational subjects has also been qualified. We have learned that in the world of quantum space-time the relation between observer and observed is problematic According to Heisenberg, "If we wish to form a picture of the nature of these elementary particles, we can no longer ignore the physical processes through which we obtain our knowledge of them (Waddington 1970, p. 105)." That is to say knowledge of such phenomena is constructed within the space-time frame of the observer, which is not to say that phenomena do not exist, but that their measurement is dependent upon the observer's position. This is not to argue that rational thought in the form of Newton's laws is no longer tenable, the lunar landing could not have occurred without them, but simply to make the point that such thought and reason is only tenable in the spaces where it can be applied and that there are contexts in which it is not effective.

Although the distinction between epistemology and ontology is problematic in that ontological structures involve epistemological positions and vice versa, it is the notion of foregrounding which is important. In summary then Lash describes two narrative paradigms, the first foregrounding a concern for epistemology and classification emerging from the Enlightenment pursuit of knowledge, the second foregrounding ontology and life-world experience(ing) emerging with phenomenology and hermeneutics during the nineteenth century. In the text of the National Curriculum for Art in England I have tried to show that although the second narrative is detectable, it is the first that is foregrounded. The text of this curriculum is concerned with cognising students within a particular epistemology, which sets out a particular understanding, classification and validation of knowledge of art practice. According to this narrative outcomes of practice are reduced to a series of normative level descriptions that are used to form students' pedagogised identities in the art curriculum. Yet it is the second narrative, which is grounded in local experiencing that for me, hints at the existential or experiential ground of art practice. This narrative is concerned with difference and with singular as opposed to normalised subjects. It is therefore not concerned with a reduction of experiencing and practice to normative classifications.

The distinction made by Lash between epistemological classification and ontological structures can be detected also when we consider the GCSE examination assessment procedures. Recently I visited a London secondary school because I was interested in the kind of work being made by students for the GCSE examination. Whilst I was photographing some of the work the external moderators were moderating the internal grades that the teachers had awarded their students. A day or so later I met one of the external moderators and he asked me what I thought of the art work. I expressed a keen interest in some of the work I had seen. His response was illuminating, he felt that some of the work was 'very conceptual' and that he found it difficult to mark and assess. The term 'conceptual' was being used, I felt, as a means of positioning some work outside of the accepted framework and understanding of art practice according to which the moderator was accustomed. Here we can see that a specific understanding of practice, generated by the assessment objective statements, invokes a particular power-knowledge formation that marginalizes the semiotic productions, and their respective visual worlds, of some students. In other words the differences of semiotic practice when considered through the gaze of GCSE assessment discourse are reduced to a particular construction and understanding of practice. Within this construction of practice some student's practices become disembodied and de-socialised because the assessment discourse anticipates a particular kind of body-in-practice and a particular organisation and production of practice. A further qualifying comment from the moderator relating to the work that was difficult to moderate was that although the teachers in the school could talk about some of the ideas behind some conceptual pieces, these ideas were not evident in the work or the planning. However, according to the moderator, other conceptual pieces did indicate a clear route from conception to final outcome and the moderators found no difficulty with such work. An interesting point, which I believe has to be considered, is, does the GCSE assessment framework create a specific epistemologising and classifying of art practice which fails to respond to the diverse ontological differences of students' art practices? Does the framework make us see and therefore conceive art practice in a particular way, so that those students who do not or cannot conform are positioned on the margins and consequently their art practice and related experience is made 'other'?

Writers on issues of gender and education are also keen to explore onto-logical issues of embodiment and power in a variety of socio-cultural contexts. In relation to education they have argued persuasively that school curriculum subjects frequently invoke forms of power-knowledge that are patriarchal (see Paechter 2000) or to put it another way, that historically the organisa-tion, curriculum content, as well as practices of learning and teaching in many school subjects have favoured boys, so that girls have occupied inferior positions as learners and consequently have come to view themselves as inferior. In other words such curriculum arrangements have disembodied girls by invoking a male embodiment of practice in certain subjects. Other research considers how masculinities and femininities are produced within school curriculum practices. Such research raises important questions relating to forms of knowledge and the organisation of the apparatuses through which they are taught in relation to ontological difference. Put another way such research questions the assumed universality of specific curriculum and pedagogic practices (which assume a particular universalised learning subject) and by foregrounding issues of gender in relation to learning practices they invoke the idea of difference and diversity thus arguing that a greater emphasis upon such ontological realities should underpin the planning and organisation of teaching and learning practices.

PRACTICE AND CHANGE

How do we begin to conceive curriculum strategies for art in education flexible enough to accommodate diverse subjectivities that emerge from a complex fusion of socio-cultural histories, practices and experiences? The exponen-tial increase in the rate of social and technological change in Western social contexts highlights the inadequacy of viewing individuals in essentialist terms born and developing within fixed and immutable cultural traditions. I have already described in Chapters 5 and 6 contemporary theorisations of subjec-tivity and identity which abandon essentialist and universal discourses in favour of a notion of subjects constituted within a network of specific practices and discourses that form their social and cultural realities. I showed, for example, how pedagogised identities are not natural formations but created within specific discourses of assessment and practice according to which both teachers and students come to understand themselves and their practice. Burgin (1986) writes:

We become what we are only through our encounter, while growing up, with the multitude of representations of what we may become – the various positions society allocates us. There is no essential self which precedes the social construction of the self through the agency of representations (p. 41).

It is our "encounter with the multitude of representations," and, "the various positions that society allocates us," which suggests the idea of individuals who are not pre-constituted but, on the contrary, who are constituted as subjects and thereby gain and expand their identities, within, or even between, specific but differing and changing contexts of social practice. Lacan's work indicates that things are even more complex when we consider the formation of subjectivity in relation to his orders of the imaginary, symbolic and Real.

The increase in the rate of social change means that our 'encounters' and 'social positionings' have increased, becoming more complex and diverse. This in turn suggests a more complicated process of subject constitution and identification within social sites such as schools. Within the art curriculum, for example, responses to increasing social and cultural complexity have included multicultural (Mason 1988; Chalmers 1997), anti-racist and gender initiatives which, in turn, have cast a critical light upon more traditional practices and forms of representation, usually to challenge and interrogate unquestioned attitudes to curriculum content, practice or representation in order to expose the hegemony of their ideological underpinnings. The search for visibility between cultures which produced multicultural art education in the 1970s, and the political thrust of anti-racist art education in the 1980s and 1990s has since shifted towards considering the idea of difference as a multi-layered phenomenon (see Dash 1999), involving psychic realities as well as local processes of subjectivity and identity. The idea of cultural hybridity, theorised in the work of Homi Bhabha (1994), suggests states of flux, fluidity and coalescence that makes it difficult to seek and determine cultural origins. Work on the idea of hybridity illustrates how earlier struggles for cultural visibility and identity in multiculturalism only exerted yet another manifestation of cultural myopia because it reinforced the idea of the other within dominant or preferred identities, so that although Afro-Caribbean and Asian communities in the UK are acknowledged they are frequently viewed as 'other'.

In England our National Curriculum states that: "It must be robust enough to define and defend the core of knowledge and cultural experience which is the entitlement of every pupil . . . (DFEE 2000, p. 3)." It is important to ask what exactly constitutes this core of knowledge and cultural experience in art education and against what or who are we to defend it? It would not be unreasonable to read this statement as implying a prescribed body of knowledge and cultural experience already in existence that is the duty of teachers to transmit to their children or students. This reflects a hermeneutics of reproduction which I described in Chapter 1. Knowledge and cultural experience are understood as pre-existent entities which can be passed on from teacher to student in order to perpetuate enduring values. This attitude takes no account of a productive understanding of culture and tradition as described, for example, by Gadamer in his hermeneutics of dialogic relations, (see Chapter 1) where culture and knowledge are always in process and where successful teaching and learning would not depend upon the transmission of preconstituted knowledge but upon a negotiation between teacher and student encapsulated by Gadamer's term, 'a fusion of horizons'. The statement also fails to acknowledge the complex social and cultural issues that affect, influence and regulate teaching and learning. The phrase, 'define and defend the core of knowledge and cultural experience,' is also interesting on the grounds that in suggesting a prescribed body of knowledge it implies that there are knowledge and practices deemed worthy and acceptable and others which are not, indicating a process of regulation and protection against the 'outside' of such prescribed practices.

In Chapter 7 I provided a brief review of different art education discourses in which I described how key terms, or Lacanian *points de caption*, fix and structure the logic of the discourse. So, for example, Witkin in the 1970s following Read in the 1940s described a pedagogy for art in education based upon ideas of self-expression, feeling and sensate experience. I argued that different pedagogical discourses and their respective practices led to the formation of contrasting pedagogised identities. Lowenfeld and Brittain's (1970) discourse on art education in *Creative and Mental Growth*, which relies heavily upon Piagetian developmental psychology, is quite different from Eisner's (1972) text, *Educating Artistic Vision*, which advocates an approach to pedagogy that concentrates on combining practice, context and aesthetic understanding. Through their contrasting ideological positions these discourses implicate contrasting pedagogised identities, that is to say they produce different ideological constructions of teaching and learning in art education. My quest is not to abandon discursive frameworks (this would be impossible) but to contemplate which discursive strategies, which *points de caption*, will enable the development of pedagogised identities in art in education that will allow students and teachers to develop art practices which include, accommodate and extend diverse forms of life and their respective semiotic practices. Key terms that reflect my earlier discussion of ontological positions and forms of life are 'difference', 'inclusion', 'experiencing' and 'identification'. Perhaps these are the *points de capiton* that might lead to a new hegemony of practice and to new directions for art in education.

EXPERIENCE AND EXPERIENCING

The notion of experience can be employed as a guiding principle for initiating and responding to art practice in schools. In the next chapter I will discuss this term in more depth in relation to Derrida's notion of presence. The term *experience* has a long history in writings about education (Dewey 1957; Edwards and Kelly 1998) and art practice (Collingwood 1979; Langer 1953). Frequently when we use the phrase, 'in my experience', it is as though we are referring to something which is not open to question. It is a phrase that is often used to justify a course of action or, for instance, to question other interpretations of, or decisions about action which, 'according to (my) experience', are incorrect. In other words this term is used frequently to refer to direct experiential knowledge that is difficult to deny, it seems indisputable because it refers to something that happened to us. Williams (1988, pp. 126–129) provides a helpful history of the term experience. He distinguishes between two historical uses, *experience past* and *experience present*. The former concerns knowledge gleaned from past events, through observation and reflection, it relates to, 'lessons of experience.' Williams makes the point that, "The general usefulness of experience past is so widely recognised that it is difficult to know who would want to challenge it (p. 127)." *Experience present* describes a state of conscious awareness that includes affective as well as cognitive states, this sense is widely employed in aesthetic discourses, it refers to a state which is immediate rather than reflective as in *experience past*. In the twentieth century *experience present* is the immediate ontological ground of study in fields such as phenomenology and ethnology that place emphasis upon 'subjective witness.' Williams discusses a further use of the term experience by referring to the social construction of experience, that is to say experience as the product of social conditions. In this latter sense factors such as race, gender, class and sexuality construct experience even though experience may appear to be natural.

The direct appeal to experience, as in Williams's experience past and experience present, frequently fails to acknowledge our imaginative semiotic construction of experience, what Kant according to Kearney (1988, p. 171) refers to as 'the imaginative synthesis of our sensible intuition.' For Kant it is the transcendental imagination that makes experience possible, according to Kearney:

The transcendental imagination is that which grounds the objectivity of the object in the subjectivity of the subject – rather than in some 'transcendent' order beyond man (woman). It preconditions our very experience of the world (pp. 167–168 my bracket).

The problem with this Kantian expression of experience however is that it fails to develop the contextualising of experience, that is to say the social and political construction of experience in relation to a semiotics of class, gender, race, disability or sexuality; in other words it fails to embody and embed experience. The subjectivist aspect of experience (present) when transferred to the domain of expression and feelings underpinned earlier curriculum rationales for art in education. In England the Gulbenkian Report, *Art in Schools* (1982), was a substantial attempt to justify art education for a pluralist society arguing that, 'significance should be attached to those activities which are concerned with the life of feeling and the development of creative powers (p. 141)'. In many ways this built upon the humanist tradition of Read's 'expression of feelings in communicable form,' Witkin's 'intelligence of feeling' and Ross's 'creative action' but Gulbenkian contextualised art practice within a plural and multicultural society. As well as focussing on practice in the arts Gulbenkian also placed emphasis upon understanding art practices from other cultures, it is still a document with much to recommend. Much of this approach to art in education developed a pedagogy in which the experience of the child or student is central to the teaching-learning relationship. On a wider front the development of inter-cultural art education is based upon a similar humanist notion of experience (present) and a concern to acknowledge, understand and legitimate the essential subjective core of different cultural traditions and practices.

The humanist idea of experience and expression when applied to art work also invokes the Kantian ideas of expression and aesthetic judgement whereby the aesthetic power of the art work rests in the ability of its formal qualities to resonate with and deepen our understanding of human experience. This understanding is a felt understanding in contrast to a conceptualised under-standing. Of course humanist ideas of experience and the idea of a subjective core or essence, which can be expressed through art practice, are challenged by post-structural theory, which in contrast denies such subjectivist notions and posits the idea of experience as a socio-cultural construction. The work of Derrida, which I will discuss in my final chapter, has radical implications for how we conceive experience and therefore, in the context of art in edu-cation, how we conceive related concepts such as perception, self-expression, self-reflection, individuality, identity, ability and representation. Derrida (1976, 1987) argues that it is not possible to gain direct access to experience or per-ception, or to use his favoured term, 'presence'. This is because any attempt to do so, to arrive at a point of origin or presence, which the terms self-expression or perception appear to suggest, always involves deferral. If we think about the term 'experiencing' we can never attain its essence or gain direct access because any attempt to do so involves the use of representa-tional or semiotic practices such as language or image, which act in mediation. This invokes an inevitable gap between experiencing and representation. In one sense this is similar to Kant's ideas on *noumena*, ontological structures that cannot be known 'in themselves' but only through narratives of reason and logic as *phenomena*.

The difference between *experience* and *experiencing* is important because it returns us to the difference between epistemology and ontology. Experience can only ever be a signifier, that is to say we can only articulate that which we experience retrospectively in discourse or image or other form of signifi-cation. Here we are concerned with *discourses of experience* and not with *experience* directly. On the other hand the term experiencing refers to states of existence which involve more than signification but of course this more can never be symbolised. Lacan's term the Real is suggestive of the extra-symbolic dimension of experiencing to which I am attempting to allude.

DIFFERENCE

The idea of difference is important in more than one sense for developing pedagogy in art education. Firstly we need to develop sensitivity to the difference of each child's or student's art practice. I have already discussed such differences in my exploration of children's drawing practices which exhibit a wide range of visual semiotic strategies and purposes. I shall shortly develop a similar exploration of secondary GCSE students' mixed media art work. Difference thus relates to the different semiotic or representational practices children and students employ and which are valid for their purposes. This suggests that we have to acquire a deep respect for the art work and this may challenge the limits of our understanding of practice. Secondly the idea of difference relates to the difference between discourse and image. In assessing art work there is the ever-present difference between the language of assessment and the visual image or construction, the relation between the two is never unproblematic and, furthermore, we can never articulate this difference!

Epistemological classifications of art practice as manifested in assessment discourses, have been contrasted with the different ontological orientations implicit to each student's art practice. The important but difficult issue is to avoid the reduction of the latter to the normalising classifications of the former. In the next section I describe art work produced by students for the GCSE Examination in England. My purpose is to discuss how each student is involved in producing visual forms of signification in order to explore their experiences and their interests in specific social issues. The work includes everyday objects and materials that are used to produce semiotic material invoking a world of intertextuality. It is not work which remains within the sphere of technical competence associated with the traditions of representational painting and drawing. As semiotic practice though I believe the work has some deep connection with children's early art practices. In my discussion of children's drawing practices I focussed upon the idea of drawings as semiotic productions, my purpose was to show that even at this early stage in their lives and using limited materials such as felt markers, pencils or paintbrushes, children are able to produce drawings and paintings which function semiotically on various levels within a piece of work. I also showed that in different pieces of work children are able to use drawing to signify a range of experiences relating to depicting action sequences, objects, narratives and playing games, all of which are important to them at this age. I also showed that such drawing practices signify a wide range of conceptual learning and understanding. In the GCSE work I will discuss shortly the semiotic activity of earlier childhood is echoed but manifested in different materials and on different scales. Essentially, I would argue, this work indicates the ability of students, aged 16, to create visual structures as signs to explore a wide range of local experiences and social issues which are relevant and important to them at this age. If young children are encouraged and supported to explore their experiences through art practices they will respond with ingenuity and similarly, if older students are encouraged and supported to explore their experiences and issues which are important to them, they will respond with equal ingenuity. The difficulty for those who support and encourage and for those who need to examine and assess is to be able to stimulate and recognise the ingenuity and to be able to respond effectively to the different ways in which this is manifested in the semiotics of visual practice.

STUDENT'S WORK

I will now describe innovative and challenging approaches to practice and pedagogy in art in education. This builds upon my description of the semiotics of drawing practices I described in Part 1 but here I focus on work that is mostly mixed media. Although this work may appear disconnected to drawing practices of younger children and secondary school students it is concerned with the manipulation of materials to act as visual signifiers. Thus the semiotic activity found in earlier drawing practices is also found in this mixed-media work. Some of this work, produced by secondary students, challenges conventional conceptions of art practice and representation in education and in doing so it raises difficulties for assessment procedures. As is the case with contemporary art practices, this work raises questions about how we understand art as a field of practice. The work certainly confronts the dominance of cultural capital associated with more traditional skills and practices and their preferred pedagogic identities and thereby offers the opportunity for developing a wider and more radical understanding of art in education and the potential of visual education for promoting and developing children's and students' comprehension of socio-cultural issues. In describing this work I will revisit the notion of *experience* in relation to the notion of *difference* in order to consolidate my argument for a more inclusive and critical approach to art practice in education and to secure the value of art practice as an educational tool for promoting personal, social and cultural understanding.

The work I present is often described as 'conceptual', a term I find inappropriate and which I suspect is used by some as a means to categorise the practices to which it refers as somehow beyond the mainstream of accepted and valued traditions of practice in art education. All art practice is in some way conceptual and so I prefer to treat this work as presenting new and different forms of visualisation or spaces of the visual, that invoke a need to ask new and alternative questions thereby avoiding the sentimentality of older forms of knowledge and practice. The work employs established media and everyday objects which is not a new technology but it does, as in the case of some contemporary art work, create challenging visual structures. Although the work I present does question more traditional attitudes towards skill and technique in art educational practice, this is not to denounce such attitudes, but rather to consider possibilities for extending our understanding of practice, skills and techniques. Simultaneously the art work I describe interrogates traditions of practice and representation and their established visualities which invoke particular practices of perception and their attendant gaze – thus deconstructing their implicit relations of power, regulation and normalisation – and in producing new spaces and practices of the visual the work demands new visualisations or ways of seeing. In the words of Rogoff (2000) such work problematises:

The structures through which the looking is done [which are] dependent on cultural narratives, projected desires and power relations, while the space in which the activity of looking takes place is animated with all the material and cultural complexities which represent the obstacles to the very idea of straightforward comprehension of what is being seen (p. 11).

For me this work demands an attitude to visual practice that attempts to embrace local subjectivities and their respective processes of visualisation rather than viewing the work through transcendent and decontextualised epistemological frameworks of representation and practice to which the work is 'subjected' and 'known'. Though this may appear contradictory the work demands an approach to the visual that is not simply concerned with the visual but rather with a space of intertextuality, which the work invokes. Some of the work raises issues of identity and subjectivity by invoking a whole field of visual productions in advertising, cinema and television, for example. In so doing such work raises potent issues of visuality and how visualities are constructed, by whom and for what purpose and in which social and cultural contexts. It raises issues about how visualities are regulated and promoted as well as which visualities are valued and which are regarded as other or are marginalized. In other words such work raises issues relating to a politics of the visible and how such a politics constitutes dominant codes of the visible.

Peirce's notion of semiosis, discussed on Chapter 1, is close to the notion of intertextuality and it is this idea which I believe is so important for developing study and practice in the field of art in education. This entails moving from a paradigm of art practice and understanding rooted within a discreet field of techniques and practices, of traditional art histories and aesthetics, towards a more complex semiotics of visual culture which includes local subjectivities, their psychic realities and the panoply of visual realities that structure and construct our subjectivities and identities. In her book, *terra infirma:geography's visual culture*, Rogoff (2000) describes the term visual culture and I will quote her at length in order to establish an important direction for practice and reflection in art in education.

How can we characterise the emergent field of 'visual culture' as an arena of study? To begin with, we must insist that this encompasses a great deal more than the study of images. At one level we certainly focus on the centrality of vision and the visual world in producing meanings, establishing and maintaining aesthetic values, gender stereotypes and power relations within culture. At another level we recognise that opening up the field of vision as an arena in which cultural meanings get constituted also simultaneously anchors to it an entire range of analyses and interpretations of the audio, the spatial, and the psychic dynamics of spectatorship. Visual culture thus opens up an entire world of intertextuality in which images sounds and spatial delineations are read onto and through one another, lending ever-accruing layers of meanings and of subjective response to each encounter we might have with film, television, advertising, art works, buildings or urban environments. In a sense we have produced a field-of-vision version of Derrida's concept of *differance* and its achievement has had a twofold effect both on the structures of meaning and interpretation and on the epistemic and institutional frameworks which attempt to organise them (pp. 28–29).

What Rogoff confronts us with is in essence an endless iteration of meaning in the field of the visual, a *visual differance* according to which visual, oral, textual and other forms interact or interweave to form ever-new structures of meaning. Thus the making of art work, constructing visual structures and visual spaces, are practices that are tied into and influenced by a range of visual, textual, oral and other semiotic processes. This process of iteration has to be acknowledged and considered when we engage in the interpretation of personal spaces of visual production and also, reflexively upon the epistemic and institutional frameworks that produce such interpretations.

The work illustrated in Figure 40 emerged from a project on identity. Prior to this piece the student had been exploring some ideas on the seven deadly sins by composing layers of text for each sin on separate sheets of paper. Thus each sheet created a textual image of a particular sin, gluttony, avarice, and so on.

She developed these ideas by relating each sin to a contemporary art work so that, for example, in her sketchbook a photograph of Rachel Whiteread's

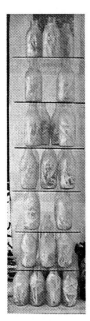

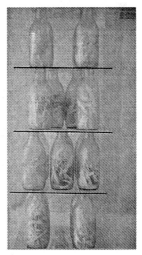

Figure 40.

concrete house installation was overlaid with a piece of tracing paper on which the term 'gluttony' and the following words are superimposed on the image:

> *This piece of work is truly amazing. Negative areas are transformed into positive, inert lumps. I have linked it to gluttony as the concrete used has greedily taken the air that was once breath and silence that was once the stuff of its rooms. It has seeped into all interior spaces that were once occupied by human activity or emotional emptiness, consuming every conceivable space – the hiding place under the bed; the secret musty atmosphere inside a wardrobe; the seductive, vacant bath. The gluttonous nature of the concrete has concealed the past lives that were once present.*

This textual-visual exploration was followed by the work on identity in which the student asked several school friends to compose a statement in which they expressed their feelings about her. The work in Figure 40 is the culmination of this project. Each glazed bottle, a metaphor for the body perhaps, contains each of her colleagues statements cut into strands and curled to fit inside the bottle. The bottles are arranged in small groups and stacked on transparent sheets of glass to approximate the height of the student. There are obvious differences between this work on identity and other more representational images. The skills required to produce it are also quite different, calling into question the very idea of skill as conceived in a more traditional sense, as well as more traditional understandings of practice. As a semiotic practice the layers of meaning are complex and they raise issues, for example, of identity construction, containment and fragmentation. It is a deceptively simple visual structure which also raises issues about the fetishising of the art work as well as the fetishising of the artist – issues which are equally problematised for example by Craig-Martin's piece entitled *Oak Tree*, exhibited at Tate Modern in London, which consists of a transparent glass shelf mounted high on the gallery wall, on top of which stands a glass of water. The work raises issues of transubstantiation in respect of the art work but it also collapses the modernist idea of the artist as a creative individual whose meaning we should attempt to decode, as a work it also fundamentally questions how we perceive and conceive art practice. This student is thus engaged in visual practice that lies beyond more traditional forms and semiotics of practice, which draw upon the semiotic practices of recent contemporary art work as well as a range of discourses and images concerned with the idea of identity.

The next piece of work in Figure 41 also makes reference to Whiteread's concrete installation but this time in quite a different way. It is the outcome of a project on homelessness and identity. It uses the form of the suitcase in order to contain mementoes of identity and personal histories. Students discussed issues of homelessness and the plight of refugees as well as people living on the streets in inner cities. In doing this they were also asked to reflect upon their lives and their material possessions. An article in *the Independent on Sunday* newspaper (28 December 1997) described and illustrated homeless

Figure 41.

peoples' possessions and this led to the students developing their ideas. Rachel Whiteread's sculptures in which everyday objects are cast in plaster or concrete in such a way as to form the empty space created by the objects became an important semiotic influence. Her well-known installation *house* is a cast of a three-story terrace house in London. The entire interior of the house was cast in concrete, filling the void left by the structure. Similarly students chose the suitcase as their container for their life mementoes. They produced a plaster cast of the inside of a suitcase that contained their memento objects. This work also taps into a wider set of discourses and visual imagery relating to diverse human experiences relating to travel, transportation, luggage, refugees, asylum-seekers and diaspora.

The next piece of work illustrated in Figure 42 was made by two 13 year old girls in Andalusia, Spain. As a work it raises many issues relating to the politics and semiotics of identity. The teacher who worked with the girls came from the UK, he had taken up a teaching post at their school on the Andalusian coast. Over the last few decades the region of Andalusia has experienced an influx of people from Madrid who have settled in the region alongside the indigenous population. On a school trip to Madrid the teacher took a group of students to see Picasso's painting, *Guernica*. Whilst some of his students were interested in the painting and why it was made others refused to even look at it and began to wander off. In another incident at the grave of General Franco some students literally wept whilst others refused to acknowledge the existence of the grave. The teacher found that the students who 'walked away' on both occasions would not discuss the matter. Shortly

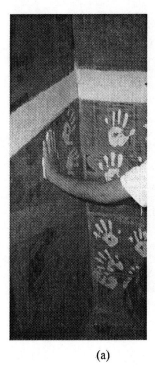

(a)   (b)

Figure 42.

after returning home an elderly relative of one of the students was killed in a bombing incident in Northern Spain but there was little talk of the incident at the school. Two girls approached the art teacher; they had been affected by the incidents on the school trip and by the recent bombing and they had noticed the lack of discussion. They wanted to make a piece of art work about the grandfather who had been killed. They found an Internet web site entitled 'White Hand', a peace movement through which one could register disagreement with violence and killing. The work they made consisted of a room in which on three walls was painted the ETA flag on top of which was superimposed a picture of the grandfather. The girls wanted to involve the school community and parents so everyone was invited to participate and they organised the entire event. Each person dipped a hand in white paint and made a handprint on top of the painted flag and superimposed image in order to produce a peace flag. The work raised many issues relating to identity, culture and allegiance. Although involved in the initial discussions for the project, the teacher played little part in the organisation and conduct of the art event. However he commented that it was, in his experience, the most moving piece of work he had witnessed in his career as a teacher. For him it raised serious questions about both the content and purpose of art in education. It made him think that if such work can achieve this level of commitment and raise such important social issues why, in his words, do we spend so much time teaching students how to draw and paint oranges? Although this is a rather blunt and perhaps rash statement it does raise some crucial issues about the purpose and content of visual education.

The work in Figure 43 needs little introduction, it is concerned with issues of feminine identity. It raises questions about how such identities are formed, conceived and perceived within socio-cultural contexts. As a visual structure it taps into contemporary discourses of the gaze and the relationship between male gazes and feminine identifications (see Mulvey 1975).

As a plaster cast it also relates back to classical antiquity and to the plaster casts kept in museums and art schools that were used frequently by western artists to study anatomy. Thus the work makes reference to contemporary portrayals and constructions of the feminine in film, television and advertising but the medium of the work also relates to historical constructions of the feminine body.

The next piece of work in Figure 44 has already been mentioned in the teacher narratives in Chapter 7. It concerns a student's response to the recent foot and mouth epidemic in England and, in her view, the mismanagement of animals for profit. The work consists of a cage in which is suspended a frozen cow's heart. The bottom of the cage is lined with a map of England

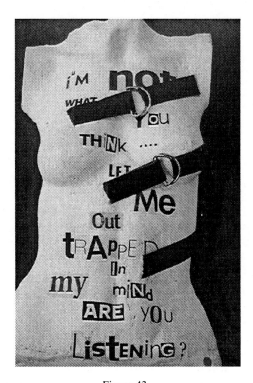

Figure 43.

Figure 44.

so that when the heart melts the blood drips and seeps into the map gradually saturating its surface. On the wall to the side of the work (not shown)
when it was exhibited was a butcher's diagram showing the animal's body
as different cuts of meat. All of these art works are accompanied by sketchbook ideas, thoughts and experiments that show the development of the
student's ideas.

The ownership of land in Zimbabwe is the subject of the work illustrated
in Figure 45. The student's grandfather is a healer and she wanted to make
a piece about the handover of land in Zimbabwe. Thus a plaster cast of her
grandfather's hands appears at the top of the sculptured-relief and underneath a cast of a younger pair of hands. They are surrounded by ears of

Figure 45.

wheat. The form of the piece is reminiscent of a gravestone perhaps suggesting the difficult political situation in Zimbabwe and the bloodshed arising from the Government's policy of land transfer.

In the next piece in Figure 46 we see a life-size model of a child's cot painted in pastel shades. Inside the cot are pillow and blankets, the pillow contains the impression of a sleeping head. But the blankets and pillow are not material, they are made of hard plaster. The head's impression is frozen in time and in the plaster cast. In fact the work is a poignant statement about the tragedy of a cot death that happened to a relative of the student.

Figure 47 is a visual comment on social constructions of femininity and in it we see a female doll and a coke bottle merging into each other. This visual production seems to associate the commercialism and the desire for Coke – 'the real thing' – with a particular image of femininity as portrayed in advertising and other media. But the doll's arms are outstretched and her body takes the form of a crucifix, which may be suggesting a struggle between

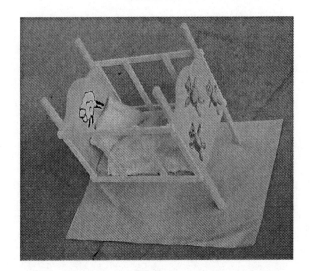

Figure 46.

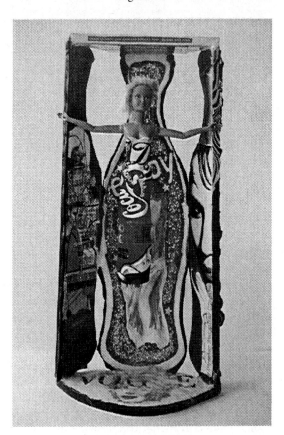

Figure 47.

an inner-self and a particular construction of femininity desired by media gazes. The relation of this piece to feminist discourses and with current interests in questions of identity generally is obvious, but the student is formulating and expressing her ideas in a particular and individual form.

These art works are semiotic structures produced by students in response to their interests that include personal, social, cultural and political issues. The work involves the struggle for visual metaphor, for a semiotics of the visual, which for each student, encapsulates his or her ideas and interests in visual form. The pieces described relate closely to contemporary art practices that frequently challenge our ideas, perceptions and conceptions of art practice, they make us question how we comprehend art as a practice. Such work illustrates quite clearly that this kind of practice is not simply about making and technique but, crucially, it is also about developing and constructing ideas in visual form. It is deeply rooted in each student's interests and developing understanding and the difficulty for others who are required to assess and examine the work is to avoid normalising classifications, to avoid epistemologising according to known and established practices what in effect is concerned with local visualisations of forms of life. To refer back to Lacan's notion of the *point de capiton*, discussed in Chapter 6, these pieces can be regarded as visual quiltings of each student's interests through the visual form of the art work, each quilting brings together a complex of discourses and images (signifiers) related to the particular theme of the work.

This work invokes a wider world of intertextuality or, to invent a visual term, a world of *intervisuality*. It is not so important to try to attain the original meaning or experience of the student even if this were possible, but rather to consider the work as generating meaning and questions in visual form. Thus essentialist notions of experience and perception, once thought to be fundamental to understanding and appreciating art practice are replaced by the student's capacity to construct visual material which has the power to function semiotically in relation to the student's interests and the wider world of discourses and images (signifiers) to which such interests relate. This is not to deny experience or perception, plainly this would be absurd, but to place more emphasis upon the generation of meaning in visual form. The value of the work I have just described therefore is that it concerns the creation of visual semiotic structures through which both students and observers are able to reflect upon those experiences and events as a consequence of which the work is made. Such work is using art practice to challenge and encourage us to think about our constructions of experience and events in different ways. I interviewed the student who made the work on the BSE epidemic in England and Wales (Figure 44). She told me that earlier in her school life art was 'all about producing realistic drawings and paintings and developing techniques like shading.' The arrival of a new art teacher, which coincided with her GCSE (16+) course, introduced her to new ways of working and thinking about what art is and can be. She told me that now 'the important thing is the idea and how to make it work.' "Yes", she said, "skills are important, but it's because they help me to get the idea across." If we compare such semiotic activity to my discussion of the semiotics of children's drawing practices there are similarities. Whereas younger children are able to create a variety of lines and other graphic configurations, such as enclosed shapes and rotations, to produce visual significations that relate to a wide range of experiences, these older students are able to employ and manipulate a range of materials to act as visual signifiers that interact and engage with a host of social discourses and practices.

In the next chapter I will conclude my study with a brief review of Derrida's critique of experience in relation to his idea of presence and then consider the implications of such ideas for art in education.

CHAPTER NINE

EXPERIENCE AND PRACTICE:
THEORISING NEW IDENTIFICATIONS

In the last chapter I contrasted the notions of epistemology and ontology with the intention of arguing that the emphasis upon the epistemologising of students art practices according to established traditions and understandings of practice within examination and assessment discourses is not without problems. The assessment criteria of the National Curriculum attainment levels as well as the GCSE assessment objectives both institute normalising descriptions of art practice, in other words they establish particular ways of knowing (epistemologising) and therefore validating art practice and, consequently, through such knowing they establish and validate students' pedagogised identities. I contrasted the notion of epistemologising practice with the notion of ontological structures, that is to say, with forms of life and their different experiencing realities. Such realities I argue constitute the phenomenological ground of each student's art practice, both in terms of experiencing and in terms of signifying experience in art media. If we acknowledge the difference of students' experiences and the diversity of their semiotic strategies then we need to be sensitive to a possible conflict between epistemological classifications and the differences of experience and semiotic practice. But this conflict appears to be even more problematic when the difference between epistemology and ontology meets the intervention of Derrida's deconstruction of *presence*, a notion that is presupposed by both epistemology and ontology.

Presence is assumed by epistemology in the sense that epistemology is preoccupied with what constitutes valid knowledge. It is therefore concerned with the search for valid meanings that establish points of origin for knowledge. Such 'points of origin' are equated with Derrida's notion of presence. Representation of the world is therefore the representation of truths and certainties in the form of knowledge, which appears unmediated. On the other hand presence is assumed by ontology in the sense of a knowing located within the immediacy of experience. Presence here refers to the presence of being and becoming, to positions of interest, intention and intuition. It is concerned with the presence of consciousness and of the unconscious. In discussing a possible conflict between the epistemologising frameworks of examination and assessment procedures, and students' or children's ontological structures of art practice this raised some difficult issues for initiating and responding effectively to children's and students' art practices. It is a conflict which can be difficult to resolve because it involves the difference between the art work as a construction in assessment discourse and the art work as grounded in the life-world context of the child or student. However, both the assessment discourse as an epistemologising of the student's art practice and the ontological orientation of child's or student's art practice presuppose a notion of presence which Derrida's philosophical interventions would dispute.

Derrida's writing on the deconstruction of the *metaphysics of presence*, the *logic of the supplement* and *differance*, reveals the fetishism of essentialist discourses, epistemological or ontological, which suggest that we can attain or regain original perceptions, meanings or intentions, (presence) in themselves. In a series of radical critiques (1973, 1976, 1978) he argues that a belief in presence, and here we can substitute the term identity as signifying a form of presence, pervades Western signification systems such as language and image. He provides a severe critique of this belief by arguing that symbolic systems never attain or uncover origins or essences (essential identities) because of the unbridgeable gap between reality and the modes of symbolisation we use to represent reality. In essence this gap can never be bridged because in order to do so we would have to rely upon further use of symbolisation. In a nutshell this describes the logic of the supplement whereby meaning is always subject to the possibility of iteration, that is to say, of further interpretation. This is close to Lacan's emphasis upon the metonymic play of signifiers in the construction of meaning. A visual illustration of this logic of the supplement can be found I believe in some of the paintings of Magritte. His painting, *Le Soir qui tombe* (1934) depicts a room with a large window and a countryside landscape of trees and fields beyond. One of the window panes is broken and the shards of glass lie on the floor beneath the window. Mysteriously the shards are not painted as pieces of transparent glass which we would expect to see lying on the floor. Rather they are painted as shards of the landscape that was previously viewed through them. Yet the landscape is still intact, there is no break in it. The painting provides a subtle and nuanced postulation that vision itself is a representation and that we can never get behind representation to a prior essential state. We expect the broken glass to be transparent, a neutral plastic medium that permits vision to occur. But by painting the shards of glass as pieces of the broken landscape, Magritte shows us that vision is always already a constructed cultural experience and not a neutral process of perception.

Reality 'in-itself' can never be accessed directly, but can only be signified in representational form. According to Boyne (1996, p. 105) 'the signified will always be a signifier.' This does not infer that experience, imagination, perception or sensation, where meaning and consciousness may fully co-exist, should be dismissed, but that we can never comprehend them 'in-themselves' because in the attempt to do so, to trace their origin or essence, to know what it is we experience or perceive at the point that we are experiencing or perceiving, we cannot avoid the mediation of representation.

What Derrida shows (. . .) is that the phenomenological desire to speak directly to the world, repudiating all metaphysical presuppositions, is founded on the assertion of an idealised moment of presence which can never be presented (Boyne 1996, p. 94).

Derrida's term, *differance*, hints at the impossibility of any direct access to presence, perception or experience. It is an amalgamation of the terms to *differ* and to *defer*, and put simply, it refers to the continual slippage of meaning from word to word, from image to image, from word to image, from signifier to signifier. *Differance* refers to an endless layering and play of meaning, and consequently to the eternal deferral of meaning in the sense that an essential point of origin is always elusive. When we think about the act of interpreting many images or texts it is fairly obvious that we cannot claim to have accessed the one true meaning or the artist's original state of being or intention. We recognise that our pursuit of meaning can never exclude the possibility of further interpretation. This is not to say that meaning cannot be established, clearly the need to act effectively demands that we are able to establish some degree of meaning, but simply to acknowledge that the formation of meaning in many social and cultural contexts is never apodictic. For Derrida the ontological states which terms such as experience or perception imply are not denied as such but simply the possibility of direct retrieval, of a hermeneutics of revelation, because all such attempts rely upon memories or traces, in other words direct experiencing as such is always mediated by forms of signification. For Lacan the *point de capiton* is the linguistic device that stops the endless play of signification whereby meaning is structured through clusters of signifiers being quilted around key signifiers. In Chapter 5 I discussed the use of the term *accuracy* as an assessment criterion, it is possible to argue that the use of this term presupposes a metaphysics of presence, in that it assumes that it is possible for the image to reproduce the presence of optical truth. It is also quite common to treat students' art practices as the expression of their intentions that we can read directly.

What Derrida shows through his notion of *differance* is that in the first instance such truth is unattainable because it is always mediated by the signifier. The application of *differance* to the term *accuracy* deconstructs the presupposition of a natural attitude to perception and representation. In the second case we are unable to gain direct access to the student's consciousness because it is always mediated by signification.

Derrida's critique of presence thus provides a difficult challenge for phenomenology and ontology. How can we begin to consider existential or phenomenological meaning, how can we think of terms such as 'the immediacy of experience', if, as Derrida claims, we can never attain the life-world realities to which such terms refer? How can we begin to consider forms of life if we are always barred access to them?

CONSEQUENCES OF THE CRITIQUE OF EXPERIENCE FOR
ART IN EDUCATION

The implications of the denial of our ability to represent or express experience or perception directly for initiating and responding to art practices in schools are disturbing. Many teachers and educators regard art practice in education as an opportunity for creative self-expression and self-reflection and therefore to deny a sense of self-presence to art practice seems rather absurd or even heretical. But is this apparent attack upon what might be referred to as a modernist idea of art practice, that is to say as the expression of self, as negative as it seems? One way of answering this question is to consider art practice as a form of enquiry or research. The modernist project of research, outlined by Usher (1997), is concerned with a search for and production of knowledge of the world, to know the world as it is through rational analysis and procedures. In this project the enquirer occupies a position of objective neutrality from which he or she is able, by adopting tried and tested methods and rational analysis, to reveal truth. In other words in this modernist project the researcher is transcendent to the world he or she researches. Usher proceeds to describe a postmodern approach to research, which in contrast to the modernist discovery of the world is concerned with 'world making'. A postmodern project of enquiry and research is always already situated in the text of the world, a crucial notion in that modernist notions of subjectivity and objectivity, knower and known, become redundant. This is because the practice of research is always already embedded within the traces of customs and traditions (texts) of research that construct both the researcher and world and so by implication this eliminates the idea of a detached neutral observer and an objective world. Thus the researcher makes the world according to the discourses and practices in which he or she is immersed, and, significantly, which he or she can modify or change. The idea of world making is therefore a semiotic production. Of course this is never a totally determined situation in the sense that when our descriptions and explanations become inadequate, usually when they fail to register with events, new or modified practices and discourses need to develop. The relation between action and understanding is thus an evolving dialectic between a semiotics of being and a semiotics of becoming.

The modernist idea of self-expression, in which art work is viewed as the expression of an underlying or inner reality of the self, and where the artist is viewed as a creative individual expressing his or her inner core, which in so called great art touches upon or expresses something of our human condition, can be equated with Usher's description of the modernist conception of research. Whereas the researcher reveals truths about the world through accepted methods and rational analysis, the artist reveals inner subjective truths and feelings and our task as observers is to try to understand the deep meaning of the work implanted by the artist. Postmodern and post-structural interpretations of art practice abandon any search for original meaning and instead would view the interpretation of work as, in Usher's term, world-making, in the sense that interpretation, echoing Gadamer, is a *productive* in contrast to a *reproductive* process. I have already argued that in assessment of art work in schools work tends to be assessed according to established codes of practice and representation, not according to perceptual truth, for example, in the case of observational drawing, (although this appears to be the case). Thus observational drawing as a semiotic practice is not understood according to its fit with 'reality' but according to established and assimilated semiotic codes (other signifiers). Denying a fit with reality opens the possibility for viewing art practice as world making in terms of resonating with semiotic traditions but also in terms of semiotic innovations or semiotic difference. Semiotic innovation or difference may cause instability and uncertainty, as I have indicated when considering drawing practices in schools and the mixed-media work discussed in the last chapter, but in doing so they entreat us to take a reflexive stance towards those semiotic codes which structure, inform and constrain our understanding of art practice.

It is possible to argue that different visualities, different visual structures construct worlds or experiences differently. This does not deny experiencing as an ontological ground of practice but accepts that experience is always already socialised, always already in semiosis. What we need to consider then is not ideas of experience or perception as something which the art work reveals, that is to say prior existential subjective realities, but to think of the art work, to use Usher's term, as a process of world making. Derrida's critique of self-presence, arguing that we cannot access such a reality without an intermediary, implies therefore that that which mediates, that is to say semiotic systems, traditions and practices, are always already *inside* and are therefore constitutive of the subject. To return to my earlier reflections on the work of Peirce in Chapter 1, the subject can therefore be conceived as a semiotic entity. This raises the difference discussed by Lacan, between the speaking subject (constituted by and through semiotic structures) and the subject who speaks. For Lacan the subject is a construction of the symbolic order, it is therefore not the same as the subject-in-itself. Lacan (1977, pp. 298–300; 1991, pp. 138–140) distinguishes between the subject of enunciation (the act of speaking) and the subject of enunciated (the subject as defined in the symbolic order). This distinction hints at the difference between what might be termed a pre-symbolic subject and the symbolic subject and the idea that the former is always repressed or de-centred by the latter. In some ways this reflects the difference I have just described between ontology and epistemology. It may be helpful here to make a short digression to a distinction, made in the previous chapter, between the terms *experience* and *experiencing*. Put briefly, we can consider the term *experience* as a signifier, that is to say, as part of the symbolic order, a *retrospective symbolic construction*. On the other hand we can think of the term *experiencing* as that which contains more than the symbolic, perhaps close to the idea of the Lacanian Real. This distinction permits a sense of agency in the sense that it does not rule out the idea of an ability to manipulate or organise the symbolic in unique or different ways. It seems to me that art action proper (see Collinwood 1979) exists on the cusp of the interface between the pre-symbolic and symbolic subject (ontological and epistemological, experiencing-experience) states. This is an important point because in much art practice in schools the child or student viewed as the subject-of-traditional-practices, presupposes an already anticipated subject of practice, which tends to predominate and repress the pre-symbolic (ontological) subject. It is the breaking through of the pre-symbolic subject, which of course is immediately lost and transformed into semiotic form, which perhaps lies at the heart of art action and the idea of world-making.

Derrida's work shows us that the idea of presence, manifested in terms such as perception and experience, has traditionally exerted a prior position to forms of signification, such as writing or drawing. His intention is to subvert this traditional hierarchy by showing the impossibility of attaining pure presence without the mediation of the signifier. The signifier in the form of discourses, images and other semiotic forms, is supplemental in that in mediation it acts as replacement and or addition. The denial of direct access to presence or experiencing through forms of representation implying that in Boyne's words, 'the signified is always a signifier', indicates that terms such as experience and perception are always already semiotic material. This takes us not into a world of subjective essence but into Barthes (1973) world of intertextuality, or in Peircian terminology, into a world of semiosis. However, although direct access to experiencing is denied by Derrida this does not mean that we abandon any notion of agency. The term world-making provides a way through this difficulty in that it stresses the point that we do work with linguistic and visual signs. Although images and discourses are powerful influences that structure our thoughts and understanding and also construct identities and subjectivities, we also manipulate such signs and in doing so form new constructions of these realities.

The Derridean critique of presence when applied to art in education thus raises difficult issues for understanding and assessing art practice. Traditional practices such as observational enquiries through drawing and painting cannot be referred back to original perceptions because they are irretrievable. This means that such work is always already located in a world of semiotic play, that is to say assessment of such work is not made according to a moment of perception but according to a particular semiotic visual code. Derrida's notion of *differance* is important here, for just as meaning in language is dependent upon the relation of words in a language and not directly upon the relation of a word to an external referent, similarly visual meaning is developed according to the relation of images to other images and texts. The work in Figure 41 in the previous chapter concerned the idea of luggage and personal mementoes, when I consider this work I ask myself how is my interpretation influenced by my previous readings of photographs of abandoned suitcases on display in the Ellis Island museum (see Rogoff 2000), or of news clips of asylum seekers? How is my interpretation affected by images of social issues in the media concerning the homeless, refugees or asylum seekers? Much of the mixed-media work described in the last chapter similarly locks into a world of images and texts, a world of media citation, iteration and dissemination, through which meaning evolves. One consequence of Derrida's deconstruction of presence does not imply that we should abandon more traditional art practices, but that we need to develop an awareness that their meaning is established within the interplay of particular semiotic codes and practices.

The impact of this Derridean deconstruction of presence and experience for art in education is that it encourages a constant vigilance towards our traditions of world making as semiotic activities so that we try to avoid, whilst simultaneously recognising the difficulty of avoiding, normalising and reductive practices of interpretation such as assessment. Put another way somehow we need to try to avoid reducing experiencing to experience. Further, the ideas of semiotic play, semiotic difference or semiotic innovation imply that different visualities or visual structures function to construct the world differently. In the domains of art practice this suggests that different worlds, or forms of life, as semiotic productions are visualised into being. Semiotic productions therefore are not ahistorical, acultural or indeed asocial, they are embedded and embodied socially, historically and culturally. Such embeddedness and embodiment are crucial factors that need to underpin our understanding and interpretation of semiotic practices in art education, in relation to the traditions through which we interpret practice and the ontological difference and innovations of practice. Assessment of art practices in schools can easily involve a clash of world making, the world-making of the assessor who functions through the normalising and reductive semiotics of assessment that construct a particular world of practice and body-in-practice and thus a particular identity of the learner, and the world-making of the child or student who functions through his or her local and embodied semiotic practices. The GCSE assessment matrix in England, which I discussed earlier, provides a particular construction of art practice in the form of six assessment objectives. Practice is conceived as a particular process, which for the sake of assessment, is split into certain inter-relating stages described in the assessment objectives. The outcome of such assessment is that students' art work is positioned according to one of five levels of ability. My point is that within this discourse a particular way of understanding art practice becomes universalised, that is to say it produces a particular totalisation of practice that reinforces particular assumptions and understandings of practice and of students as learners and practitioners. As such it is likely to legitimate and sanction particular approaches to and outcomes of practice and marginalise or reject others. The training video for GCSE assessment produced by EDEXEL Examination Board for 2000–2002 is also instructive here. In helping teachers to understand assessment procedures they need to employ, the art work that is assessed on the video is limited to more conventional practices, beginning with observational investigations that lead to a final outcome. The video does not refer to work which reflects contemporary art practices. The subjectification of art practice to particular ways of conceiving and understanding such practice whilst simultaneously wanting to acknowledge innovation raises a difficult dilemma which Bourdieu (1993, pp. 225–226) discusses in relation to what he terms 'the readability of contemporary art (p. 225).' He refers to the clash between established codes of interpretation and new art work which employs new semiotic structures. The difficulty arises when such work is read through established codes of perception and which are precisely those against which the art work has been created. Although Bourdieu is referring to the context of contemporary art practices his comments are relevant to the contexts of art in education and the interpretation of children's and student's art practices.

As new technologies and their respective practices become more evident in art education they create new conditions for teaching and learning through art. Computer generated imagery provides the possibility for creating new visualities and a revolutionary way of working with image and text. Such technology means that we need to consider and re-evaluate terms such as *self-expression, originality* or *uniqueness*. Derrida's critique of presence may have radical implications for understanding art practice in digital technology which suggests a different notion of the body-in-practice. New digital technology means we have to reconsider our understanding of skill, technique, expression and representation. Such technology changes the way in which we have traditionally understood the notions of epistemology and ontology because it introduces new ways of understanding time and space through the notion of virtuality. This technology allows us to manipulate multiple times and spaces which contrast with the temporalities of drawing and painting using traditional media; it presents us with a multi-modal semiotic experience. In other words this technology introduces unimaginable possibilities for world-making in the context of art education. In many ways this book could be described as limited because it does not deal with issues of identity and practice in art education in relation to new technology. I have to accept this charge and in my defence I can only state that the speed of change brought about by technological innovations makes it extremely difficult for me to comprehend its effects upon teaching and learning in art education. However it is possible to recognise that such technology implies different ways of conceiving art practice and pedagogised identities, and it problematises traditional understandings of art practice to the extent that we can no longer be so certain what the term art practice means. In a strange and ironic sense though new digital technology and its construction of a virtual reality, implying that prior to its invention we were dealing with some kind of direct reality, alerts us to the fact that the latter was always already virtualised (see Zizek 1996, p. 194). This has been a central point in my explorations of our interpretations of art practices and experience through the work of Lacan and Derrida.

*   *   *

In this book the art practices of children and students have been considered as powerful semiotic activities in which they construct meaning in visual form. I have also provided a critical perspective on the discourses in which we tend to understand such art practices particularly in assessment discourses. I have shown that it is in such discourses that pedagogic identities of both teacher and student are formed. Thus my focus has been upon practice and discourses in which practice is understood and valued. An important aspect of art in education, which I have not discussed, is that concerned with initiating and extending children's and students' understanding of the work of artists, craftspeople or designers. This requires substantial study and is the subject for another book. However I would like to comment briefly upon this area of art in education because the hemeneutic strategies I have outlined and applied here are directly relevant. In the UK the term 'critical studies' (see Thistlewood 1990; Dawtrey, Jackson, Masterton and Meecham 1996) is often used to describe this aspect of art in education and it is an important part of the National Curriculum for Art. In the USA, Discipline-Based Art Education (DBAE, see Eisner 1988) includes art criticism, art history and aesthetics. Essentially critical studies in the English National Curriculum for Art, and art history, art criticism and aesthetics in DBAE, are concerned with developing visual literacy, that is to say, with developing an ability to under-stand how art works signify and communicate. In other words such study is concerned with exploring how artists and others manipulate materials and use visual media as semiotic material. This might mean for example, exploring the iconography of medieval or early renaissance painting, the symbolism of Australian Aboriginal painting, the structure of cubist painting or the sym-bolism of Afante flags or Navajo sand pictures, and so on. The purpose is to provide children and students with skills and techniques for interpreting the visual. This is a hermeneutic activity and as such demands a consideration of different hermeneutic strategies.

There are those who would view critical studies in terms of a hermeneu-tics of reproduction whereby children and students should be introduced to valued art works that, in the Arnoldian sense, exemplify 'all that is great and good'. Students should therefore study art works that have stood the test of time, which transcend history and biographical location and which signify the artist's genius. Given the right method, students should be able to discover the artist's intentions. There are those who argue for a strategy of a dialogue with traditions along the lines of Gadamer's hermeneutics (see Cox 2000) in which meaning is produced in an ongoing dialogue between child/student and art work but channelled and encouraged by the teacher. There are those who would wish to interrogate art work in order to expose issues of identity such as gender and race (see Pollock 1988; McEveilley 1992) to deconstruct paintings and other art work in order to expose their ideological content. The work of Foucault, Butler, Walkerdine, Lacan and Bourdieu I have discussed is relevant to such hermeneutic strategies. Both Lacan's work on identity and Derrida's critique of presence denies any form of original or absolute meaning and is therefore a challenging intervention for any hermeneutic activity such as critical studies in art education. Derrida's work introduces notions of endless iteration and play of meaning and this must include a constant vigilance of the very discourses in which meaning is formed and reformed. Lacan's theory of the *point de capiton* illustrates how meaning is quilted by key signifiers that establish ideological discourses within which identifications are formed.

All these interpretational strategies are concerned, in their different ideological positions, with the semiotics of art practice and the formation of meaning. The act of looking and interpreting is not neutral but one which is socially and culturally situated. Thus we need to consider not just what is being looked at but who is looking, as Pollock (1995) states:

The question now is who is looking at what, at whom, with what effects in terms of power (p. 40).

We are concerned therefore with a politics of looking and interpreting and the construction of particular kinds of viewers or interpreters. In the school context we are concerned with the development of pedagogised viewers and interpreters where children and students are guided and informed in their looking by teachers and by official educational agencies that specify curriculum content relating to critical studies. Who decides, for example, what should be looked at and why, and in which way should children's and students' looking be guided and informed? In a plural society such questions raise important pedagogic questions *vis a vis* critical studies and children's and students' entitlement. Which art and artists are considered will effect the formation of children and students as critical subjects and their understanding of art as practice. Hopefully we are past the time when Western male artists dominated the content of critical studies. However it is important not only to introduce children and students to art practices from different historical, social and cultural contexts but also to introduce them to different strategies of reading in which meaning is produced.

END PIECE

The idea of identity is complex and perhaps is better conceived rather in terms of a series of identifications. In Western societies even the notion of home identity is a problematical concept when we consider that the television screen transmits all kinds of information from different places into our living rooms (Morley 2000). The outside thus becomes firmly embedded within our daily experiences of home. In our homes we eat food from different countries, listen to world music and in some cases have access to global communication systems. All such developments affect who and what we are and the way in which we perceive others.

When we think of pedagogised identities in the context of art in education in a world of rapid change perhaps we need to consider closely the ways in which such identities are formed in our schools within the kind of practices we teach. In this book I have attempted to illustrate how such identities are constructed in assessment practices and as a consequence what such constructions may leave out. I have also attempted to expose the myth of essentialist ideas of ability and perception which contribute to the formation of pedagogised identities in art education by revealing that such ideas do not refer to natural capacities but to ideological constructions. The idea of practice has to be commensurate with the idea of difference and thus to the different ways in which children and students, if encouraged and supported, can do work with visual signs. In early drawing practices and in later mixed media work I have argued that they are capable of quite extraordinary visual semiotic practices that lead to the production of diverse forms of world-making. These visual productions are simultaneously personal spaces but also social spaces, they create ways of understanding in visual form. From early drawings in which children explore their worlds to later mixed media constructions and installations in which teenagers explore and comment upon their worlds, these visual productions are an important means by which children and students enter and expand the world of visual culture. The processes and outcomes of visual practice provide them with an opportunity to develop a form of action and comprehension that evokes a form of learning that is valuable and profound but which it is impossible to encapsulate in words.

Throughout this book I have advocated the need for a hermeneutic understanding, which is commensurate with the diversity and ingenuity of children's and students' art practices. I have employed a series of hermeneutic strategies in order to interpret their art practices and also to interrogate the discourses in which we understand art practices. Simultaneously I have argued for the need for constant vigilance of our interpretational frameworks within which pedagogised identities are formed. I have shown that the relationship between the logic of assessment discourses and the diverse ontological grounds of art practice can be problematic. A recent telephone conversation with an old friend, Bill Brookes, who supervised my doctoral studies at The University of Southampton, generated some further thoughts on this issue. When we were discussing the issue of assessment discourses and assessment criteria Bill advised that we need to remember that, 'a logic is an endomorphism on a language.' His advice highlights many of the issues with which I have been struggling. In a nutshell it begs the question in my mind, 'is all that we wish or need to assess susceptible to assessment criteria?' The point is that any assessment logic operates a reduction, in language, of that which it addresses and by implication such reduction will inevitably omit those things, those forms of life, which do not fit. We are then left with a process of mapping practice, retrospectively, in relation to what has to be declared according to the assessment discourse. When we contemplate the far greater space of children's and student's art practices how much does assessment miss or ignore. In truth we have some ways of understanding processes of children's and student's art practices but our understanding of these intricate processes could never be said to be total. If we view art teaching not as a transmission of ready-made knowledge and practice but rather as the creation of new conditions for learning it is possible to argue that as educators we need to know how to ignore what we already know.

There are numerous challenges for art in education at the beginning of the twenty-first century and I am reminded of the final pages of Herbert Read's book, *Education Through Art*. When writing of a world full of social inequalities and the tragedies of war he saw art practice as a means for developing a more sensitive understanding and appreciation of difference. Although somewhat idealistic there is a sense in which Read's concerns are relevant to recent events in the UK; in Northern Ireland, Burnley, Bradford, Bolton, Leeds and London. Can art practice be utilised for exploring and developing children's and student's understanding of difference, co-existence and cooperation? I can think of no more powerful form of practice for trying to achieve such ends, but understanding their relationship to the signifiers they create is a challenging task.

REFERENCES

Abbs, P. (1987) *Living Powers: The Arts in Education*, London: Falmer Press.

Abbs, P. (1989) *The Symbolic Order*, London: Falmer Press.

Allen, D. (1994) 'Teaching visual literacy: some reflections on the term.' *Journal of Art and Design Education*, Vol. 13, No. 2, pp. 133–144.

Allen, D. (1996) 'As well as painting.' In *Critical Studies and Modern Art*, eds. Dawtrey, L., Jackson, T., Massterto, M. and Meecham, P. Milton Keynes: Open University Press.

Althusser, L. (1977) *Lenin and Philosophy and Other Essays*, London: New Left Books.

Apple, M. (1990) *Ideology and Curriculum*, London: Routledge.

Aronowitz, S. and Giroux, H.A. (1993) *Postmodern Education*, Minneapolis: University of Minnesota Press.

Atkinson, D. (1987) *Form and Action in Art Education: A Reflection upon Theory and Practice in the Teaching of Art*, unpublished PhD Dissertation, University of Southampton.

Atkinson, D. (1991) 'How children use drawing.' *Journal of Art and Design Education*, Vol. 10, No. 1, pp. 57–72.

Atkinson, D. (1993) 'Representation and practice in children's drawing.' *Journal of Art and Design Education*, Vol. 12, No. 1, pp. 85–104.

Atkinson, D. (1995) 'Discourse and practice in the art curriculum and the production of the pupil as a subject.' *Journal of Art and Design Education*, Vol. 14, No. 3, pp. 259–270.

Atkinson, D. (1998a) 'The production of the pupil as a subject within the art curriculum.' *Journal of Curriculum Studies*, Vol. 30, No. 1, pp. 27–42.

Atkinson, D. (1998b) 'The cultural production of drawing ability.' *International Journal of Inclusive Education*, Vol. 2, No. 1, pp. 45–54.

Atkinson, D. (1999a) 'A critical reading of the national curriculum for art.' *Journal of Art and Design Education.* 'Directions' Vol. 13, No. 1, pp. 107–113.

Atkinson, D. (1999b) 'Art in education: identity and the pedagogised other.' In *Art Education Discourses*, Vol. 2. Birmingham: ARTicle Press, pp. 97–113.

Atkinson, D. (1999c) *A Critical Reading of the National Curriculum for Art in the Light of Contemporary Theories of Subjectivity*, Birmingham: ARTicle Press.

Atkinson, D. (2001) 'Assessment in educational practice: forming pedagogised identities in the art curriculum.' *International Journal of Art and Design Education*, Vol. 20, No. 1, pp. 96–108.

Ball, S. (ed.) (1990) *Foucault and Education*, London and New York: Routledge.

Barrett, M. (1979) *Art Education: A Strategy for Course Design*, London: Heinemann.

Barthes, R. (1973) *Mythologies*, London: Granada.

Barthes, R. (1977) *Image, Music, Text*, London: Fontana.

Bateson, G. (1980) *Mind and Nature*, London: Fontana.

Berger, J. (1972) *Ways of Seeing*, London: Penguin.

Bergson, H. (1913) *An Introduction to Metaphysics* (Trans. T.E. Hulme).

Bhabha, H. (1994) *The Location of Culture*, London and New York: Routledge.

Bignell, J. (1997) *Media Semiotics*, Manchester: Manchester University Press.

Bourdieu, P. and Passeron, J. (1977) *Reproduction in Education, Society and Culture*, London and Beverley Hills: Sage.

Bourdieu, P. (1992) *Language and Symbolic Power*, Cambridge: Polity Press.

Bourdieu, P. (1993) *The Field of Cultural Production*, Cambridge: Polity.

Bowie, M. (1991) *Lacan*, London: Fontana.

Boyne, R. (1996) *Foucault and Derrida*, London and New York: Routledge.

Brookes, W.M. (1976) *Philosophy and Action*.

Brown, T. (2001) *Mathematics Education and Language: Interpreting Hermeneutics and Post-Structuralism*, Dordrecht: Kluwer Academic Press.

Brown, T. and Jones, L. (2001) *Action Research and Postmodernism: Congruence and Critique*, Milton Keynes: Open University Press.

Bryson, N. (1988) 'The gaze in the expanded field.' In *Vision and Visuality*, ed. Foster, H. Seattle: Bay Press.

Bryson, N. (1983) *Vision and Painting: The Logic of the Gaze*, London: Macmillan.

Bryson, N. (1991) 'Semiology and visual interpretation.' In *Visual Theory*, eds. Bryson, N., Holly, M.A. and Moxey, K. Cambridge: Polity Press.

Bryson, N., Holly, M.A. and Moxey, K. (1994) *Visual Culture: Images and Interpretations*, Hanover and London:Wesleyan University Press.

Buchanan, I. (2000) *Michel de Certeau*, London: Sage.

Burgin, V. (1986) *The End of Art Theory*, London: Macmillan.

Butler, J. (1993) *Bodies that Matter*, London: Routledge.

Butler, J. (1997) *The Psychic Life of Power*, Stanford: Stanford University Press.

Carr, W. and Kemmis, S. (1989) *Becoming Critical: Education, Knowledge and Action Research*, London: Falmer Press.

Caputo, J.D. (1987) *Radical Hermeneutics: Repetition, Deconstruction and the Hermeneutic Project*, Bloomington: Indiana University Press.

Chalmers, G.F. (1996) *Celebrating Pluralism: Art, Education and Cultural Diversity*, Los Angeles: The Getty Education Institute for the Arts.

Clarke, K. *Civilization*, BBC Television Series.

Collingwood, R.G. (1979) *The Principles of Art*, Oxford.

Colluney, T. (2001) 'Computer graphics – fine art or novelty toolbox.' In *A'N'D The Newsletter of the National Society for Education in Art and Design*, Summer 2001, p. 12.

Coward, R. and Ellis, J. (1977) *Language and Materialism*, London: Routledge and Kegan Paul.

Cox, M. (1998) 'Drawings of People by Australian Aboriginal Children: The Intermixing of Cultural Styles.' *Journal of Art and Design Education*, Vol. 17, No. 1, pp. 71–79.

Cox, M. (1993) *Children's Drawings*, Harmondsworth: Penguin.

Crary, J. (1996) *Techniques of the Observer: On Vision and Modernity in the Nineteenth Century*, London and Massachusetts; MIT Press.

Cunliffe, L. (1999) 'Learning How to Learn, Art Education and the "Background".' *Journal of Art and Design Education*, Vol. 18, No. 1, pp. 115–121.

D.F.E.E. (1995, 2000) *The National Curriculum for Art*.

Dash, P. (1999) 'Thoughts on a Relevant Art Curriculum for the 21st Century.' *Journal of Art and Design Education*, Vol. 18, No. 1, pp. 123–127.

Davey, N. (1999) 'The Hermeneutics of Seeing.' In Heywood, I. and Sandywell, B. (eds) *Interpreting Visual Culture: Explorations in the Hermeneutics of the Visual*, London and New York: Routledge.

De Certeau, M. (1984) *The Practice of Everyday Life*, trans. Steven Randall. Berkeley: University of California Press.

Derrida, J. (1973) *Speech and Phenomena*, trans. David B. Allison, Evanston IL: Northwestern University Press.

Derrida, J. (1976) *Of Grammatology*, Baltimore: John Hopkins University Press.

Derrida, J. (1978) *Writing and Difference*, trans. A. Bass. London: Routledge and Kegan Paul.

Derrida, J. (1987) *Positions*, London: Athlone Press.

Dewey, J. (1957) *Experience and Nature*, New York: Dover.

Dilthey, W. (1976) *Selected Writings* (edited and translated by H.P. Rickman), Cambridge: Cambridge University Press.

Dubery, F. and Willats, J. (1972) *Drawing Systems*, London; Studio Vista; New York: Van Nostrand Reinhold.

Eagleton, T. (2000) *The Idea of Culture*, Oxford and Massachusetts: Blackwell.

Easthope, A. (1991) *British Post-Structuralism Since 1968*, London and New York: Routledge.

Easthope, A. (2002) *Privileging Difference*, London: Palgrave.

Eco, U. (1976) *A Theory of Semiotics*, Bloomington: Indiana University Press.

Ed Exel (2000) *Training Video GCSE Art*.

Edwards, G. and Kelly, A.V. (1998) *Experience and Education: Towards an Alternative National Curriculum*, London: Paul Chapman.

Efland, A., Freedman, K. and Stuhr, P. (1996) *Postmodern Art Education: An Approach to Curriculum*, Virginia: The National Art Association.

Elliott, J. (1991) *Action Research for Educational Change*, Milton Keynes: Open University Press.

Eisner, E. (1972) *Educating Artistic Visio*.

Evans, D. (1997) *An Introductory Dictionary of Lacanian Psychoanalysis*, London and New York: Routledge.

Evans, J. and Hall, S. (1999) *Visual Culture: The Reader*, London, Thousand oaks and New Delhi: Sage and Open University Press.

Evernden, N. (1992) *The Social Creation of Nature*, Baltimore: John Hopkins University Press.

Foster, H. (ed.), (1988) *Vision and Visuality*, Seattle: Bay View Press.

Foster, H. (1996) *Return of the Real*, Cambridge, Mass.: MIT Press.

Foucault, M. (1970) *The Order of Things: An Archaeology of the Human Sciences*, London: Tavistock Publications.

Foucault, M. (1967) *Madness and Civilisation*, London: Tavistock.

Foucault, M. (1972) *The Archaeology of Knowledge*, London: Tavistock Publications.

Foucault, M. (1977) *Discipline and Punish: The Birth of the Prison*, London: Allen Lane.

Foucault, M. (1980) *Power/Knowledge*, London: Harvester Wheatsheaf.

Foucault, M. (1987) *The Use of Pleasure*, Harmondsworth: Penguin.

Freud, S. (1984) *On Metapsychology, trans. James Strachey*, Harmondsworth: Penguin Freud Library.

Gadamer, H.G. (1989) *Truth and Method*, trans. Joel Weinsheimer and Donald G. Marshall. New York: Crossroad Press.

Gallagher, S. (1992) *Hermeneutics and Education*, Albany: State University of New York Press.

Gardner, H. (1980) *Artful Scribbles*, New York: Basic Books.

Goodnow, J. (1977) *Children's Drawing*, Cambridge, Mass: Harvard University Press.

Gombrich, E. (1984) *The Story of Art*, Oxford: Phaidon.

Grossberg, L. (1996) 'Identity and Cultural Studies: Is That All There Is?' In Questions of Cultural Identity, eds., Hall, S. and Du Gay, P., London: Sage Publications.

Gruber, H. and Voneche, J. (1977) *The Essential Piaget*, London: Routledge.

Gulbenkian, C. Foundation (1982) *The Arts in Schools: Principles*, Practice and Provision, London: Oyez Press Ltd.

Habermas, J. (1972) *Knowledge and Human Interests*, Boston: Beacon Press.

Habermas, J. (1984) *Theory of Communicative Action*, Vol. 1, trans. Tony McCarthy. London: Heinemann.

Habermas, J. (1987) *Theory of Communicative Action*, Vol. 2. Cambridge: Polity Press.

Hall, S. (1996) 'Who Needs Identity?' In *Questions of Cultural Identity*, eds. Hal, S. and Du Gay, P., London: Sage Publications.

Harvey, D. (1989) *The Condition of Postmodernity*, Oxford: Blackwell.

Hawkes, T. (1977) *Structuralism and Semiotics*, London: Routledge.

Heidegger, M. (1962) *Being and Time*, trans. John Macquarrie and Edward Robinson. New York: Harper Row.

Heidegger, M. (1977) *Basic Writings*, trans. David F. Krell. New York: Harper and Row.

Henriques, J. et al. (1984) *Changing the Subject*, London and New York: Methuen.

Heywood, I. and Sandywell, B. (eds.) (1999) *Interpreting Visual Culture: Explorations in the Hermeneutics of the Visual*, London and New York: Routledge.

Hirsch, E.D. (1987) *Cultural Literacy: What Every American Needs to Know*, Boston: Houghton Miflin.

Hockney, D. (2002) *Hidden Knowledge*, London: Thames and Hudson.

Hughes, A. (1998) 'Reconceptualising the Art Curriculum,' *Journal of Art and Design Education*, Vol. 17, No. 1, pp. 41–49.

Inner London Education Authority ILEA (1986) *GCSE Art and Design: Video 1, Session: Differentiation*. ILEA Learning Resources Branch Television and Publishing Centre, London. Produced in collaboration with the University of London Schools Examinations Board and Norman Binch, ILEA Staff Inspector for Art and Design.

Jay, M. (1994) *Downcast Eyes: The Denigration of Vision in Twentieth-Century French Thought*, Berkeley and London:University of California Press.

Jakobson, R and Halle, M. (1956) *Fundamentals of Language*, The Hague: Mouton.

Jenks, C. (ed.) (1995) *Visual Culture*, London: Routledge.

Kearney, R. (1988) *The Wake of Imagination*, London: Hutchinson.

Kress, G. and Hodge (198) *Social Semiotics*.

Kristeva, J. (1986) ed. Toril Moi, The Kristeva Reader, Oxford: Blackwell.

Lacan, J. (1936) 'The mirror stage as formative of the I as revealed in psychoanalytic experience.' In Lacan, J. Ecrits, London: Routledge (1977).

Lacan, J. (1977) *Ecrits*, London: Routledge.

Lacan, J. (1988) *The Seminar. Book 1 Freud's Papers on Technique 1953–54*, trans. J. Forrester, New York: Norton; Cambridge University Press.

Lacan, J. (1991) *Four Fundamental Concepts of Psychoanalysis*, London: Penguin.

Lacan, J. (1993) *Jacques Lacan The Seminar Book III The Psychoses 1955–56*, Jacques-Allain Miller (ed.), trans. Russell Griggs, London: Routledge.

Langer, S. (1953) *Feeling and For,*. London: Routledge and Kegan Paul.

Lash, S. (1999) *Another Modernity A Different Rationality*, Oxford: Blackwell.

Levi-Strauss, C. (1966) *The Savage Mind*, London: Weidenfeld and Nicolson.

Lowenfeld, V. and Brittain, L. (1970) *Creative and Mental Growth*, New York: Macmillan.

Luquet, G.H. (1927) *Le Dessin Enfantin*, Paris: Alcan.

Mason, R. (19 88) *Art Education and Multiculturalism*, Beckenham: Croom Helm.

Matthews, J. (1994) *Helping Young Children to Draw and Paint in Early Childhood*, London: Hodder and Stoughton.

Matthews, J. (1999) *The Art of Childhood and Adolescence*, London: Falmer Press.

Mead, G.H. (1934) *Mind, Self and Society*, Chicago: University of Chicago Press.

Meleau_Ponty, M. (1962) *Phenomenology of Perception*, trans. Colin Smith. London: Routledge and Kegan Paul.

Mitchell, W.J.T. (1995) *Picture Theory*, Chicago: University of Chicago Press.

Moore, A. (1999) *Teaching Multicultured Students*, London: Falmer Press.

Morley, D. (2000) *Home Territories: Media, Mobility and Identity*, London and New York: Routledge.

Mulvey, L. (1975) 'Visual pleasure and narrative cinema,' *Screen* 16.3, pp. 6–18.

NACCCE (2000) *All Our Futures: Creativity, Culture and Education*, London: NACCCE.

Paechter, C.F. (2000) *Changing School Subjects: Power, Gender and Curriculum*, Buckingham: Open University Press.

Panofsky, E. (1991) *Perspective as Symbolic Form*, New York: Zone Books.

Pascall, D. (1992) *The Cultural Dimension in Education, Speech delivered to the National Foundation for Arts Education at the Royal Society of Arts*, London: 20th November 1992.

Peirce, C.S. (1931–35) *Collected Papers*, Volumes 1–6. Harvard: Harvard University Press.

Peirce, C.S. (1966) *Selected Writings: Values in a Universe of Chance*, New York: Dover.

Peters, M. (ed.) (1998) *Naming the Multiple: Poststructuralism and Education*, Wesport, Connecticut and London: Bergin and Garvey.

Piaget, J. (1950) *The Psychology of Intelligence*, London: Routledge and Kegan Paul.

Piaget, J. and Inhelder, B. (1956) *The Child's Conception of Space*, London: Routledge and Kegan Paul.

Pile, S. and Thrift, (1995) *Mapping the Subject*, London and New York: Routledge.

Read, H. (1943) *Education Through Art*, London: Faber and Faber.

Ricoeur, P. (1966) *Freedom and Nature: The Voluntary and the Involuntary*, Evanston: North Western University Press.

Ricoeur, P. (1976) *Interpretation Theory: Discourse and the Surplus of Meaning*, Fort Worth: Texas Christian University Press.

Ricoeur, P. (1981) *Hermeneutics and the Human Sciences*, trans. John B. Thompson. Cambridge: Cambridge University Press.

Ricoeur, P. (1991) 'Life: A story in search of a narrator.' In *A Ricoeur Reader: Reflection and Imagination*, ed. Valdes. J. M. London: Harvester Wheatsheaf.

Rogoff, I. (2000) *Terra Infirma: Geography's Visual Culture*, London and New York: Routledge.

Ross, M. (1978) *The Creative Arts*, London: Heinemann Educational Books.

Ross, M. (1980) *The Arts and Personal Growth*, London: Pergamon Press.

Ross, M. (1983) *The Arts a Way of Knowing*, London: Pergamon Press.

Ross, M. (1984) *The Aesthetic Impulse*, London: Pergamon Press.

Ross, M. (1995) 'National Curriculum Art and Music,' *Journal of Art and Design Education*, Vol. 14, No. 3, pp. 271–276.

Saussure, F. (1959) *Course in General Linguistics*, trans. W. Baskin. New York: The Philosophical Library Inc.

Schools Council (1975) *Arts and the Adolescent: Working Paper 54*. London: Evans and Methuen.

Schools, Arts, Crafts Councils (1981–84) *Critical Studies in Art Education Project*.

Schools Council and Assessment Authority (SCAA, 1996) *Consistency in Teacher Assessment: Exemplification of Standards*. Hayes, Middlesex: SCAA.

Schutz, A. (1962) *Collected Papers 1: The problem of Social Reality*, The Hague: Martinus Nijhoff.

Sebeok, T.A. (1969) (ed.) *Approaches to Semiotics*, The Hague: Mouton.

Stavrakakis, Y. (1999) *Lacan and the Political*, London: Routledge.

Steers, J. (1999) 'A Manifesto for Art in Schools.' *Journal of Art and Design Education*, Vol. 18, No. 1, pp. 7–13.

Swift, J. (1999) 'A Manifesto for Art in Schools.' *Journal of Art and Design Education*, Vol. 18, No. 1, pp. 7–13.

Taber, A. (1978) 'Art in a Multicultural School.' *New Approaches in Multiracial Education*, Vol. 7, No. 1, 1–5.

Taber, A. (1981) Art and craft in a multicultural school.' In Lynch, J. (ed.) *Teaching in the Multicultural School*, London: Ward Lock Educational, pp. 57–75.

Taylor, R. (1986) *Educating for Art: Critical Response and Development*, Harlow: Longman.

Thistlewood, D. (1984) *Herbert Read: Formlessness and Form*, London: Routledge and Kegan Paul.

Thistlewood, D. (1990) *Critical and Contextual Studies in Art and Design Education*, Harlow: Longman.

Thomas, G.V. and Silk, A.M.J. (1990) A*n Introduction to the Psychology of Children,s Drawings*, London and New York: Harvester Wheatsheaf.

Thompson, J. B. (1992) *'Editor's Introduction,'* to *Language and Symbolic Power*, Bourdieu, P. Cambridge: Polity Press.

Usher, R. and Edwards, R. (1994) *Postmodernism and Education*, London: Routledge.

Usher, R. (1997) 'Telling a story about research and research as story-telling.' In *Understanding Social Research: Perspectives on Methodology and Practice*, eds. McKenzie, G. Powell, J. and Usher, R. London: Falmer pp. 27–41.

Valdes, M. J. (1991) *A Ricoeur Reader:Reflection and Imagination*, London: Harvester Wheatsheaf.

Vygotsky, L.S. (1962) *Thought and Language*, Cambridge, Mass.: MIT Press.

Vygotsky, L.S. (1978) *Mind and Society*, Cambridge, Mass.:Harvard University Press.

Waddington, C.H. (1970) *Behind Appearance*, Cambidge, Mass.: MIT Press.

Waddington, C.H. (1977) *Tools For Thought*, London: Paladin.

Walkerdine, V. (1984) 'Developmental psychology and the child-centred pedagogy: The insertion of Piaget into early education.' In *Changing the Subject*, eds. Henriques, J. et al. London: Methuen.

Walkerdine, V. (1990) *Schoolgirl Fictions*, London: Verso.

Walerdine, V. and Blackman, L. (2001) *Mass Hysteria: Critical Psychology and Media Studies*, Houndmills Basingstoke: Palgrave.

Willats, J. (1997) *Art and Representation*, New Jersey: Princeton University Press.

Williams, R. (1977) *Marxism and Literature*, Oxford: Blackwell.

Williams, R. (1980) *Keywords*, London: Fontana.

Wittgenstein, L. (1953) *Philosophical Investigations*, Oxford: Blackwell.

Witkin, R. (1974) *The Intelligence of Feeling*, London: Heinemann Educational Books.

Wolf, D. and Perry, M.D. (1988) 'From endpoints to repertoires: some new conclusions about drawing development.' *Journal of Aesthetic Education*, Vol. 2, No. 1, pp. 17–34.

Wollheim, R. (1973) *On Art and the Mind*, London: Allen Lane.

Wollheim, R. (1987) *Painting as an Art*, Princeton: Princeton University Press.

Zizek, S. (1989) *The Sublime Object of Ideology*, London: Verso.

Zizek, S. (1991) *Looking Awry*, Cambridge, Mass.: MIT Press.

Zizek, S. (1996) *The Indivisible Remainder*, London: Verso.

Zizek, S. (1997) *The Plague of Fantasies*, London: Verso.

SUBJECT INDEX

NAME INDEX

Printed in the United States
60508LVS00002B/9